New Ways of Working in Mental Health

Edited by

James Dooher

QUAY
BOOKS

A division of MA Healthcare Ltd

Quay Books Division, MA Healthcare Ltd, St Jude's Church, Dulwich Road, London SE24 0PB

British Library Cataloguing-in-Publication Data
A catalogue record is available for this book

© MA Healthcare Limited 2006

ISBN 1 85642 290 9

Printed by Gutenberg Press Ltd, Gudja Road, Tarxien, Malta

Contents

Contents

Foreword

Since the publication of the National Service Framework for mental health, we have seen a huge amount of activity to make mental health services more responsive to the needs and wishes of the people who use them. At the time of writing, we are halfway through a ten-year programme to implement the National Service Framework and the benefits of accelerated reform are becoming evident for both service users and staff.

The creation of specialist community mental health teams offering home treatment, early intervention or intensive support for people with complex needs has been the central plank of our modernisation programme. Improved provision in the community helps prevent inpatient admissions where possible and reduces the length of inpatient stays by supporting people intensively in the least restrictive environment consistent with their needs. This in turn leads to less pressure on the existing beds, higher staff-patient ratios and better outcomes for service users.

Facilitating new people to work in mental health services without joining one of the traditional professions has been the other central·concept of reform. This was behind the proposal to employ graduate workers in primary care to deliver brief psychological therapies and help people to find the help they need elsewhere. Together with the significant increases we have seen in the numbers of conventional staff, there are now signs that we are on course to developing the mental health workforce that we need to deliver effective treatment and care, reduce unfair variation, raise standards, and provide quicker, more convenient services.

While we cannot yet claim that the historical problems that have affected mental health services have been solved, the past five years have shown us that we can create a mental health service that our service users deserve. This, I believe, is a milestone in the history of mental health care and our goal to create a service that we are all proud of is finally within our reach.

Rt Hon Patricia Hewitt MP
Secretary of State for Health

This book is dedicated to Sally, Millie and Libby

Contributors

Dr Elizabeth Anderson

Senior Lecturer in Shared Learning, Department of Medical and Social Care Education, University of Leicester

Elizabeth completed a degree course in nursing at St Bartholomew's Hospital and City University London. Working as a Midwife and Health Visitor in Leicester she progressed with an academic career and now works in the department of medical and social care education in the University of Leicester, establishing new teaching models for interprofessional education at the pre- and post-qualified levels. She chairs the regional interprofessional education strategy group for Leicestershire, Rutland and Northampton Strategic Health Authority. Her research interests reflect her previous nursing work as a health visitor focused on child health issues and recently within health and social care education. She is a board member of the UK Centre for the Advancement of Interprofessional Education.

Claire Armitage

RMN, Dip. Healthcare Research, MA

Claire is Senior Nurse and Service Clinical Governance Lead for Adult Mental Health Services, working within an NHS trust. She is a mental health nurse by background and has previously held clinical posts within rehabilitation and challenging behaviour settings. More recently she has developed experience in quality improvement, practice development and clinical governance. Claire has an MA in Quality Management and Improvement and a Postgraduate Diploma in Healthcare Research. Her particular interests include user and carer involvement, patient safety and suicide prevention.

Janet Couloute

Social Work Tutor, Department of Medical and Social Care Education, University of Leicester

With a background in social work practice and education, particularly in the field of mental health, Janet currently works as a social work tutor. Janet previously worked on two research projects with Dr Liz Anderson on a parent evaluation of the impact of a local Sure Start project and on the evaluation of professional views on team working.

Tim Davis
RMN, Dip. C, BA (Hons)
Tim is the Team Manager for the Leicestershire Counties Crisis Resolution and Home Treatment Service. He has worked in Adult Mental Health Services for Leicestershire since 1987. He was involved in setting up the Crisis Service from January 2004.

James Dooher
RMN, MA, FHE Cert Ed, Dip. HCR, ILTM
James is a principal Lecturer and Academic Lead for Mental Health Nursing at De Montfort University, Leicester. He is course leader for the Graduate Mental Health Worker Programme and has written extensively on the subjects of user empowerment, practice development and clinical supervision.

Lois Dugmore
RMN, BA (Hons) MSc, MBA, Nurse Consultant – Dual Diagnosis
Lois works as a nurse consultant for Leicestershire partnership NHS Trust and has been a nurse consultant in dual diagnosis for the last two years. Her role is both clinical and strategic, aimed at incorporating and developing a multi-agency approach to dual diagnosis. Lois sits on the national Nurse Consultant Group and has a particular interest in research, audit and risk management. Lois also works for the healthcare commission and is an experienced CHI reviewer. Lois has experience in a wide variety of mental health services and specialises in addictions and mental health. Lois has had work published in development and change of services.

Martin Fahy
RMN, BA Health, PG Dip. PSI
Martin is the Team Manager for the PIER Team (Early Intervention in Psychosis Service) within Leicestershire Partnership Trust.

Martin has been working in the mental health field for the past 16 years. He has experience within areas ranging from Forensic, Community, Rehabilitation and Adult Acute (PICU) mental health services and is completing his final year of a MSc in PSI at Sheffield University. Martin joined the Leicester Early Intervention Team in Sept 2004 and is responsible for this newly established county-wide Early Intervention team (covering Leicester City, Leicestershire and Rutland).

Kath Ferguson
MSc, BSc, RGN, RMN, PG Dip. Ed., Adv. Dip Counselling
Kath Ferguson works as a Senior Mental Health Practitioner and as a counsellor within a day care setting for people with mental health problems. She has also worked for many years in higher education, and currently teaches for the Open University. During the past few years, she and Sara Owen have worked together on a number of research projects which have been used to inform the work of the Mental Health Care Group Workforce Team.

Barry Foley

Barry's role as the Mental Health Workforce Designer, developing later into Lead Workforce Designer and now Associate Director for New Ways of Working (NWW) with Care Services Improvement Partnership (CSIP)/National Institute for Mental Health in England (NIMHE), has changed to reflect the size, depth and breadth of the work of involved, and in 2006 Barry will take on a similar position in New Zealand.

Dave Kingdon

RMN, MEd Counselling, MBACP Accred.

Dave has been involved in developing and implementing the Common Mental Health Problem Service within PCTs across Leicestershire, and is a Senior Practice Therapist providing psychological interventions with patients in GP surgeries. He spent one year seconded to De Montfort University, Leicester, as Lecturer Practitioner to deliver the Postgraduate Certificate in Primary Care Mental Health, and to facilitate the introduction of Graduate Mental Health Workers. His particular interests are in the field of primary care mental health and the development, access and delivery of psychological therapies.

Dr Aftab Laher

BA, MSc, PhD, C. Psychol., AFBPsS, UKCP, Chartered Consultant Clinical and Health Psychologist, Accredited Cognitive-Behavioural Psychotherapist, Associate Fellow of the British Psychological Society, Honorary Lecturer in Clinical Psychology (University of Leicester)

Aftab qualified as a chartered clinical psychologist in 1994 through successfully completing a three-year postgraduate level professional training course in clinical psychology run jointly by Trent Regional Health Authority and the University of Leicester. He worked as a clinical psychologist within a medical psychology service for adults in Leicestershire. In 1997 Aftab took up a post as Lecturer in Clinical Psychology at the University of Leicester while maintaining a contract as Honorary Clinical Psychologist. In 2000 he was appointed as Consultant Clinical Psychologist within the Southern Derbyshire NHS Mental Health Services, with a main remit to develop and lead a multidisciplinary pain management service for adults with pain conditions. He completed a PhD in 2000, and in September 2003 formed his own company, Laher Human Solutions Ltd, offering a portfolio of psychological services to a range of individual and corporate clients.

Dr Sara Owen

PhD, BA, BEd, SRN, RMN, RNT

Sara is a Reader in Mental Health in the School of Nursing at Nottingham University. She has worked with Kath Ferguson on a number of research projects for the Mental Health Care Group Workforce Team, including projects on the clinical activity of mental health lecturers and recruitment to the mental health professions.

Samantha Mackintosh

RMN (Dip.)

Samantha qualified as a Registered Mental Health Nurse in Leicester in 1994. Prior to qualifying she worked for some time as a nursing assistant on a long-stay mental health ward and also in learning disabilities. Samantha worked as an RMN on an adult general mental health ward serving a busy city catchment area for five years before the development of the current unique Link Nurse role.

Petrina South

BSc (Hons), PG Cert. Mental Health Work

Following the completion of her undergraduate studies in psychology, Petrina undertook the role of a Graduate Mental Health Worker, studying at De Montfort University and working in Primary Care placements. Petrina currently works as a Prescriptions for Healthy Learning Advisor at nextstep Leicester and Leicestershire.

Dr Sarah Supple

Sarah completed her undergraduate degree in psychology and sociology at the University of Bath. Following this she worked in a variety of residential settings with both children and adults within the mental health services. She studied for a doctorate in psychotherapeutic and counselling psychology at the University of Surrey, and since graduating has worked for Northamptonshire Health Care NHS trust. Sarah works in a split post with a community mental health team and an outpatient adult mental health psychology department.

Lynne Ward

BA (Hons) Humanities, RMN, Diploma in the Care and Management of Suicidal and Parasuicidal Behaviour

Lynne trained and has worked in the mental health services in Leicestershire since 1985. At the time of the pilot Lynne was the Ward Manager on Fosse Ward and worked together with Sam to develop the role of the link nurse.

Lynne is currently the Modern Matron at the Bradgate Unit.

Dr Jo Wright

Jo is an inner city GP and has worked in secondary care mental health services in both Australia and the UK. Current work includes GP training (she is a Course Organiser on a Vocational Training Scheme) and working with asylum seekers. She is currently studying for a BSc in Family Therapy.

Introduction

Working with users of mental health services in the 21st century demands enthusiasm and flexibility, the ability to improvise, empathy, and a willingness to help your clients reach their optimum potential. When we overlay the public demand for expertise and a personal service which is timely and effective, the weight of responsibility resting upon those defined as 'professionals' is clear. This book provides an examination of our respective disciplines' core values and roles with the aspiration to provide holistic care that ensures equality and the meeting of diverse needs. It considers some of the new roles and explores how creative and dynamic change has and will promote better quality care.

The fashion for collaborative working has acknowledged the overlap of roles and responsibilities from within uniprofessional groups, and has encouraged the sharing of ideas, skills and knowledge often fiercely protected by distinct professional tribes. Professional tribalism is now, or should be, dead, and the world of cooperative multidisciplinary education and practice is the 'new way'.

This has been achieved in part through the recognition by professionals that the quality of services will be improved by greater collaboration and that shared care is safer in terms of accountability. Employing organisations have played their part through role and job redesign and consideration of new ways of working (Department of Health, 2005c). The skill mix of the NHS workforce has been under constant review from the late 1980s and changes have been made which build on a growing body of evidence, experience and good practice. Improved partnerships have enabled local mental health communities to take a joined-up approach to improving service users' experiences by redesigning the way services are delivered at all stages of the service user's journey. The NHS Improvement Plan (Department of Health, 2004a), set out the way in which the NHS needs to change in order to become truly patient-led. These changes are far reaching and they impact upon organisations and the ways in which different professional groups view themselves and work with each other.

The Government has been firmly at the centre of driving these developments and, through its modernisation programme, has embarked on a massive, complex strategy to change and improve the way in which NHS services are delivered. The essential aims are to cut down waiting times and make the most effective use of existing resources, with new money to improve the patient's experience as a recipient of healthcare. This is being achieved through the setting of standards, organising staff to achieve their potential and giving patients more authority.

> The extra money coming into Health and Social Services gives us the opportunity to make real improvements. We can expand through recruiting new staff, developing new services and creating new facilities. Even more importantly, we can transform the quality of services by raising standards, tackling inequality, becoming more accessible and flexible and designing our services around the needs and choices of the people we serve (Crisp, 2003, p. 2).

Access to psychological therapies has been considered by the Labour Government's No. 10 Policy unit, resulting in the Layard Report. Lord Layard (2005) suggests that around 10,000 mental health professionals are needed to treat common mental health problems using psychological therapies. This therapeutic workforce will comprise a new career pathway, alongside retrained or newly recruited staff taking traditional professional routes. Roughly half of these people will undertake a two-year diploma, and they will be drawn from the graduate psychology base, nursing, social work or occupational therapy professions. In addition, Layard proposes doubling the number of psychiatrists and clinical psychology training places.

These numbers are based on an assumption that over the next five years, to provide 10 therapy sessions for an estimated one million at-risk individuals per annum, 250 teams, each comprising approximately 20 therapists, will be required.

The plan suggests a hub and spoke model, and in keeping with NHS strategies Layard supports a cognitive behaviour therapy (CBT) based approach, and promotes treatment choice for patients. These ideas dovetail into other elements of the NHS agenda in several ways.

For example, the 'substantial proportion' of individuals on incapacity benefit who have underlying and treatable mental health problems could be targeted. If treatment results in an earlier return to work, there are long-term economic and health gains to be achieved by shifting resources from the benefit system to the health system.

However, although these increased numbers will no doubt improve the accessibility of therapeutic services, the constraints of the favoured CBT model will undermine the scope and range of therapeutic interventions on offer. For anxiety disorders or depression, NICE guidance suggests that the efficacy of the CBT approach is comparable to that of medication. The model is well established, but the choice seems to be limited to medication or CBT. Clearly combinations of the two will emerge, but the marginalisation of other therapeutic schools may see them withering on the vine that is the NHS, and regerminating in the field of private enterprise. This said, these developments will go some way towards obviating the lack of access, issues of stigma, and poor recognition of psychological disorders in primary care, and to reducing the prevalence of untreated mental health problems in the community.

It is suggested that therapy would be available through specialist centres, where groups of therapists, usually headed by a clinical psychologist, would work together.

The debate about whether management should be integrated or separated from Community Mental Health Teams is ongoing, although I suspect that a fair proportion of existing CMHT workers will self select into these new teams, resulting in staff shortages and depleted expertise within the indigenous CMHT workforce.

There are some significant benefits to this development. In that this is a true opportunity for multiprofessional education in the role of Associate Psychologist it will create a new strand of clinical career for psychologists and the benefits of multi-professional supervision will add weight to the quality of the treatment.

These far-reaching changes have seen the balance of power shifted to the front line (Department of Health, 2001). According to Bywaters (2005), staff at the centre of organisations have been reduced in number, the bulk of the money has been given to Primary Care Trusts with no strings attached, and those working at a national level feel almost impotent. She goes on to suggest that those involved in public mental health in local communities do not feel correspondingly empowered. Clearly the government has not set out to disempower any particular professional group or managerial tier; however, when significant change occurs there will inevitably be some sections of the workforce who feel they have become casualties of that change. The process of consultation, production of guidance and subsequent change is relentless, as we see from the plethora of papers emanating from the Department of Health over the few years: for example, Department of Health (1994, 1998a,b, 1999a,b,c, 2000a,b,c, 2001a,b,c,d, 2002, 2003a,b,c), 2004a,b,c, 2005a,b,c. The NHS Chief Executive, Sir Nigel Crisp (2005), has suggested that

> The past five years have been about building capacity and capability. The next will be about improving quality, making sure that we give the very best value for money and use the new capacity and capability to build a truly patient led service.

Most recently, Chief Nursing Officer Chris Beasley launched the consultation regarding the future development of mental health nursing in England. The consultation is part of the review of mental health nursing launched in February 2005, the provisional outcomes of which should be available in late 2005.

This is clearly an important development, as nursing is the largest professional group in mental health services, with 47,000 qualified nurses working in the NHS in England and another 30,000 support staff working with them. This consultation sought views as to how mental health nurses should contribute to a wide range of issues, including:

■ Services for people from black and ethnic minority groups
■ The delivery of psychological therapies
■ Health promotion
■ Meeting the needs of carers

The NHS Modernisation Programme has seen a growth in the number of bodies set up to organise and monitor this increase in capacity and capability. The range of groups and their associated acronyms is overwhelming, and to the ordinary worker who is who, and who does what, can easily blur into a homogenised whirl of useful sources of help to do one's job and stick-wielding quality and standard controllers. Extrapolating today's most useful information is a lifelong learning task in itself, and the resulting passivity may not be due to any lack of interest, but to limited capacity of time and reduced capability to focus specifically, owing to the sheer volume of material emanating from these bodies. Individual workers may take some solace from the fact that strategic planners are also struggling to keep pace with the demands of modernisation. Clearly this is counterproductive, and there seems to be no holiday from the relentless outpouring of new aspirations and benchmarks. This view may be seen as resistive to change, although I would suggest that it has its basis in my own attempts to keep informed and develop a thoroughly modern perspective.

This observation is supported in part by criticisms of Local Implementation Plans, in that some localities are struggling with workforce planning in all its forms, and in some cases it is not being prioritised. Department of Health (2001e) included observations which pointed out that poor workforce planning was due to such factors as:

■ lack of robust data on numbers, types of staff, skills mix and needs
■ lack of local strategies across the statutory authorities and the non-statutory sector
■ lack of effective links to the service planning and delivery process
■ lack of enthusiasm to implement flexible working across professions and disciplines

This book suggests that despite the difficulties, staff delivering care do have enthusiasm for change, and are willing to improve their links, contribute to the evidence base and provide a robust quality service. The contributors capture the urgency of providing best practice now, today and within the resources available. They explore their roles, attitudes and professional aspirations in a way that encourages the reader to take up new ideas and become an active part of the 'New NHS'.

References

Bywaters, J. (2005) *Carpe diem*: seize the day. *Journal of Public Mental Health*, **4**, 7–9.

Crisp, N. (2003) *Improvement, Expansion and Reform: the Next 3 Years Priorities and Planning Framework 2003–2006*. London, HMSO.

Crisp, N. (2005) *Creating a Patient-led NHS – Delivering the NHS Improvement Plan*. London, HMSO, pp. 3–4.

Department of Health (1994) *Working in Partnership: The Review of Mental Health Nursing*. London, HMSO.

Department of Health (1998a) *A First Class Service, Quality in the New NHS*. London, HMSO.

Department of Health (1998b) *Modernising Social Services*. London, HMSO.

Department of Health (1999a) *Making a Difference. Strengthening the Nursing, Midwifery and Health Visiting Contribution to Health and Health Care*. London, HMSO.

Department of Health (1999b) *Clinical Governance, Quality in the New NHS*. London, HMSO.

Department of Health (1999c) *A National Service Framework for Mental Health*. London, HMSO.

Department of Health (2000a) *Meeting the Challenge: A Strategy for the Allied Health Professions*. London, HMSO.

Department of Health (2000b) *An Organisation with a Memory. Report on an Expert Group on Learning from Adverse Events in the NHS*. London, HMSO.

Department of Health (2000c) *The NHS Plan. A Plan for Investment, a Plan for Reform*. London, HMSO.

Department of Health (2001a) *Essence of Care. Patient-focused Benchmarking for Health Care Practitioners*. London, HMSO.

Department of Health (2001b) *Involving Patients and the Public in Healthcare. A Discussion Document*. London, HMSO.

Department of Health (2001c) *Investment and Reform for NHS Staff – Taking Forward the NHS Plan*. London, HMSO.

Department of Health (2001d) *Shifting the Balance of Power Within the NHS: Securing Delivery*. London, HMSO.

Department of Health (2001e) *Mental Health NSF (and the NHS Plan): Workforce Planning, Education and Training – Underpinning Programme: Adult Mental Health Services. Final Report by the Workforce Action Team, August 2001*. London, HMSO.

Department of Health (2002) *Delivering the NHS Plan. Next Steps on Investment. Next Steps on Reform.* London, HMSO.

Department of Health (2003a) *Improvement Expansion and Reform: The Next 3 Years. Planning and Priorities Framework 2003–2006.* London, HMSO.

Department of Health (2003b) *Inside Outside: Improving Mental Health Services for Black and Minority Ethnic Communities in England.* London, HMSO.

Department of Health (2003c) *Women's Mental Health Strategy.* London, HMSO.

Department of Health (2004a) *The NHS Improvement Plan. Putting People at the Heart of Public Services.* London, HMSO.

Department of Health (2004b) *National Standards, Local Action: Health and Social Care Standards and Planning Framework 2005/06–2007.* London, HMSO.

Department of Health (2004c) *Choosing Health: Making Healthier Choices Easier.* London, HMSO.

Department of Health (2005a) *Delivering Race Equality in Mental Health Care: An Action Plan for Reform Inside and Outside Services and the Government's Response to the Independent Inquiry Into the Death of David Bennett.* London, HMSO.

Department of Health (2005b) *The 2004/05 National Survey of Investment in Mental Health Services.* London, HMSO.

Department of Health (2005c) *Improvement Leaders' Guide Redesigning roles: Personal and Organisational Development.* London, HMSO.

Layard, R. (2005) *Mental Health: Britain's Biggest Social Problem?* London: Strategy Unit, Cabinet Office.

CHAPTER 1

Making it better for patients and better for staff

A personal reflection of new ways of working, including examples of support time recovery workers and mental health pharmacy and consultant psychiatrist roles

Barry Foley

Making it better for patients and better for staff was the guiding principle of the Changing Workforce Programme's (CWP) work on new and changing roles across all care groups, including mental health.

My role as the Mental Health Workforce Designer, developing later into Lead Workforce Designer and now Associate Director for New Ways of Working (NWW) with Care Services Improvement Partnership (CSIP)/National Institute for Mental Health in England (NIMHE), has changed to reflect the size, depth and breadth of the work of the complex task of promoting innovation and creativity throughout a spectrum of healthcare arenas.

The Changing Workforce Programme has its focus on 13 pilot sites looking at:

- Mental health
- Anaesthesia, critical care and pain management
- Care of the older person
- Diabetes
- Emergency care
- Diagnostic care
- Generalist and specialist care
- Primary care
- Scientists – cancer
- Senior House Officer and equivalent roles
- Stroke care
- Technical and other support staff
- Allied health professionals

I commenced involvement in July 2002. At this time, there was a Director, three lead managers and a group of eventually 12 designers (including myself). The team believed change could grow by small incremental steps in pilots sites by creating toolkits, tools, videos, and guidance, gaining support and momentum. We anticipated that later we could use spread techniques such as the national accelerated development programmes to consolidate this work.

An important aspect was to build capacity in and for workforce development and change into Trusts, Strategic Health Authorities and other organisations. Four years on, this approach, with the support of many other agencies, has been enabled and immense change has taken place and local support created.

The areas of work and teams appointed to undertake the different aspects of new ways of working were initially the Changing Workforce Programme, joined later by the

- European Working Time Directive Team
- Recruitment and Retention Team
- Agenda for Change Team
- Consultant Contract Implementation Team

These and other programmes were part of the Modernisation Agency (MA).

Mental health was, and still is, at the heart of these changes. It began with appointments to project manager posts and the establishing of chosen pilot sites, developing project development plans, steering groups and areas for work. A starting point for me was to work with the Chief Executive and his team in Northumberland, which had a reputation for partnership working and interest in different approaches to mental health care and how it works.

Timing and important drivers have been vital to the success of the work. At the initial meetings with staff, service users and carers, it was clear that work was needed across the range of professions, including psychiatrists. It was also clear that Northumberland had an advantage and was not an average Trust. It was agreed that support should be given to what is now the North Cumbria Mental Health and Learning Disabilities Trust, which had recently been the subject of an investigation of its older people's ward, and it should join as a national pilot working with Northumberland.

Meetings and small focus groups identified that work was needed around:

- *Consultant roles* – examples of users having seven locums in a year causing lack of continuity of care, frequent medication change and unhappiness for consultants and users and their carers.
- *Psychology* – had long waiting times, in some cases 18 months.
- *Nursing* – had little time for talking to users.
- *Support services* – such as housekeeping, administration and clerical posts – did not exist in many areas.

- *Occupational therapy* – there was dissatisfaction with occupational therapy availability and its timeliness.
- *Community psychiatric nurses* – need for a new approach in primary care to create open access clinics in general practice.

Across the workforce, high vacancy rates, recruitment, retention issues and a need to make better use of highly skilled, experienced, professional staff was driving a move to look at new ways of doing things. It was also clear from the initial pilot sites and meetings I had with key stakeholders that we could recruit to mental health for assistant, clerical, administration and support staff in most places. Staff present from these roles at early meetings were willing and happy to explore taking on new and changed roles.

I met a large number of individuals and groups and identified that others were beginning to work on new roles. Some work had emerged from the Workforce Action Teams report, from user and carer demands for a range of new workers and from the implementation of new services such as:

- The Support, Time and Recovery (STR) worker
- Gateway workers
- Graduate primary care workers
- New approaches arising from the National Service Framework for Mental Health.

In early January 2003 I met Roslyn Hope, who was leading local work in the West Midlands and undertaking development work on the soon to be formed National Institute for Mental Health in England. Many of our approaches seemed to be similar and agreement was reached to work together. This developed into joint working and aligning CWP programmes into the NIMHE MH National Workforce Programme. More recently the CWP team moved into CSIP/NIMHE to continue and complete our programmes until March 2007. I had also had meetings with colleagues at the Department of Health (DoH) and was invited to join the Support Time Recovery (STR) Guidance Group. It was agreed that as well as the pilot site work in two trusts, the CWP should lead on establishing seven STR pilot sites across England.

Drivers for change and background to the setting up of the National Steering Group

The NSFs, the NHS Plans and changes in populations of the countries that comprise the UK and the Western world, together with the European Working Time

Directive, have created new challenges for the workforce by transforming the demand and supply of mental health care. Furthermore, challenges set by the Wanless Report in England and in Wales, which stress community services and emphasise health promotion, are going to have fundamental effects on the pattern of statutory sector-funded services in the UK. Service users in secondary care are cared for by specialist teams and other new types of service, thereby creating greater expectations and the need for new ways of working. The limited supply of staff in all professional groups means that a review of their roles, responsibilities and working practices across the role boundaries between the professions is essential.

Several contemporary pieces of work put in hand by different bodies identified similar requirements for a wider UK-wide review: the Northern Centre for Mental Health had undertaken an initial role analysis; the BMA's Central Consultant Specialist Committee had established a sub-group to look at the role of consultant psychiatrists in multidisciplinary teams; and the Royal College of Psychiatrists had established its scoping group on the roles and values of psychiatrists. Several other groups at the Royal College and the Department of Health had begun to explore the need for new and changing roles for consultant psychiatrists and other professionals engaged in mental health care. The latter included work that is being undertaken in the then Modernisation Agency's Changing Workforce Pilots in Newcastle, Northumberland and Tyneside and North Cumbria. A project to learn more about what consultants do and the pressures on them by shadowing consultant psychiatrists gave particular insights, which reinforced the need for new ways of working. Finally, a large number of psychiatrists attended two national conferences, held in the spring of 2003, as a joint initiative involving NIMHE, the BMA, the Royal College of Psychiatrists, CWP and the GMC, and again their responses provided strong support for the urgency of a review.

In parallel, a letter to Jacqui Smith MP, then Minister responsible for Mental Health, from Dr Mike Shooter, President of the Royal College of Psychiatrists, and supported by the National Director of Mental Health, Professor Louis Appleby, led to a review of the role of psychiatrists and their interface with other professionals who provide mental health care.

Therefore, a National Steering Group with two subgroups was established. Dr Shooter and Professor Sheehan (then Chief Executive of NIMHE) jointly chaired the Steering Group. This group comprised representation of all the key professions and related staff groups involved in mental health care, together with service users and carers.

The Steering Group met for the first time at the end of February 2003. Beforehand, Professor Anthony Sheehan contacted the relevant presidents, heads of other organisations or colleges and lead officers to seek their advice, support and nominations for the National Steering Group. As a result, the group has a wide membership.

The aims of the Steering Group are to:

- Review the current roles of psychiatrists and produce recommendations for more effective and satisfactory modern roles and career paths
- Explore the professional role of psychiatrists in the context of multidisciplinary working including all groups working in mental health care
- Commission projects to identify challenges and solutions, test new ways of working and support dissemination
- Oversee an initial first year's programme of work

The two subgroups were formed to undertake the work needed:

- *The Consultant Roles Subgroup*
  This group, looking specifically at the role of consultants, has adopted a focus on workforce design. It has examined, reviewed and recommended an action plan for the emerging new and changing roles of psychiatrists.

  This group is jointly chaired by Professor Richard Williams, from the Royal College of Psychiatrists, and Barry Foley, Mental Health Lead from the Changing Workforce Programme. It has a wide membership, including professionals, organisations and users of mental health services.

- *Working across Professional Boundaries Subgroup*
  This group, looking at the existing roles of all professions and non-professionally affiliated staff, is exploring the flexibility of roles and responsibilities and the potential for multidisciplinary working in new and changing models of mental health care.

  The group is jointly chaired by Dr Matt Muijen, Director of the Sainsbury Centre for Mental Health, and Roslyn Hope, Director of National Workforce Programme for NIMHE. Its membership is representative of organisations and involves users and carers.

The two original pilot sites had by now agreed programmes.

Northumberland

In Northumberland the goals were to extend the roles of support staff and to recruit and release pharmacists to work with ward teams. Three people were recruited to vacancies and major changes were made to other pharmacy staff to enable them to work differently and establish clinical pharmacy in wards, which led to some releasing of doctor and nurse time. This has led to a national spread programme involving initially 16 further pilot sites and has resulted in 44 sites undertaking development work in pharmacy across England.

Following a consultation with senior staff it was established that the role of the consultant psychiatrist needed to change. This echoed what had been said in the staff, user and carer stakeholder groups in the focus groups. It was to be the start of what is now a major national programme for new and changing roles of consultant psychiatrists and other professions.

Newcastle

A three-year review of the mental health services in Newcastle had commenced which the CWP began to support the workforce elements. As the need for service change was identified and cross-boundary working changed, the need for team and consultant roles to change started to be discussed, with a view to consultants undertaking a more functional approach to meet service users' needs.

The journey to a changed service can be a challenging one, which the following study shows, but change can occur even with the merging of trusts and when dealing with major financial problems. It identified the need to keep communicating with PCTs, GPs, mental health staff, and service users and their carers and showed that it was crucial to check and make sure that they have chance to discuss and understand what is proposed and that plans need to be regularly reviewed and refocused to achieve the direction of change.

The Newcastle approach has been seen as very important to the development of different ways of doing things, and for using consultants' high level of knowledge, skills and experience in a new way. This work will continue, and caseloads, support roles and lessons to be learned will be shared as the programme progresses.

Brief outline of work so far

On 13 September 2004, 13 consultant psychiatrists changed their roles following three years of preparation. The role changes are part of a much larger service change – 'the pathways through care project'. Since November 2003, an evaluation of the change of roles has begun and all the baseline data has been collected.

The change of roles is from that of a traditional consultant psychiatrist role to more specialised roles: initially inpatient and community. Eventually it is envisaged that specialist roles will develop in primary care liaison, acute integrated treatment and specialist community roles, e.g. personality disorder, psychosis, anxiety and depression.

Evaluation pre- and post-change includes:

- CMHT activity
- The organisational change process
- The changes in the pathways through care
- Job satisfaction of professional groups
- Team functioning
- Working patterns and the role of consultant psychiatrists
- Referrals to CMHT
- Inpatient admissions
- Waiting times
- Sickness and absence
- Grievances
- Recruitment
- Complaints
- Serious untoward incidents

Part of this work involved the shadowing of consultants, which was found to be a useful method of taking stock of how individuals approach their roles. It was then possible to feed back observations, giving the consultants time to reflect and to following up with key points for action. A year on, repeat shadowing showed that most had undertaken changes to their roles and felt the process was supportive and helpful.

Case study: Redefining how the needs of service users can be reflected in the role of consultants and in new ways of working within teams

Avon & Wiltshire Mental Health Partnerships NHS Trust has began to redefine the consultant's role in a multidisciplinary context. This Trust has fostered the development of New Ways of Working (NWW) for consultants by providing a central steer and then supporting local initiatives. One of these, in West Wiltshire, became one of the first pilot sites, and the changes there are now being rolled out more widely.

AWP's approach has been to encourage the development of NWW in the following way:

1. **Support from the Executive Team and the Board.**
2. **Defining the boundaries of the role of the consultant.** The Trust produced its own 'Trust Guidance on the Role of the Consultant Psychiatrist'

in response to requests for more clarity from staff. In this document, it sought to interpret the currently available national guidance, clarify what is law and what is guidance, and define the responsibilities of individuals (including consultants) and teams. The guidance supports a model of distributed responsibility, and has led to a number of practical changes that have emphasised the new approach (e.g. defining episodes of care by team rather than by consultant; PCTs no longer commissioning GP to consultant referrals). Legal advice and the endorsement of the CNST (Clinical Negligence Scheme for Trusts) were obtained before the document was approved by the Trust Board. This guidance is recommended for use by other Trusts developing NWW, and appears as an appendix in the Interim Report of the National Steering Group (2004).

3. **Defining the boundaries of the work of the team**. A Trust-wide workshop was held, with commissioners, users and carers, to produce a 'framework' for the development of entry and exit criteria for services and teams. The framework was then modified according to local/speciality need.

In West Wiltshire, a project was then launched to move from a traditional referral and outpatient model to a new multidisciplinary assessment clinic. On receipt of the electronic referral (using the local acute hospital system), a senior practitioner in the team makes the decision to assess the patient, and the letter inviting the patient to ring to book an appointment is sent. The patient is assessed by two clinicians from different professions; one does most of the assessment while the other types the information into a standard template which is considerably shorter than the usual 'core assessment', risk assessment and CPA. The management plan is decided upon and agreed with the patient, who receives a copy of the form; this is then emailed to the GP.

There is not space for giving anything but a flavour of some of the NWW in mental health and brief sections of guidance produced for new and changing roles.

Examples of new roles

Support, time and recovery workers

In 2001, the Workforce Action Team (WAT) produced its Final Report and, as a result of looking at the non-professionally affiliated workforce, suggested that a new type of worker should be introduced into the mental health workforce – the Support, Time and Recovery worker (STR worker).

An STR worker is someone who works as part of a team that provides mental health services and focuses directly on the needs of service users. STR workers are based in one organisation but work across others, and provide support and negotiated time to the service user working with them towards recovery.

When new STR posts are advertised we encourage people who would not traditionally have applied for jobs in health and social care to apply – for instance service users.

As with any staff we recruit to work with service users, STR workers must be respectful to service users and fellow colleagues. They must be able to listen, communicate appropriately, show by their body language that they are encouraging and actively listening, and communicate in writing.

For STR workers to be effective they require a range of skills, which include being:

■ Compassionate, patient and able to empathise
■ Able to deal sensitively with distress
■ Non-judgemental
■ Flexible
■ Able to think and act calmly
■ Knowledgeable about when to seek help or supervision
■ Creative in their approach to problem solving
■ Practically skilled
■ Able to promote the rights responsibilities and recovery of service users
■ Able to promote good physical health
■ Able to promote anti-discriminatory practice and equal opportunities and treat service users and colleagues with dignity and respect
■ Able to maintain confidentiality according to the organisation's policies
■ Able to work safely and to know their local community resources

STR workers work as part of a team under the care programme approach, and demonstrate a range of abilities that promote independence and provide companionship and support with daily living for service users through practical tasks.

This role is designed to help people live ordinary lives by promoting healthy living and by enabling users to access appropriate resources. In addition, STR workers collaborate with service users to identify early signs of relapse, liaising with families, carers or significant people when appropriate. They take an empowering role to promote service users to develop active participation in their care, treatment or support package (Dooher and Byrt, 2002, 2003).

Testing and service user involvement

A national steering group of key people was set up, and many focus groups were convened across the country comprised of staff and service users. Healthy debate in the STR role was a feature of these events. The guidance was revised eight times before the final document was produced.

Department of Health targets set out an aspiration to establish 3000 STR workers in post across England by December 2006, and the Changing Workforce Programme encouraged the implementation of STR workers, supporting the original pilot sites with programme managers and the Accelerated Development Programme (ADP). ADP is a model for rapid widespread implementation of a tested role. Although the STR role had not been tested in detail, it had been subject to intensive development through focus groups and the ADP model was amended to suit. Mental health has a strong and proud history of service user involvement in and it was essential to ensure that this was an integral part of the ADP.

There were six original pilot sites. These pilot sites carried out some early testing and development, particularly around education and training processes, using equal opportunities to integrate into the organisation.

Current position

The Support, Time and Recovery worker Accelerated Development Programme continued into its fourth wave in April 2005, extending upon the 66 existing partnership sites across England. At that time there were 630 STR workers in post, 113 in the process of recruitment procedures and a further 825 identified with funding for future conversion or recruitment from teams within the ADP (cf. the target of 3000 workers in post by December 2006).

A very successful celebration event was recently held in Newcastle upon Tyne where STR workers, managers, service users, practitioners, and carers or supporters participated in an interactive day.

There was a strong service user presence at the event with two service user-led sessions on recovery and a very useful question/discussion session.

The STR ADP collects anonymised data on each individual site's success in attracting people who have lived experience of mental health problems to become STR workers (at present this is around 20% of new workers recruited, which is very encouraging). A number of the sites have commissioned evaluations of the impact of STR workers. For instance, in Hambleton and Richmondshire, a small survey in a rural organisation revealed that 78% of service users felt that they managed their own life, and were valued more, as a result of the implementation of STR workers.

Other key outcomes from the ADP include good practice guidance for occupational health departments on supporting people with mental health problems, creative approaches to retention and recruitment, and work in developing a modular recovery package. Teams and project leads involved in the ADP report a very positive experience from working collaboratively in teams with all stake-holders involved.

Mental health pharmacy staff roles

The roles of Clinical Pharmacist, Medicines Management Technician and Dispensing Assistant already exist within the NHS. However, the extent to which the roles operate vary from organisation to organisation. For example, a few mental health trusts operate a fully integrated clinical pharmacy service, but most fall somewhere on a spectrum between little or minimal clinical pharmacy services to the full integrated service (with many Trusts having variations across their services and localities).

Although in other programmes the focus tends to be on developing new roles, such as the Support, Time and Recovery worker, and extending/amending existing roles, the pharmacy programme focuses predominantly on supporting pharmacy staff work in a way that uses their existing skills and training to deliver clinical pharmacy services.

For clinical pharmacists this is about being an essential part of the multidisciplinary team alongside other professionals, such as doctors, nurses and occupational therapists. For the patient, accessing the pharmacists is as important as seeing their doctor.

With the programme focusing on existing roles and (in most cases), existing skills a key component is the process of implementing change. Staging a national programme to implement existing roles may seem unnecessary when the issue 'appears' to be lack of resources and profile of pharmacy services; however, raising this profile and encouraging integrated business cases is a key learning objective of this programme.

For example, one mental health NHS Trust routinely considers the amount of pharmacy time required when developing new teams, but this does not appear to be common practice across the country.

Whilst the concept of integrated clinical pharmacy services goes as far back as the 1960s and 1970s, with many organisations striving to develop their services, in many cases the current situation of inequity, nationally and locally, exists.

Background to the programme

The CWP mental health pilot (2002–2003) in Northumberland supported a programme that involved all three roles across pharmacy. Up until the pilot, the pharmaceutical services in the Trust essentially concentrated on 'supply and dispensing' functions, with only limited ward input.

Following the original pilot, the CWP supported further work through its Replication Programme and it is currently running a National Spread Programme, with the key aim to support improved delivery of medicines management and clinical pharmacy through the utilisation of the pharmacy roles.

Although emphasis is placed on the development of integrated clinical pharmacy services, a key to the programme was to engage with local needs and priorities. In some Trusts the case was and is to focus on improved supply and dispensing functions of the pharmacy service. This may be done through developing the dispensing assistant role, with the eventual desired impact further along the spectrum of 'freeing up' the technician and pharmacist roles. In other Trusts the supply and dispensing service is already well developed and the focus is to increase the input of the technician and pharmacist, i.e. patient counselling, MDT attendance, side-effect monitoring or intervention monitoring services.

The key themes developed in both these subsequent programmes involve:

- MDT inclusion/integration of pharmacists
- Mental health pharmacist role to work within secondary/primary care interface – i.e. improving discharge process
- Phlebotomy role for technicians
- 'Checker' role for technicians
- Side-effect monitoring
- Supporting service user self-administration schemes
- Medicines histories
- Service user concordance
- Monitoring roles – impact for training and education
- Service users, carers and other MDT members access to medicines information
- Re-designing supply pathways – individual patient supplies, satellite services
- Developing protocols
- Utilising technology
- Drug specific needs, i.e. anti-epilepsy drugs
- Reducing waste – Patient Drugs Schemes
  These themes are developed across organisations and care areas such as:
- Partnership working across specialist mental health services, PCT and Acute Trusts.
- Mental health service users' medicines needs in prisons
- Work across teams – adult acute inpatient services and CMHT
- Forensic services
- New teams, such as Crisis Resolution Teams

Implementation process

Phase two of the Changing Workforce Programme aimed to support other organisations to deliver improved clinical pharmacy/medicines management through one or more of the pharmacy staff roles.

With other Replication Programmes in 2003–04, the test of 'replicability' was to show that other organisations could confidently adopt the roles tested originally and that they would be likely to obtain similar benefits. In the case of the mental health pharmacy roles, the focus of success would be more about supporting change and sustaining the change.

Engaging service provider organisations in the replication programme was an informal process that required mainly linking into current networks (and not based on a demographic or any formal selection process); the links were made mainly with or through a Mental Health Trust's Chief Pharmacist. Aspects of clinical pharmacy/medicines management were identified as requiring local development, matched against the pharmacy roles to deliver that change.

Momentum has been gained by supporting a systematic and larger scale national spread programme for 2004–05, with the aim of engaging a minimum of 33 service provider organisations that provide pharmaceutical services to mental health service users. With extra resources provided, 44 organisations signed up to the programme, although the reality is that more organisations are involved, as in individual sites in some cases two or three organisations might be working in partnership.

The National Spread Programme has worked in close partnership with the CWP national team and the NIMHE RDC workforce leads to ensure robust support networks. To support the sites each has access to small amounts of enabling resources for implementation of the new and changed ways of working.

The National Spread Programme commenced in the autumn of 2004 with a national launch event and four regional implementation events. The target for site implementation was November 2004 onwards through to November 2005, with a report and review to be completed by March 2006.

There are many other examples of new roles such as the Associate Mental Health Practitioner in Hampshire, the Mental Health Practitioner in Avon and Wiltshire, and the Assistant, Practitioner, Advanced Practitioner, Consultant model in Greater Manchester.

Work is under way as part of the national workforce strategy with a range of professions such as psychology and social work.

The final report of the National Steering Group will be useful further reading for those involved in mental health care and workforce design and development. It will give advice, guidance and an implementation plan for new and changing roles. In addition, joint guidance on the employment of consultant psychiatrists has been produced as part of this work and will provide a platform for innovative working in the next decade and beyond.

References

Dooher, J. and Byrt, R. (2002) *Empowerment and Participation: Power Influence and Control in Contemporary Healthcare.* Wiltshire: Quay Books.

Dooher, J. and Byrt, R. (2003) *Empowerment and the Health Service User.* Wiltshire: Quay Books.

National Steering Group (2004) *Guidance on New Ways of Working for Psychiatrists in a Multi-disciplinary and Multi-agency Context.* London: Department of Health.

CHAPTER 2

Black and minority ethnic Community Development Workers

James Dooher

The Department of Health responded to the demand for improved services for black and minority ethnic (BME) people with the production of a document entitled *Inside Outside*. The call for change was noted in the National Service Framework for Mental Health (Department of Health, 1999), which identified that services were not adequately meeting the needs of black and minority ethnic service users, and that black and minority ethnic communities lacked confidence in mental health services. The extent to which this factor has excluded individuals from within these communities is incalculable, as is the number of people affected. Nearly 6.4 million people in England belong to ethnic minority communities, which represents a significant proportion of the population and equates to about 1 person in 9.

The strategy for improving mental health services for these communities has its basis in the Government's aim to improve the lives of all service users (Department of Health, 1999, 2000; Winterton, 2005), and as part of the solution an innovative new role has been created. Community Development Workers (CDWs) will be introduced into the mental health workforce to enhance the capacity within black and minority ethnic groups in dealing with the burden of mental ill health and tackling the inequalities inherent in the services provided. The plan is to employ 500 CDWs by December 2006. The recognition that something needs to be done to address the imbalance in care provision for black and minority ethnic communities has been fuelled by the results of the inquiry into the death of David Bennett in 1998 (Norfolk, Suffolk and Cambridgeshire Strategic Health Authority, 2003) in which the Government produced a blueprint to tackle and eradicate discrimination in mental health services over the next five years.

The main elements of the blueprint are intended to provide a clear and comprehensive action plan for making sure that progress continues to accelerate and includes:

- Primary Care Trusts providing more responsive services based on the needs of the local population, helped by local demographic data.
- NHS trusts being assessed by the Healthcare Commission on their performance in challenging discrimination and providing equality of access.
- A new commitment to reduce the disproportionate rates of compulsory detention of black and ethnic minority mental health patients and preventing deaths in mental health services following physical intervention.
- New focused implementation sites where Strategic Health Authorities and organisations will work together, on a local level, to drive change in mental health services for black and ethnic minority people and develop best practice.
- Creating a workforce that has the knowledge and skills to deliver equitable care to black and minority ethnic populations with support from the Royal College of Psychiatrists and better race equality training.
- An important role for the independent sector, supported by a £2 million national community engagement scheme to help Primary Care Trusts identify black and minority ethnic voluntary and community organisations that can advise them, and, in some cases act as partners in delivering services. Primary Care Trusts will be supported by 500 new community development workers.
- NHS Direct providing a national interpretation and translation service and Primary Care Trusts providing directories of NHS and social services targeted at black and minority ethnic people.
- Working with the Home Office and police to improve local liaison and the National Patient Safety Agency (NPSA) to reform the process of independent inquiries and issue guidance on creating safer environments on acute psychiatric wards.

The role and scope of these 500 new Community Development Workers will contribute to Primary Care provision and the efforts of workers will be targeted towards seeking out the strengths and capabilities within particular communities around issues of mental health, perhaps with workers themselves being drawn from the communities to which they serve. Workers will to bridge the gap between Western models of care and the values and norms of the community they serve, enabling mental health organisations and in particular, supporting community groups and networks. It is hoped that workers will have an understanding of funding arrangements within health and social care and promote their communities ability to access that money, making better and more effective use of its distribution. A key role for workers is to facilitate community participation and ownership in mental health provision and they will be given a voice to combat health inequalities, and act as an advocate for the community itself. It is hoped that workers will challenge the significant and unacceptable inequalities in the access to mental health services that black and minority ethnic patients have, in their experience of those services, and in the outcome of those services.

As Minister of State for Health, Smith (2003) proposed that mental health services should be appropriate to the needs of those who use them and non-discriminatory. She went on to suggest that tackling ethnic inequalities within mental health services, in terms of prevention, early detection, access, diagnosis, care and quality of treatment and outcome is one of the greatest challenges facing us. As health care workers we have an obligation to meet this challenge and tackle racism at every opportunity, to identify and challenge institutional discrimination and to promote equality within mental health services. Whilst these ideas are robust in themselves, the process of delivery raises some interesting questions. For example, the notion of equity implies that the basis of a non-discriminatory service should be 'colour blind' in that it provides the same provision to all the population, yet discrimination is inevitable when certain sections of society, based on ethnicity or colour for example, receive their own discrete service. Such organisational behaviour could be seen to contradict the basic value of equity that is the cornerstone of the NHS. It may also be seen as necessary positive discrimination designed to redress the imbalance born of years of institutional racism.

The Government as a whole is committed to public services tailored to individuals' needs and circumstances and to greater choice for, and empowerment of, service users and those seeking help (Johnson, 2004).

She suggests that it is important for all those who manage and work in the NHS to be on their guard to identify and root out personal racism and discriminatory policies and practices within the organisation. These policies and procedures may unwittingly and unfairly discriminate against certain individuals or communities, and the Department of Health has a role to play in ensuring that the whole population is treated with respect and can access effective and appropriate health and care services.

The segregation debate is currently being played out within education circles, where it has been observed that good results are being attained in the USA by schools who teach black boys separately. A significant argument against the replication of separate education for black boys is that the UK is less racially segregated and that importing the US model would create divisions where they do not presently exist (Sale, 2005). In addition, and with regard to mental health provision, there is often the assumption that everyone from a particular culture has the same needs, and this leads to a blanket policy approach that may well be culturally specific, but which lacks the individual flexibility required to meet personal preferences. This argument would be supported by the Director of the Department of Health's Mental Health Black and Minority Ethnic Programme, Kamlesh Patel, who suggests that it is not possible to adequately address improvements in access, experience and outcomes for BME mental health patients without taking a mainstream approach (Patel, 2005). The development of flexibility in services will no doubt be perceived by some as inequality, and this rather blunt term does not overtly encompass the possibility for different services which are flexible. This said, the call for the identification of inequality has led the Department of Health to develop a comprehensive programme of work to tackle those inequalities. An important part of the strategy is the development of a programme called Delivering Race Equality in Mental Health Care – an Action Plan for Reform Inside and Outside Services. 'DRE', as it is known, was published on 11 January 2005, along with the Government's response to the independent inquiry into the death of David Bennett.

The BME Mental Health Programme is an integral part of the Department's wider programme for race equality in the NHS. The Programme Board brings together many of the key individuals and organisations responsible for making change happen for BME users of mental health care.

This programme is the largest of the current National Institute for Mental Health in England (NIMHE) programmes, and reflects the priority of BME issues within mental health services and outside of those services.

This programme aims to enhance the quality of life and challenge exclusion through improved mental health services and health outcomes. It has identified a need for the development of culturally competent services and outlined a need for more specific education and training, together with support for staff to enable the confident delivery of services. The programme hopes to develop existing links within black and minority communities and to build capacity where it is not currently available, making best use of the voluntary sector to promote good mental health and improve the range of options for those suffering from mental ill health.

The emergence of mental ill health is seen to emanate from the often neglected and marginalised needs of people from ethnic minorities. The myth prevails that such communities 'look after their own', but this is not the case and some ethnic minorities are over-represented in the acute psychiatric system.

Community Development Workers are central to the roll-out of these ideas, and will be at the forefront of promoting good mental health. These new appointments will take on a variety of roles, dictated as far as possible by the particular and identified needs of the communities from which they are drawn. In addition to promoting health they will be charged with the responsibility for developing channels of communication, promoting diversity and enhancing co-terminosity with statutory services. To do this, however, there are many barriers to overcome, which may include:

- A lack of knowledge among ethnic minority communities about the availability of support.
- A lack of appropriate services.
- Poor-quality services.
- Insufficient choice of services.
- Workers who cannot communicate effectively.

- Workers without the experience and skills needed to work with diverse communities.
- Direct and institutional discrimination.

Clearly the worker who attempts to induce such changes would struggle if undertaking this task without explicit organisational support that has designed and which provides services based on what people want; implements policy and monitoring frameworks to promote diversity; actively involves service users in planning and delivering services; and has robust monitoring systems.

These factors become acutely obvious when we consider that BME Community Development Workers will work with asylum seekers. This group present a range of particular issues which will test the skills and abilities of workers, in that asylum seekers will present with needs resulting from war, human rights abuses and persecution on grounds of politics, religion, gender or ethnicity. They may have issues of loss, including cultural identity, family, friends and previous profession or work identity. Interpreting language and dialect may impact upon the person's ability to recount their story effectively, and their very residence in the UK will have affected their aspirations for the future.

According to Bracken (2002), the practical difficulties facing asylum seekers when they arrive in this country can be more harmful to their mental health than the pain and suffering that they fled, fuelled by the uncertainty of their future, the psychological and practical adjustment necessary to adapt to the UK lifestyle and the hardship caused by financial poverty. Asylum seekers may be the subject of racism as it has been noted that Islamic communities and other vulnerable groups have been the subject of increased racism following the terrorist attacks on the USA of 11 September 2001 and the London bombings of 7 July 2005. The European Monitoring Centre on Racism and Xenophobia (EUMC) noted that a greater sense of fear among the general population has exacerbated already existing prejudices and fuelled acts of harassment and aggression across Europe (EUMC, 2002; Bunting, 2005).

Tribe (2002) suggests that mental health of asylum seekers is adversely affected by traumatic life events, multiple change, stereotyping by the host community and unknown cultural traditions. Black and minority ethnic CDWs will need a significant range of skills to address some of these issues and engage with a person who may be extremely anxious about the security of personal information and reluctant to engage in a trusting relationship.

The range of skills needed and the scope of practice expected of black and minority ethnic CDWs is highlighted by reports that less than a quarter of people with learning difficulties from ethnic minority groups are known to services (Ahmed, 2005). In particular, a report by the Valuing People Support Team found this group to be marginalised not only due to their learning disability, but also because of their ethnicity; a paucity of specific provision and a lack of planning have left people struggling without support.

Over the years, concerns have been raised about inaccessible and inappropriate services. Changes in the demographic profile of the ethnic minority population and this report by the Valuing People Support Team criticised learning disability partnership boards for 'a lack of strategic leadership and action' over ethnic minority issues, with only 10% reporting that all their strategies routinely considered people from ethnic minority groups. The rationales for the lack of planning and poor record-keeping, and the consequent inadequate support, have been blamed on a variety of factors. Partnership boards identified obstacles to improving services, including limited resources, lack of staff time, a lack of organisational commitment and difficulties in engaging ethnic minority groups. The report said:

> Poor information, small numbers of people from minority ethnic communities in the local area and a lack of engagement with local minority ethnic communities seemed to be given as reasons [by partnership boards] for not pursuing strategic action, rather than as factors stimulating such action.

There is an expectation that black and minority ethnic CDWs will rectify this situation. Working in conjunction with other primary care staff they will be expected to bridge the gaps left by policy planners. The outcome of this strategy is an expectation that by 2010 that we will see a service characterised by a reduction in the disproportionate rates of admission and compulsory detention of black and minority ethnic patients, a more balanced range of effective therapies, increased patient satisfaction, and less fear of services among black and minority ethnic communities (Winterton, 2005).

References

Ahmed, M. (2005). Ethnic minorities unknown to services. *Community Care*, 24 August.

Bracken, P. (2002) *Annual Meeting: Psychiatry Today*. 24–27 June, Cardiff International Arena, Cardiff.

Bunting, M. (2005) Throwing mud at Muslims. *The Guardian*, 22 August.

Department of Health (1999) *A National Service Framework for Mental Health*. London: HMSO.

Department of Health (2000) *The NHS Plan. A Plan for Investment, A Plan for Reform*. London: HMSO.

Department of Health (2004) *Community Development Workers for Black and Minority Ethnic Communities Interim Guidance*. London: Department of Health Publications.

Department of Health (2003) *Delivering Race Equality: A Framework for Action.* Mental Health Services Consultation Document. London: Department of Health Publications.

EUMC (2002) *The European Monitoring Centre on Racism and Xenophobia Newsletter.* Issue 13.

Johnson, M. (2004) Speech by Melanie Johnson MP, 27 October 2004: Mary Seacole Awards. http://www.dh.gov.uk/NewsHome/Speeches/Speeches-List/SpeechesArticle/fs/en? CONTENT_ID=4093015&chk=yfMVI8.

Norfolk, Suffolk and Cambridgeshire Strategic Health Authority (2003) *Independent Inquiry into the Death of David Bennett.* Cambridge: Norfolk, Suffolk and Cambridgeshire Strategic Health Authority.

Patel, K. (2005) In: Government response to David Bennett inquiry. New blueprint to tackle and eradicate discrimination in mental health services over the next five years. *Department of Health Press Release*, No. 2005/0008.

Population Trends (2005) *Population Trends 120.* Palgrave Macmillan and http://www.statistics.gov.uk/.

Sale, A.U. (2005) We don't want no separation. *Community Care*, 1–7 September, pp. 34–35.

Smith, J. (2003) *Inside Outside: Improving Mental Health Services for Black and Minority Ethnic Communities in England.* London: Department of Health

Tribe, R. (2002) The mental health of refugees and asylum seekers. *Advances in Psychiatric Treatment*, **8**, 240–248.

Winterton, R. (2005) In: Government response to David Bennett inquiry. New blueprint to tackle and eradicate discrimination in mental health services over the next five years. *Department of Health Press Release*, No. 2005/0008.

CHAPTER 3

The link nurse

An approach to seamless discharge from a mental health unit

Claire Armitage, Sam Mackintosh and Lynn Ward

After listening to service users' frustrations on issues surrounding re-integration into the community, a trust in Leicester City created a link nurse role to help. Now, with the scheme having been identified as an area of good practice, we evaluate the success of this role.

Staff on Fosse Ward, an acute mental health inpatient unit in Leicester, recognised that patients' discharges can be delayed due to factors such as limited family and social support networks and a delay in input from community mental health teams. Delayed discharges lead to an unnecessary pressure on beds, and prolonged admission can adversely affect the confidence of patients re-engaging with the community. In 2000, the team on Fosse Ward piloted an approach to alleviating this problem by developing the role of link nurse to act as a bridge between hospital and re-integration into the community. The link nurse offers time-limited input to support patients throughout the discharge process and during the difficult first weeks at home. The input ranges from mental health monitoring, to offering practical support with issues such as shopping and debt management, to facilitating re-integration with community networks. The approach has been evaluated and was found to be valued by service users and their families, and by colleagues in inpatient and community settings.

Background

Fosse Ward, part of Leicestershire Partnership NHS Trust's adult mental health services, is a 21 bedded acute admission ward. It serves an urban area of Leicester City which has high rates of deprivation and unemployment.

A high percentage of the ward's patients present with challenging behaviours and around 50% of the male patients have a dual diagnosis of mental health problems and substance misuse (Connell, 2001). A recent local study highlighted the challenges faced by wards in Leicester's city catchment areas (Sainsbury Centre for Mental Health, 2003). These are characterised by inpatient bed occupancy levels well in excess of 100% (achieved by the process of 'hot-bedding', in which the bed of a person who is on leave is occupied by another person during the period of leave, resulting in occupancy levels which appear to exceed bed capacity) and overstretched community teams.

Leave

Leave periods are crucial in the lead-up to discharge and re-integration into the community. Delays in being able to facilitate leave cause delays in discharge, which runs counter to current policies encouraging the targeting of resources to secure earlier discharges from hospital. The Department of Health (2002) identifies that a lack of overall service system coordination and coherence contributes to the existing pressures on inpatient wards, such as poor throughput and delayed discharge.

Planned leave in the run-up to discharge and immediately post-discharge can be particularly anxiety-provoking for service users and, where applicable, their families. Staff were concerned that episodes of leave would often have to be delayed until weekends, when family would be available to support, monitor and give their perception of the success of the leave. For the significant proportion of service users in the locality who do not have family, particular caution had to be exercised with leaves.

The team and service users looked at the perceived gaps in the process leading to discharge and identified a range of needs that were not being effectively addressed, including:

- Anxieties around returning to the environment in which the service user had recently become distressed.
- Overwhelming worries about how to start to address practical problems such as bills, rent, shopping and outstanding debts.
- Isolation and lack of social support systems either as a result of, or as a precursor to, the period of illness.
- General lack of self-confidence and self-esteem that inhibited service users from developing social, leisure or employment opportunities following the period of illness.

Nursing staff were acutely aware of these gaps in service and delays in discharge, but felt unable to address them due to existing work pressures. They were nevertheless keen to consider how their service could maximise connections to community services and, with this aim in mind, the ward manager and an experienced staff nurse introduced the role of link nurse in 2000. The role was funded within the ward's existing nursing budget.

The link nurse role

The link nurse is an established role in many services, such as infection control, tissue viability and diabetes (see, for example, Tinley, 2000; Teare *et al.*, 2001; and Lowe and Davies, 2001). Some link nurses are mental health nurses who provide advice and support to staff working within other specialties, including residential homes and acute general hospitals (Crouch, 1997).

The role of the nurses who work to bridge the gap between hospital and community services within acute mental health is less well documented. Cleary *et al.* (2003) identified a need for the further development of strategies to improve the continuity of services between hospital and community mental health settings in Australia. Bowles (2002) expressed concern that acute wards were not set up to provide high levels of engagement, with staff and patients ending up with low expectations that contribute to 'a pact of apathy'. Rippon and Rae (2002) suggested that effective engagement with service users to encourage positive relationships was a key role for nurses in the acute environment, and that opportunities to develop specific roles for nurses in these settings should be explored.

The link nurse initiative on Fosse Ward focuses on clients with severe mental illness who would benefit from confidence building and further assessment prior to leave or discharge from hospital. The role, which was piloted for a 12 month period, was set up to provide a service to cover gaps patients often experience during the transition from hospital to home.

The aims of the role are to:

■ Facilitate earlier discharge from hospital for severely mentally ill patients who would benefit from inpatient support on re-engaging in the community.
■ Monitor patients during the high-risk post-discharge period.
■ Support clients who are ready to have a trial period of leave from hospital but have limited family and social support.
■ Develop and maintain links with community support and resources.

- Work closely with the community mental health team and day unit to facilitate a seamless discharge process.
- Work closely with patients, carers, families and the multidisciplinary team in developing a pre- and post-discharge plan of care.

The overarching goal is to work with service users for a limited period pre- and post discharge. Firm boundaries need to be maintained to ensure the caseload is limited to around 10–12 service users to enable them to get the necessary focused support from the link nurse; the agreed maximum caseload is reviewed in frequent supervision sessions offered by the deputy clinical team leader.

Clearly defined referral criteria were developed by the multidisciplinary team. Clients with a primary diagnosis of alcohol or substance misuse were excluded, as were patients with brain damage or other organic disorders, learning difficulties and situations involving domestic violence. The team also identified the need to exercise caution in accepting clients with assessed dependency issues, and service users with a diagnosis of borderline personality disorder were excluded. This approach was evaluated as the role developed, and service users with borderline personality disorders and those with alcohol problems have subsequently been incorporated into the scheme, with some early successful outcomes.

The service focuses largely on individuals with mental health problems characterised by features of depression and anxiety. There is also a recognised need for service users who may not require an enhanced Care Programme Approach (CPA) but who need short-term, proactive support to assist them in returning to and re-engaging with community life. The Care Programme Approach is the process through which individuals' needs are assessed and care delivered depending on the severity and complexity of their needs. Support and interventions can be from either a single professional discipline (standard CPA) or a number of professional disciplines (enhanced CPA) to enable an individual to function in the community.

Assertive outreach services and intensive community support workers employed by the city social care and health directorate provide a complementary service for those with enduring mental health problems and who are identified as requiring enhanced CPA input.

Impact of the link nurse role

The impact of this role will be felt primarily by the service user. However, the perceptions of clinical colleagues working within the multidisciplinary team will dictate the future developments and maintenance of this type of worker. Some comments about the impact of the role suggest a positive perception from colleagues:

> The link nurse provides more flexibility and responsiveness in care, which fills a gap with community services and helps reduce dependency on the hospital. (*Consultant Psychiatrist*)

> I believe the link nurse role is a central pillar in the work of Fosse Ward... (*Social worker who has liaised closely with the link nurse over recent months to facilitate successful reintegration into the community*)

> She's an experienced nurse with a balanced range of therapeutic skills, and she's very good at building rapport with patients and networking with other agencies... (*Ward staff nurse*)

Since the role was introduced, the link nurse appears to have become a much-valued member of the core team.

At the end of the first year, she worked closely with the service users and the trust's clinical audit department to evaluate the role. She found that 93% of ex-patients who had accessed her support had an understanding of her role and felt that her input had helped them.

'She took me out into the world and I felt like a normal, even likeable, person', said one ex-patient. 'I would probably still be lying in bed on Fosse Ward now, instead of which, having enrolled on a course with her help, I am employed in teaching literacy to adults, and it's the most rewarding job I've ever done.'

Another stated that 'the use of experienced and qualified personnel meant that it was an integral part of care rather than an appendage of hospital treatment. Early contact with the link nurse meant a confidence in the procedure'.

The link nurse plans to build on this small, qualitative study by analysing quantitative outcome data such as comparisons of readmission and recovery rates.

The role has also been discussed with staff in other areas of the service who are keen to look at how they can develop a similar approach to the discharge process.

'The link worker scheme is an excellent example of clinical governance in action', the trust's service director believes. 'The initiative came about as a result of staff listening to the frustrations expressed by service users and looking at how they could use their existing resources to make changes that could help, and I think the audit of the service demonstrates how successful the team has been.'

The City Adult Mental Health Service has now identified the scheme as an area of good practice that should be rolled out across all inpatient wards, and the service is currently exploring how this could be achieved. Due to the large number of referrals to the link nurse service, a graduate worker will be working alongside her to help cope with the high demand. The success of the link nurse role has also inspired the development of six similar link worker roles in one of the trust's crisis resolution teams.

The decrease in the number of institutional beds available continues to place additional pressure on mental health professionals to expand their professional boundaries and expertise (Jones and Ward, 1997). The link nurse's role, in common with some of the other new ways of working that the organisation has embraced (such as assertive outreach and crisis resolution), aims to assist clients to engage, or remain engaged, with community life and draw on the resources available to them. Although it is acknowledged that individuals may have difficulty in accessing mainstream social activities, education and employment, this approach can serve to minimise the potential for stigmatisation and affirmation of the sick role (Stickley, 2005). By helping people to establish some kind of meaningful position in society, such as volunteer, student or neighbour, the service is assisting clients to develop a social role through which they can gain a sense of self-esteem, responsibility and reward.

The role in practice

The link nurse works in partnership with the rest of the multidisciplinary team on the ward. She attends ward rounds, meets regularly with key workers and documents her care programmes in the integrated multidisciplinary records. She takes an active role in mental state assessment, risk assessment and care planning, feeding back areas of need that may be less apparent or more difficult to assess within the ward environment. The link nurse has also worked hard to develop contacts with colleagues across health and social care and the voluntary sector.

In practice, the work tends to focus on assistance with practical problems, anxiety management techniques and liaison with other agencies, particularly community teams, day units and community resources. Assisting patients to develop employment, education, voluntary and leisure links is also a significant focus of the role.

The link nurse and other colleagues have responded to service users' perceived needs for evening support by setting up the Tomonari Group (the name is derived from the Japanese word for developing friendships). The group started in May 2003 and has been running successfully since this date. It is registered as a voluntary organisation and has been awarded funding from the Community Chest Fund (a government charitable small grant programme aiming to regenerate deprived areas of the city). The link nurse has also applied successfully to the City Council Small Grants Scheme

A day in the life of a link nurse

The morning
No two days are the same for me, but they all begin at 8 am; routinely the first hour or so is usually spent on the ward or in the office, where I catch up with paperwork, make referrals, spend time either receiving or giving clinical supervision and receive a handover from ward and day unit staff about any of my patients. This is also a time when I liaise with other agencies, both voluntary and statutory, and the relatives and carers involved in the patient's care as well as throughout the rest of my day. After this first hour anything can happen.

Today, I left the ward at 10 a.m. I am currently seeing a woman who has been discharged from the ward for a couple of weeks. I collected her from her home and accompanied her to a community centre where she attends a support group for women. She has had problems engaging in such groups in the past due to anxiety and lack of confidence. Her problems with low mood and associated drinking are due to feelings of isolation and loneliness. I have arranged with the community staff to accompany her and stay with her for the duration of the group.

We spent the morning with a group of women from her housing estate. She chatted and learned how to knit. She was able to befriend another woman in the group and arranged to meet for coffee. She also put her name down for a planned trip to a local soap factory. Afterwards, I gave her a lift home and returned to the ward.

It remains important to document nursing input and the patient's mental state. Copies of my notes are sent to the day unit staff and the consultant involved in her care. A copy is also kept on the ward. This enables staff to identify what input she has had and her recent mental state if the patient rings the ward for support.

One-to-one session
Later on, I saw another recently discharged patient for a one-to-one session in the outpatient department. We have agreed to meet for eight sessions post-discharge. He is going through a marital separation and consequently has some interpersonal issues we have been exploring. I am able to utilise my psychodynamic therapy training during this work; generally, I access supervision as required by the specialised psychotherapy services and cognitive behavioural psychotherapy service.

Last patient of the day
My last intervention of the day is to take an inpatient home for a period of overnight leave. This also involves practical help with transport, as he lacks

any support network. We explored any anxieties he may have held about the leave period and tried to identify ways to resolve them. We discussed coping strategies and contingencies should he require support during the leave period. I usually spend a period of time at home with such patients. This gives an opportunity for them to feel more relaxed and confident and to adjust to their environment, and gives me time to check on more mundane matters such as an adequate food supply, electricity, gas and water.

The last hour of my day tends to be similar to the first – writing up notes and liaising with staff and other agencies.

My job is hugely enjoyable, which I generally attribute to the diversity involved.

I take an eclectic approach, drawing on a number of different working styles. I use general mental health assessments alongside psychodynamic and cognitive behavioural approaches and employ problem-solving strategies while helping out with practical issues. I think the job is successful because of this flexible approach. The ability to adapt to what is often a challenging patient group has led to increased patient satisfaction, earlier discharges and a reduction in readmission rates. The rewards, however, are not just related to the knowledge of improved clinical performance. The integral role I play in empowering patients during their move from the ward environment into the community has, on a personal level, been the biggest reward.

Samantha Mackintosh, Link Nurse

for extra funding, all of which will subsidise trips and evenings out for the group.

Case study

K is a 60-year-old recently retired factory worker. She is a widow and lives alone in what was previously the family home. Her husband, to whom she had been very happily married, had died suddenly from a heart attack seven years ago. She has four grown-up daughters, who all live close by, and eight grandchildren. The family is close and K described them as very supportive.

K had an uneventful upbringing and schooling, although her mother suffered with depression. This had required three admissions, one following a serious suicide attempt. Despite this K described her childhood as very happy. K had been employed in the same company, as a machinist, for the last 30 years of her working life. K had no ongoing significant medical problems.

K had been seen in outpatients by the consultant psychiatrist for a six-month period leading up to this admission. Her difficulties began shortly after her retirement. She had been treated with anti-depressant medication. She had not had any previous admissions to a mental health unit.

K was admitted to the ward feeling very anxious and low in mood. These feelings had been significantly worse for the two weeks leading up to admission.

She was very nervous and agitated in her presentation. She was periodically tearful and visibly trembling. Her thinking was very negative, expressing feelings of hopelessness and ideas that she was useless. She had morbid thoughts with some fears about dying. This featured daily in her thinking and had a consequential effect on her activity levels. She started to avoid any activities that she feared might result in failure or a fatal accident. She was also overwhelmed by guilt, feeling that she had no reason to be so unwell. She had begun to have some suicidal thoughts. K had struggled with a lack of motivation to carry out her normal daily activities and had begun to neglect her self-care. Her sleep was poor, with early morning waking, and her appetite had significantly reduced with some weight loss. There appeared to be some issues of unresolved grief over the loss of her husband some years earlier.

K was admitted to the ward for just over a month. She was referred for Link Nurse input within the first week, and involvement continued for a five-month period after discharge. The initial reasons for referral were to assist and support with a programme of leave from the ward, and to begin developing access to resources within the community for the post-discharge period.

Initially input was three times weekly, starting with some short periods of escorted home leave. This gradually developed into a structured and supported package of care that was formulated collaboratively with other team members, K's carers and K herself.

K was taught distraction and relaxation techniques and how to monitor her activities and thoughts using a diary. There was a consistent emphasis on education, with the link nurse helping K to have an understanding of her illness and to find ways to manage her symptoms. She was assisted in re-establishing attendance at a local support group, which she had disengaged from several weeks prior to admission. She was also referred by the Link Nurse to attend a fortnightly evening support group. She soon began developing much-needed links and support networks within her local community. The Link Nurse also referred her to a community education project. With practical support and encouragement she began attending two classes a week.

In conjunction with this support and mental health monitoring, more formalised cognitive behavioural work was also undertaken in order to help manage K's low self-esteem and the effect of her negative thinking on her mood. The Link Nurse had supervision from a clinician from the Cognitive Behavioural Therapy team. She worked with K, who kept a diary of her panic symptoms and negative thoughts. She slowly learnt to identify, challenge, and rationalise these. Some exposure work with K was also carried out in the various places that she had previously felt compelled to avoid. K also agreed to an assessment with a bereavement counselling service, though unfortunately she did not find this helpful.

K's progress was slow. However, gradually her anxiety levels became less intense and more episodic. Her confidence and motivation improved. Her panic became more manageable and less intrusive in her increasingly active social life. Her social functioning significantly improved as she established social network independent of her family. K was also encouraged to consider voluntary work. She was supported by the Link Nurse in applying, and at interview, for a catering post in a charitable organisation. With continuing psycho-education, her insight and understanding of her illness developed, and she was able to identify symptoms without viewing them as a fault.

As there seemed to be a clear need for long-term monitoring and support, after discussion with K's Consultant Psychiatrist she was referred to the Community Mental Health Team. The Link Nurse and allocated Community Mental Health Nurse carried out joint visits initially, until a rapport was established and a smooth transition of care had been achieved.

At the point of discharge by the Link Nurse, K was being seen on a regular basis in the Outpatient Department by her consultant, and at home by a Community Mental Health Nurse. She was engaged with both a daytime and evening support group. She was also attending classes at a community educational centre once a week and had settled in to her voluntary work.

Some key learning points for organisations considering the implementation of this type of role suggest that a lack of overall service coordination and coherence in discharge policies negatively contributes to the pressures on inpatient wards. This may manifest itself in reduced throughput and delayed discharge, for example.

The discharge of service users can be delayed due to a number of factors which form the basis of an important paradox. Service users who are admitted to hospital to improve their mental health find that following a prolonged admission, their ability to re-engage with the community is adversely affected. The approach can serve to minimise the potential for stigmatisation and affirmation of the sick role, and reduce the need for further hospital admissions The link nurse needs to work in close partnership with the rest of the multidisciplinary team, playing an active role in mental state assessment, risk assessment and care planning and feeding back areas of need that may be less apparent, or more difficult to assess, within the ward environment.

The overarching aim of the link nurse role is to work with service users for a limited period pre- and post-discharge, to assist them to re-engage with community life and draw on the resources available to them. However, the link nurse's caseload should be capped to approximately 10–12 service users, and clearly defined referral criteria may leave some service users unable to access the service. An essential element of the role is the development of close links with colleagues across health and social care and the voluntary sector, as well as employment, educational and leisure providers.

Acknowledgements

This chapter has been adapted from a paper that appeared in *Mental Health Practice*:

Armitage, C., Mackintosh, S. and Ward, L. (2004) The link nurse: an approach to seamless discharge from a mental health unit. *Mental Health Practice*, **8**(2), 20–23.

References

Bowles, N. (2002) A solution-focused approach to engagement in acute psychiatry. *Nursing Times*, **98**(48), 26–27.

Cleary, M., Horsfall, J. and Hunt, G. E. (2003) Consumer feedback on nursing care and discharge planning. *Journal of Advanced Nursing*, **42**(3), 269–277.

Connell, M. (2001) *Audit to Establish the Extent of Alcohol and Drug Abuse by Patients during Admission on an Adult General Psychiatric Ward*. Unpublished audit project.

Crouch, J. (1997) The missing link... community psychiatric nurses... a service for people aged over 65 living in nursing or residential homes. *Nursing Times*, **93**(8), 57.

Department of Health (2002) *Adult Acute In-patient Care Provision, Mental Health Policy Implementation Guide*. London: Department of Health.

Jones, M. and Ward, M. (1997) Community-led services for mental health care: a study. *Nursing Standard*, **11**(41), 35–39.

Lowe, C. M. and Davies, M. J. (2001) A ward-based link nurse scheme to improve diabetes in-patient care. *Journal of Diabetes Care*, **5**(5), 147–150.

Rippon, S. and Rae, M. (2002) Reshaping adult acute in-patient services. *Mental Health Practice*, **5**(9), 4–5.

Sainsbury Centre for Mental Health (2003) *Leicestershire Partnership NHS Trust Future Bed Requirements Report*. Unpublished.

Stickley, T. (2005) Developing a social inclusion strategy for people with ongoing mental health problems. *Mental Health Practice*, **8**(6), 12–15.

Teare, E. L., Peacock, A. J., Dakin, H., Bates, L. and Grant-Casey, J. (2001) Build your own infection control link nurse. *Journal of Hospital Infection*, **48**(4), 312–319.

Tinley, P. (2000) The link nurse system in relation to the speciality of tissue viability. *British Journal of Nursing*, **6**(19), 59–62.

CHAPTER 4

The role and function of contemporary mental health education

Sara Owen and Kath Ferguson

Introduction

This chapter explores some of the changes which have taken place recently in mental health care and policy, and considers how educationalists can best prepare a workforce which is ready to meet the challenges of providing present and future mental health services. The focus of this chapter is on the role of Higher Education Institutions, who are responsible for the professional pre- and post-qualification education of psychiatrists, occupational therapists, social workers, clinical psychologists and mental health nurses. Increasingly, due to recent problems of recruitment to the traditional mental health professions, Higher Education Institutions are also involved in the training of new types of mental health workers, such as graduate primary care mental health workers (Department of Health, 2003a) and associate mental health practitioners (Kingdon, 2002).

Our interest in this field has been influenced by working in mental health as lecturers, practitioners and researchers. We have also completed a number of research projects on behalf of the Mental Health Care Group Workforce Team, including studies about recruitment to mental health professions (Owen *et al.*, 2004), the clinical activity of mental health lecturers (Ferguson *et al.*, 2003a), and a review of a mapping exercise into education and training of mental health staff (Ferguson *et al.*, 2003b). These experiences have reinforced our belief that mental health education and training should be rooted in practice and informed by contemporary research. This is the key to preparing a mental health workforce that we can be proud of, who will be capable of providing the highest standard of care to service users and their carers in continually evolving services.

The first part of the chapter provides the context to the role and function of contemporary mental health education. This includes a brief overview of policy developments, the current national mental health workforce programme, and the concerns that have been raised about the quality and appropriateness of mental health education and training currently being provided in Higher Education Institutions. In the second part we suggest a range of strategies that can be adopted by Higher Education Institutions to enable lecturers to develop and update the requisite knowledge, skills and attitudes they will require to educate the current and future generation of mental health workers. These strategies are presented within a tripartite model of practice, research and education.

Context

Mental health care is in the midst of a period of great change, which has huge implications for the education and training of mental health staff. Major and far-reaching reforms have been unveiled to modernise health and social care in the form of the *NHS Plan* (Department of Health, 2000) and *Modernising Social Services* (Department of Health, 1998a). After being a poor relation in health care for many years, mental health care currently represents one of the top clinical priorities in the National Health Service. A radical programme of reform has been outlined in *Modernising Mental Health Services* (Department of Health, 1998b) and the *National Service Framework for Mental Health* (Department of Health, 1999a), which set standards for mental health care across the spectrum of provision. The Care Programme Approach has been introduced as a way of better supporting vulnerable individuals (Department of Health, 1999b), risk assessment tools have been developed and a new Mental Health Act is on the horizon. The past few decades have also witnessed a shift in the provision of mental health services from the hospital setting to a range of diverse services in the community, and an increasing emphasis on user-centred care and evidence-based practice. Much of mental health provision is moving into partnership trusts and joint health and social care services are being established. There is also a growing emphasis on collaborative working and management systems.

The importance of modernising education and training to ensure that the workforce is properly equipped to deliver the new mental health agenda is acknowledged as part of the process of reform. The *Pulling Together* report highlights the need to ensure that the skills, knowledge and attitudes of both existing and future mental health staff are appropriate to the demands of this changed environment, and that they are prepared to function in continuing evolving services (Sainsbury Centre for Mental Health, 1997). Staff are increasingly required to work across both statutory and non-statutory agencies, in interdisciplinary teams, to liaise with primary care staff, to use research to inform their work and to keep abreast with policy developments.

A developing programme of work on workforce issues is currently being undertaken by a variety of key stakeholders including the Changing Workforce Programme and the Department of Health, coordinated through the National Institute of Mental Health (England) National Workforce Programme on behalf of the Mental Health Care Group Workforce Team. A number of key documents have also been published that will impact on the future education and training of mental health staff; notably, the *Ten Essential Shared Capabilities* (NIMHE, 2004) and the *National Continuous Quality Improvement Tool for Mental Health Education* (Northern Centre for Mental Health 2003). Most recently, the *National Mental Health Workforce Strategy* was published in 2004 (NIMHE/MHCGWT, 2004). This document aims to provide some coherence to the complex and dynamic issues facing all staff involved in workforce planning, design and development. One of the key priorities of this strategy is to develop the workforce through revised education and training at both pre- and post-qualification levels, and to improve the quality standard setting and monitoring of Higher Education Institution programmes.

Recent reports suggest, however, that many existing and newly qualified staff are currently inadequately prepared for present-day services. Particular shortfalls have been identified in training for care of the severely mentally ill (Holmshaw *et al.*, 1999), for roles in primary care (Department of Health, 2001a), for acute care (Department of Health, 1999c), and for personality disorder (NIMHE, 2003) amongst others. Current courses are often inappropriate and not relevant to support the implementation of the *National Service Framework* (Department of Health, 2001b; Brooker *et al.*, 2002), and there is evidence of poor relationships between Trusts and Higher Education Institutions (Department of Health, 1999d).

Crucially, concerns have been expressed about the competency of mental health lecturers to deliver these radical new approaches, and a need identified for them to update their own skills and knowledge in line with the competencies expected of the workforce (Sainsbury Centre for Mental Health, 1997). Practice staff consider that lecturers lack robust recent clinical experience, are not regarded as clinically credible, have little experience in the skills and interventions they are required to teach, are out of touch with developments in service delivery, and are clearly perceived to have training needs of their own (Brooker *et al.*, 2002; Department of Health, 2001b; Lindley and Lemmer, 2001; Department of Health, 1999c).

Strategies for developing mental health education

A recent report on the ideal learning environment that should exist in Higher Education Institutions (Department of Health, 2002) provides a useful framework for thinking about strategies for developing mental health education. The report argues that in addition to improving the research base of learning environments by investment in the development of research capability, lecturers also need to develop their clinical and teaching skills. Crucially, the report suggests that not all lecturers need to develop in each of these areas, but a vibrant learning environment would see some staff developing in each domain.

We believe that this tripartite model of research, education and practice provides an excellent framework for teams of lecturers wanting to develop a coherent and comprehensive approach to the delivery of mental health education. Arguably these three areas are mutually enhancing and complementary, although we recognise that whilst the role of mental health lecturers encompasses all three to a degree, it is unrealistic for individual lecturers to be an expert in each. Ideally, mechanisms need to be established in Schools or Departments to provide opportunities for lecturers to focus on and develop a particular expertise in clinical practice, teaching or research. Staff should be encouraged to build on their strengths and may choose to prioritise different aspects of their role at varying stages of their career. Importantly, each area of work needs to be equally valued within Higher Education Institutions.

We will now suggest a range of strategies that lecturers specialising in each of the three areas could use to keep up to date with developments in mental health, thus enabling them to deliver education and training which is contemporary and relevant to evolving services. These will be presented under the headings of education, practice and research.

Education

Lecturers who are responsible for developing new mental health curricula and for updating existing ones at pre- and post-qualification levels can often feel overwhelmed by the volume of guidance documents that have been recently published. Courses not only have to meet the specific requirements of professional bodies such as the Nursing and Midwifery Council and the British Psychological Society, but they also need to incorporate the mental health requirements specified in a number of key documents. The purpose of this section is to highlight the documents that lecturers need to become familiar with in order to ensure that curricula are relevant to the current NHS and Social Care modernisation agenda.

To begin, it is important to be familiar with the content of the following four guidance documents: the *Ten Essential Shared Capabilities* (NIMHE, 2004), the *Capable Practitioner Framework* (Sainsbury Centre for Mental Health, 2001), the *Knowledge and Skills Framework* (Department of Health, 2003b), and the *Mental Health National Occupational Standards* (http://www.skillsforhealth.org.uk/). It is also important to recognise three things about them. Firstly, although complementary, all four frameworks were developed separately. This is partly due to the way they were commissioned and partly historical. Secondly, they do not all cover the same issues. Thirdly, whilst the Ten Essential Shared Capabilities, the Capable Practitioner Framework, and the Mental Health National Occupational Standards have all been produced specifically for mental health services, the Knowledge and Skills Framework has a National Health Service focus. The Knowledge and Skills Framework is not mental health specific and is designed to help provide the basis for an added dimension; for example, pay progression as part of the National Health Service Agenda for Change initiative using a skills escalator approach. A brief summary of each of these documents will now be given.

The Ten Essential Shared Capabilities document sets out the shared capabilities that all staff working in mental health services should achieve as part of their education and training. Whilst elements of the Ten Essential Shared Capabilities can be found amongst a variety of capability and competency frameworks, it is the one framework that provides a single, concise list of essential capabilities being asked for by staff and service users. The ten essential capabilities are:

- Working in partnership
- Respecting diversity
- Practising ethically
- Challenging inequality
- Promoting recovery
- Identifying people's needs and strengths
- Providing service user-centred care
- Making a difference
- Promoting safety and positive risk taking
- Personal development and learning

The intention of this document is to make explicit what should be included as core in the curricula of all pre- and post-qualification training for professional and non-professionally affiliated staff as well as being embedded in induction and continuing professional/practitioner development. The document also offers practical examples of each of the capabilities, with suggestions for the content of curricula. Further work is currently under way to ensure the successful implementation of the Ten Essential Shared Capabilities. This includes developing a database of training and education resources and curricula that will be available on the NIMHE Knowledge Community web site (http://www.nimhe.org.uk/).

The Capable Practitioner Framework sets out the skills, knowledge and attitudes required within the mental health workforce to effectively implement the National Service Framework for Mental Health. It was intended to be used in a variety of ways, including providing lecturers with a guide for the content of mental health education and training programmes at both pre- and post-qualification levels. Capability for modern mental health practice is divided into five areas, namely ethical practice, knowledge, process of care, interventions, and application as they apply to specific service settings or functions. Each of these five categories is further subdivided into specific statements of capability for mental health practice. The document provides considerable detail for educationalists developing or updating mental health curricula.

The Mental Health National Occupational Standards are designed to provide a measurement of output or performance by setting out detailed descriptions of competence required in providing mental health services in three key areas. These are: operating within an ethical framework; working with and supporting individuals, carers and families; and influencing and supporting communities, organisations, agencies and services. There is an expectation that the knowledge and understanding set out in the Mental Health Occupational Standards should be developed as part of pre- and post-qualifying education and training.

Finally, the Knowledge and Skills Framework is another form of competency framework, which staff should take account of in mental health services where it applies. The concept behind the Knowledge and Skills Framework is that as part of pay progression, a member of staff needs to move up a skills escalator so that as the person gains more skills and knowledge this may be reflected in a higher level of pay. Whilst the Knowledge and Skills Framework sets the context for a particular skill or knowledge, the evidence for mental health purposes that this function is being carried out effectively comes from the Mental Health National Occupational Standards.

There are a range of additional developments that mental health lecturers need to be aware of. Work is currently under way to develop criteria for measuring the degree to which the Ten Essential Shared Capabilities are present within educational curricula. These criteria will become part of the National Continuous Quality Improvement Tool for Mental Health Education (Northern Centre for Mental Health, 2003) which will in turn become part of the Teaching Quality Assurance Assessment process. It is important that lecturers familiarise themselves with the National Continuous Quality Improvement Tool for Mental Health Education, as in the future it will be used by Workforce Development Directorates to commission education and training programmes, and as a mechanism for ensuring that mental health programmes include an objective rating of quality in relation to their relevance to the implementation of the NHS and Social Care modernisation agenda. The tool focuses on the following key areas:

■ The degree of collaboration between Workforce Development Directorates and service and education providers in planning the content of programmes.

■ The relevance of programmes to the NHS and Social Care modernisation agenda, to include the explicit links of programmes to the Capable Practitioner Framework, the Mental Health National Occupational Standards, and the Ten Essential Shared Capabilities.

■ The meaningful involvement of mental health service users and their carers in the planning, design, delivery and evaluation of programmes.

■ The assessment of the impact of the programme; for example, how education and service providers together measure the acquisition of capabilities and ensure that these are assessed in the practice area.

The implementation of the tool is intended to be facilitative and can be used by lecturers as a useful template for effective partnerships between a range of key stakeholders in the planning and development of new programmes.

A strong theme running through all the guidance documents is user and carer involvement in mental health education and training. By virtue of their direct experience of mental distress and professional responses (both helpful and unhelpful), service users and carers have valuable knowledge and expertise to offer. Their involvement has the potential to enrich student learning by offering a more stimulating and challenging educational experience that can equip students to practice more effectively.

Although the principle of involving users and carers in education and training programmes is now widely accepted, many lecturers are in the early stages of the process. *Learning from Experience* (Tew *et al.*, 2004) is a comprehensive good practice guide for involving service users and carers. The guide contains a general introduction to the topic and draws on a range of current initiatives as pointers towards good practice in relation to effective involvement. A range of evaluation tools are also offered which can be useful in charting progress and identifying the next steps to be taken. Lecturers can use the guide as a companion to the National Continuous Quality Improvement Tool for Mental Health Education, or simply for ideas and tips illustrated by a range of examples from current practice.

Finally, the Mental Health in Higher Education Project is an invaluable resource for lecturers keen to keep abreast with the huge and continuing changes in the mental health education and training agenda. The project set out to enhance learning and teaching about mental health across the disciplines and professions in Higher Education. Progress of the project to date is summarised in the *Mental Health in Higher Education Report of Activity 2003–2004* (Anderson, 2004). The web site contains a wealth of information including future workshops, case studies of learning and teaching in mental health, good practice guides, and links to a wide range of additional resources (http://www.mhhe.ltsn.ac.uk/).

Practice

The past few decades have witnessed significant and rapid changes in most areas of mental health service delivery. Consequently, many lecturers are likely to have worked in care environments which are very different from those that their students practise in now. Concerns have been expressed in recent policy documents about the extent to which mental health lecturers have managed to keep up to date with these developments, and their clinical credibility has been brought into question (Sainsbury Centre for Mental Health, 1997).

A national research project, conducted by the authors, which consisted of a questionnaire, focus groups and semi-structured interviews with mental health lecturers, representing each of the five main professional groups, provides useful information on their current clinical/practice activity (Ferguson *et al.*, 2003a). On the basis of these findings, strategies are suggested to ensure that lecturers remain clinically credible, so that departments are able to deliver teaching which is relevant and pertinent to contemporary practice.

The project revealed clear agreement amongst mental health lecturers of all disciplines about the importance of keeping up to date with developments in clinical practice. However, the notion of what is meant by 'clinical activity' and 'clinical credibility' aroused considerable debate. This was especially in relation to whether lecturers actually needed to be involved in direct therapeutic work with clients. There were inconsistencies, both within and between disciplines, in the extent to which they were expected to do this. Whilst most psychologists and psychiatrists had a clinical role, usually having an honorary contract with a Trust, social work and occupational therapy lecturers most often had a predominantly academic role, although they worked closely with practice teachers. In nursing, the picture was much more mixed, with some staff doing direct work with clients, whilst others were involved in a whole range of other practice-related activities. These included supporting and assessing students in practice areas, auditing placements, staff support and supervision and sitting on policy-making committees.

A number of barriers were identified which made it difficult for lecturers to engage in practice activities, in particular pressure of work and balancing competing demands of research, teaching and administration. The need for lecturers to maintain contact with clinical/practice areas and developments was not always valued or recognised by Higher Education Institutions, and this was reflected in the criteria used for promotion. Higher Education Institutions tend to place greater emphasis on teaching and research in response to pressures of the Research Assessment Exercise and Teaching Quality Assessment exercises.

Clearly, if mental health courses are to produce students who are fit to practice in modern mental health services, Higher Education Institutions need to ensure that lecturers are supported in maintaining and developing clinical and practice skills, as well as their expertise in teaching and research. Clearly, the model used in clinical psychology and psychiatry of a lecturer being active in clinical work, research and teaching may be seen as an ideal, with all three aspects of their role being mutually enriching. However, it may not be practical or desirable for all lecturers to try to juggle all of these roles. For example, in departments where staff:student ratios are not so good, where there are large numbers of students to be supported in practice, or where staff have a heavy teaching/administrative load, it is seldom feasible for lecturers to also spend part of their week working as practitioners. In addition, it may be difficult for practice areas to identify a role for a member of staff who only visits for a short time each week. Taking account of this, the tripartite model is a helpful one, whereby departments would have a percentage of their lecturers involved in regular direct therapeutic work with clients, and those staff would take particular responsibility for skills and clinical/practice teaching (Department of Health, 2002). Although the remaining lecturers would not have a direct clinical role, they also need to keep up to date with recent developments in practice so that their teaching and research are relevant to contemporary mental health care. Based on the findings of Ferguson *et al.* (2003a), a number of ways in which mental health lecturers can keep abreast of developments in their field are suggested, either through direct engagement in therapeutic work or through other related activities. These ideas may serve as inspiration to departments struggling with this issue.

Central to addressing the problems of maintaining the clinical credibility of mental health lecturers is the concept of partnership between academic and practice areas. Higher Education Institutions, Trusts and Workforce Development Directorates need to work closely together in order to maximise opportunities for lecturers to retain their clinical/practice skills. They also need to address organisational and resource issues, which may act as barriers to keeping in touch with practice.

Arguably, those staff who are responsible for teaching clinical aspects of courses, should be involved in direct work with clients. This can be achieved in a number of ways:

- Joint appointments, where the lecturer has an honorary contract with the Trust as well as a University contract. These may be at Lecturer, Senior Lecturer, Reader and Professorial levels.
- Secondment of Trust staff to teach, and also secondment of academic staff into practice areas.

- Job swaps for part of the week or for a set period of time.
- Sabbaticals with opportunities to update in practice areas.
- Participation in clinically related courses to develop particular therapeutic skills.

Non-clinically active staff also need to retain regular and effective contact with practice but may achieve this in ways other than direct therapeutic work with clients. This includes:

- Clinically related research.
- Supporting and assessing students in practice areas in collaboration with practitioners.
- Working with mentors/practice teachers.
- Practice development activities.
- Working with students on enquiry-based learning/work-based learning.
- Involvement on committees/Boards at Trust level.
- Involvement on national policy making committees.
- Team teaching with practitioners.
- Staff supervision.
- Multidisciplinary update courses.
- Conferences/training.

In addition, Trusts, professional bodies and Higher Education Institutions need to work together to ensure that clinical/practice work is valued as an essential part of the work of mental health lecturers, and that this is reflected by the establishment of clear career progression routes for staff who wish to retain a clinical role. Efforts also need to be made to address organisational and resource difficulties which make it difficult for individual staff to maintain a clinical role. These include sorting out pay differentials, work on contracts, cover, development of joint appraisal systems and addressing the practical difficulties associated with trying to juggle different roles. Across the country, some departments have made considerable progress with addressing this problem. Efforts need to be made to disseminate their experience in terms of both the models used and the strategies they have adopted to address some of the difficulties.

Research

There is an expectation that contemporary mental health education must be informed by evidence-based practice, the outcomes of research in general and user-led research in particular (Anderson, 2004). In order to facilitate access to and deliver the best quality evidence-based, values-based health and social care interventions to meet the needs and aspirations of service users and their carers, students emerging from mental health programmes need to be able to:

- Appreciate research and its importance in the development of high-quality services (Department of Health, 2002).
- Understand the notions of evidence-based and values-based best practice as enshrined in the National Institute of Clinical Excellence guidelines, for example (NIMHE, 2004).
- Seek out and critically appraise contemporary and emerging research (Department of Health, 2002; Sainsbury Centre for Mental Health, 2001).
- Understand a range of research methods so they can support research being undertaken in the services in which they may work in the future (Department of Health, 2002).
- Conduct audits and evaluations of services, ideally incorporating user-focused monitoring (NIMHE, 2004).

Arguably, students will be best able to develop critical appraisal skills, an appreciation of research and the importance of a robust evidence base for practice in Higher Education Institutions with a research active environment. Such environments provide lecturers with the time and opportunity to conduct and disseminate their research, and to reflect on the links between their research and teaching. Research-active lecturers are a valuable asset to the teaching team in two key ways. Firstly, they are familiar with the range of research and evidence-based knowledge and skills to be taught. Secondly, being involved in clinical, practice-based or educational research provides an ideal opportunity to develop an awareness and understanding of developments in service delivery locally and nationally. Thus students are being taught by lecturers who are up to date and actively engaged in the generation of an evidence base to support mental health service and educational delivery.

The role of a research-active mental health lecturer is becoming increasingly pressurised. The demands of the Research Assessment Exercise, for example, require that lecturers generate research funds, publish high-quality research papers in peer-reviewed journals, and supervise postgraduate students. Most lecturers are required to do this alongside their other teaching, practice and administrative responsibilities. The move towards preferential funding of proposals by large and/or established multidisciplinary research groups and consortia also militates against individual researchers trying to develop programmes of research alone. In order to compete in this environment, mental health lecturers need to plan their research careers thoughtfully by establishing collaborative links with other researchers, developing a programme of research rather than a series of 'one-off' projects, and keeping abreast with the current research priorities within the mental health community. Despite these demands, an increasing number of mental health lecturers are enthusiastic and keen to develop their research profile, but may be unsure of how to go about it. Some useful tips and suggestions can be found in papers by Jones (2000) and Owen and Maslin-Prothero (2001). Each covers a range of issues, including writing for publication, time management, finding an academic mentor and seeking research funding.

Finally, researchers must consider mechanisms for ensuring that mental health service users and their carers are involved in all stages of the research process. Useful and practical information about initiating and sustaining user and carer involvement can be found in *Learning from Experience* (Tew *et al.*, 2004). This includes issues such as user training, employment, contracting, payment and expenses. The National Institute of Mental Health in England is also currently developing and evaluating approaches to involving service users and carers in research (http://www.nimhe.org.uk/). Further information is provided by the Service User Research Group for England (SURGE) which supports user involvement in research projects (http://www.hsr.iop.kcl.ac.uk/sure/).

Conclusion

The role and function of contemporary mental health education is clear. It plays a vital part in preparing the current and future workforce with the requisite knowledge, skills and attitudes necessary to deliver the changed and continuously evolving mental health services. This cannot be achieved, however, if mental health lecturers remain divorced from practice and out of touch with developments in service delivery. At the same time, lecturers need to acknowledge their unique contribution in terms of research expertise and educational innovation. We argue that teams of mental health lecturers are best able to contribute to the current agenda by organising themselves within the tripartite model of research, education and practice outlined in this chapter.

Key learning points:

- Relevant and appropriate education and training is vital to ensure that the current and future workforce is equipped to deliver the new mental health agenda.
- A tripartite model of research, education and practice provides a framework for teams of lecturers wanting to develop a coherent and comprehensive approach to the delivery of mental health education.
- Lecturers responsible for developing new mental health curricula need to be cognisant of the specific requirements of professional bodies, the range of recently published mental health workforce documents, and the need to involve service users and carers at all levels and stages.

■ All lecturers have a responsibility to engage with practice to some degree, although mental health practice skills must be taught by those involved in regular therapeutic work with service users.

■ Research-active lecturers have a role in preparing students to work within the contemporary culture of evidence-based practice, and in the generation of an evidence base to support mental health service and educational delivery.

References

Anderson, J. (2004) *Mental Health in Higher Education: Report of Activity 2003–2004*. London: The Higher Education Academy.

Brooker, C., Gournay, K., O'Halloran, P. and Saul, C. (2002) Mapping training to support the implementation of the National Service Framework for Mental Health. *Journal of Mental Health*, **11**(1), 103–116.

Department of Health (1998a) *Modernising Social Services: Promoting Independence, Improving Protection, Raising Standards*. London: Stationery Office.

Department of Health (1998b) *Modernising Mental Health Services: Safe, Sound & Supportive*. London: Department of Health.

Department of Health (1999a) *National Service Framework for Mental Health: Modern Standards and Service Models*. London: HMSO.

Department of Health (1999b) *Effective Care Co-ordination in Mental Health Services: Modernising the Care Programme Approach*. London: Department of Health.

Department of Health (1999c) *Report by the Standing Nursing & Midwifery Advisory Committee (SNMAC). Mental Health Nursing: Addressing Acute Concerns*. London: HMSO.

Department of Health (1999d) *Making a Difference: Strengthening the Nursing, Midwifery and Health Visiting Contribution to Health Care*. London: Department of Health.

Department of Health (2000) *The NHS Plan*. London: HMSO.

Department of Health (2001a) Primary care key group report. In: *Final Report by the Workforce Action Team – Mental Health National Service Framework, Workforce Planning, Education and Training*. London: Department of Health. http://www.doh.gov.uk/mentalhealth/wat.htm#report

Department of Health (2001b) *Workforce Action Team – Key Area H: Mapping of Education and Training*. London: Department of Health.

Department of Health (2002) *Funding Learning and Developing for the Health-care Workforce: Consultation on the Review of NHS Education and Training Funding and the Review of Contract Benchmarking for NHS Funded Education and Training*. London: Department of Health.

Department of Health (2003a) *Fast-Forwarding Primary Care Mental Health: Graduate Primary Care Mental Health Workers. Best Practice Guidance*. London: Department of Health.

Department of Health (2003b) *The NHS Knowledge and Skills Framework and Related Development Review: A Working Draft*. London: Department of Health.

Ferguson, K., Owen, S. and Baguley, I. (2003a) *The Clinical Activity of Mental Health Lecturers in Higher Education Institutions*. Report prepared for the Mental Health Care Group Workforce Team, Department of Health.

Ferguson, K. and Owen, S. (2003b) *A Review of the National Mental Health Mapping of Education and Training Exercise*. Report prepared for the Mental Health Care Group Workforce Team, Department of Health.

Holmshaw, J. *et al.* (1999) Fitness to practice in community mental health. *Nursing Times*, **95**(34), 52–53.

Jones, F. (2000) How to succeed in research. *The Psychologist*, **13**(6), 311.

Kingdon, D. (2002) The mental health practitioner: bypassing the recruitment bottleneck. *Psychiatric Bulletin*, **26**, 328–331.

Lindley, P. and Lemmer, B. (2001) *Clinical Effectiveness Training: A Role Development Programme for Lecturers in Mental Health*. Sainsbury Centre for Mental Health, London.

Northern Centre for Mental Health (2003) *National Continuous Quality Improvement Tool for Mental Health Education*. Durham: Northern Centre for Mental Health.

NIMHE (2003) *Personality Disorder: No Longer a Diagnosis of Exclusion. Policy Implementation Guidance for the Development of Services for People with Personality Disorder*. London: Department of Health.

NIMHE (2004) *The Ten Essential Shared Capabilities: A Framework for the whole of the Mental Health Workforce*. London: Department of Health.

NIMHE/MHCGWT (2004) *National Mental Health Workforce Strategy*. London: Department of Health.

Owen, S. and Maslin-Prothero, S. (2001) Developing your research profile. *Nurse Education in Practice*, **1**, 5–11.

Owen, S., Ferguson, K., Beswick, S. and Baguley, I. (2004) *Choosing to Work in Mental Health: the Recruitment of Health and Social Care Professionals*. Report prepared for the Mental Health Care Group Workforce Team, Department of Health.

Sainsbury Centre for Mental Health (1997) *Pulling Together: The Future Roles and Training of Mental Health Staff*. London: Sainsbury Centre for Mental Health.

Sainsbury Centre for Mental Health (2001) *The Capable Practitioner: A Framework and List of Practitioner Capabilities Required to Implement the National Service Framework for Mental Health*. London: Sainsbury Centre for Mental Health.

Tew, J., Gell, C. and Foster, S. (2004) *Learning from Experience: Involving Service Users and Carers in Mental Health Education and Training*. Mental Health in Higher Education Project, Trent Workforce Development Confederation.

CHAPTER 5

Interprofessional perspectives in mental health

Liz Anderson and Janet Couloute

Introduction

In mental health, as in all health and social care delivery, team working is accepted as the gold standard. Major changes to modernise health and social care delivery have seen new forms of working emerge, as partnerships between statutory and voluntary bodies offer new cultures for collaborative working, to support effective interprofessional team working to address service user needs. For today's practitioners both excellent uni-professional skills and team working skills are now required. Central to the new modern way of collaborative working is the need to work in partnerships with the service user. The National Service Framework for Mental Health (Department of Health, 1999b) presents challenges and opportunities for statutory and non-statutory workers, as they join together to provide a truly responsive, user-centred interprofessional team-based service. In this chapter we will outline the current evidence for collaborative practice in mental health, the extent to which partnerships are being formed, the extent of team working and the role of interprofessional education in shaping the new horizon for effective patient centred, interprofessional working.

Terminology

There are a plethora of terms to depict health and social care professionals working together. For clarity of understanding we will outline some of the most

Table 5.1: Terms for health and social care professionals working together.

Terms	Meanings
Team work	group of people organised to work together (*Oxford English Dictionary*)
	combined efforts and organised co-operation, that is a group of people coming together to get things done (Firth-Cozens, 1992)
	a group who share a common health goal and common objectives, determined by community needs, to the achievement of which each member of the team contributes, in accordance with his or her competencies and skill and in coordination with the functions of others (WHO, 1984)
Interprofessional Interdisciplinary	a group of colleagues from two or more disciplines who coordinate their expertise in providing care to patients (Farrell *et al.*, 2001)
	The key term that refers to interaction between the professionals involved, albeit from different backgrounds, who have the same joint goals in working together. (Leathard, 2003)
Multi-professional Multidisciplinary	Several different professional groups working together. (Payne, 2000)
	multidisciplinary work usually refers to the coming together and contribution of different academic disciplines (Leathard, 2003)
Partnership	the state of being a partner or partners, a pair or group of partners, a joint business (*Oxford English Dictionary*)
	is a shared commitment, where all partners have a right and an obligation to participate and will be effected equally by the benefits and disadvantages arising from the partnership (Carnwell and Buchanan, 2005)
Collaborative practice	to co-operate traitorously with an enemy: to work jointly (*Oxford English Dictionary*)
	A relationship between two or more people, groups or organisations working together to define and achieve a common purpose. (Hornby and Atkins, 2000)

Terms	Meanings
Network	A group of people who exchange information, contacts, and experience for professional or social purposes (*Oxford English Dictionary*)
	Networking may more aptly describe collaboration across agencies and working settings, although the notion is less defined and less tested than team working (Barr, 2002)
Multi-professional education	occasions when two or more professions learn side by side for whatever reason (Barr, 2002)
Interprofessional education	occasions when two or more professions learn from and about each other to improve collaboration and the quality of care (Barr, 2002)

accepted definitions that underpin our use of terminology throughout this chapter (Table 5.1).

Evidence for collaborative practice in mental health

Collaborative practice within mental health has been evolving for over 25 years (Department of Health, 1975, 1995, 1999a, 2001) and is likely to be further endorsed with the awaited reform of the Mental Health Act 1983 (Department of Health, 1983):

> As part of its commitment to a modern, decent and inclusive society the Government has set out clear proposals to modernise the NHS and Social Services, requiring these agencies to work in partnership and to provide integrated services which will improve the quality of life for all citizens (Department of Health, 1999a)

Following the closure of psychiatric hospitals and the ideological shift in the organisation of mental health services from the acute or hospital settings to the community, new models of working were required. Reflecting these changes, Community Mental Health Teams (CMHTs) were viewed by the Department of Health in England as the 'most effective' way of delivering multidisciplinary services for people with enduring mental health. Ideally these teams would be truly interprofessional, consisting of a range of professions including medicine, nursing, social work, therapies and others. In reality they have mainly been made up of community psychiatric nurses, clinical psychologists, occupational therapists, social workers, support workers and psychiatrists, and have proved to be the starkest example of mental health care delivered in an interprofessional way (Norman and Peck, 1999). More recently, CMHTs have acted as a template for other models of service delivery, such as Crisis Resolution Teams, Acute Hospital Teams and Early Intervention Teams. In the evolution of these new teams the range of members has broadened: for example, membership can go beyond traditional staff composition to include youth workers and family therapists.

Joint working between health and social services is not new and has been operating throughout the UK for decades. It is now pivotal within the government agenda for joint working, underpinned by a partnership approach, at both the operational and strategic level (Department of Health, 1997a). Translating this into reality and successful collaborative practice requires structure, especially where working together involves the overlap of professional roles and responsibilities. Models for collaboration vary from simplistic exchanges of information to coordinated team working and joint commissioning (Hudson, 1998). How best to coordinate collaboration remains a puzzle, but depends on the aims of the work. In some cases user models of coordination work best, as they are designed to empower the user, but ultimately organisations must be able to work together and professional agreement will be required (Leathard, 2003).

The major response to a coordinated approach within mental health services has been the emergence of joint assessments. These link together the health, social care, voluntary and private sectors to identify and meet individual needs. Mainly this is referred to as the 'Care Programme Approach' as used by health workers and/or the 'Care Management Approach' as used by social care practitioners. These modes of delivering community care are now merging to form one 'Care Programme Approach' (CPA), which embraces the principles of a collective assessment and collective decision making for optimal user-centred care. This philosophy has been outlined in the NHS and Community Care Act (Department of Health, 1990) and in Effective Care Co-ordination in Mental Health Services (Department of Health, 1999a) The coordinated steps involve:

- Arrangements for assessing the health and social needs of people accepted into mental health services.
- Formation of a care plan to identify the health and social care services required to meet needs.
- The appointment of a care coordinator to keep in touch with the service user and to monitor and coordinate care.
- Regular review and monitoring and, where necessary, agreed changes to plans.

This type of coordinated collaborative approach benefits users, especially those with complex needs which affect every aspect of their lives, e.g. finance, employment, housing, education and family dynamics.

Early movements towards team working in mental health placed service users on the margins with the emergence of professionally dominated teams. However, recent empowerment models of team working have begun to embrace the user as a valued team member. Forming partnerships with service users and carers is one of the most challenging aspects of collaborative partnerships in mental health, where care is at times experienced as coercive, and where the credibility of service users is undermined by experts. Millar and Rose (1986) suggest that therapeutic interventions that encourage service user involvement showed better outcomes than those which lacked this mode of working. Describing users and carers as experts in the knowledge of their lives and needs, the National Service Framework demands that all mental health services listen to their views in an attempt to involve both groups in decision-making processes, education and research. All carers supporting service users on CPA should have their needs assessed on an annual basis, with a care plan independent of the service user (Department of Health, 1999b).

> The process of the CPA is clearly intended to deliver care to meet the individual needs of service users. However, those needs often relate not just to their own lives, but also to the lives of their wider family. The CPA should take account of this, in particular the needs of children and carers of people with mental health problems (Department of Health, 1999a)

The success of coordinated approaches varies. In the UK there are regional variations in the extent of the implementation of team working both at the strategic and operational levels (Department of Health, 1997b). Failures mostly result from difficulties of working across the health and social care sectors. The evidence suggests significant points of divergence in the ideology and work of the two sectors (Sheppard, 1990). These problems include differences in the model of mental illness that professionals aspire towards, and professional differences in attitudes and values, underpinned by stereotypical ideas effecting role clarification and the cultures surrounding service commissioning (Barnes *et al.*, 2000; Hannigan, 1999). Interprofessional team working also has highlighted service gaps, as in the need for greater interface between adolescent and adult care services, where there exists a need for a specialist team consisting of education, social services, health and non-statutory services (Richards and Vostanis, 2004). Partnerships are also developing between health, prison and police services where greater cooperation benefits defendants (Home Office, 1990). In the Midlands a new integrated health and social care community model is achieving joined-up services for individuals with enduring mental health problems (Glasby, 2004).

In a review of the extent of collaboration and partnerships within mental health care services, acknowledgement is made of the benefits and potentials of joined-up working; however, problems remain, especially in identifying service users views and establishing partnerships in areas of historical difficulty (Glasby and Lester, 2004). There are no easy solutions to promoting greater inter-agency collaboration (Sainsbury Centre for Mental Health, 2000).

The extent of team working

Team working definitions vary (see Table 5.1), as do individuals' beliefs about what a team is and does. Teams within health and social care practice are complex entities and something to which we aspire in health and social care rather than achieve:

> The aspiration is of some perfect, seamless robe or shared endeavour, when different people, from different organisations, act in different ways, according to different knowledge bases, cultural traditions and objectives. (Payne, 2000)

The theory of team working – why it optimises working practice, how it develops and evolves, and the processes supporting its function – is beyond the scope of this chapter. Evidence is drawn strongly from psychology in the exploration of interpersonal and individual preferences and from the business world of management now adopted within health and social care. Team work trends have emerged to:

■ Increase the use of teams – multidisciplinary and interagency – as an approach to problem solving as people from different departments and professions are brought together to pool expertise, insights and ideas.
■ Flatten organisations, as the responsibility of operational management is given to teams, who are facilitated and empowered rather than controlled.
■ Increase distinctions between core and peripheral teams and the value of networks.
■ Link to the process of total quality management and service users' views in implementing improvements.

Teams are felt to be more creative and productive when they can achieve high levels of participation, cooperation and collaboration among members.

Effective teams gain mutual trust, a sense of group identity (in that the group is unique and worthwhile), and a sense of group efficacy (in that group members work better together than apart) (Druskat *et al.*, 2001).

Examples of team working in mental health are growing. There are several examples of social workers working in General Practice. In a Manchester-based project the reconfiguration of a new Primary Care Trust enabled a team of mental health social workers to be based in a GP practice. They offered a different perspective for the care of mentally distressed people in an inner city area (Firth *et al.*, 2003). In a similar study in Solihull the attachment of a social worker to a GP practice led to faster access users and improved appreciation of the roles and responsibilities of the primary health care team (Eaton, 1998). An evaluation of a community mental health team highlighted how an integrated team approach improved the dissemination of information, encouraged sharing of expertise and decision making to result in a more responsive service (Cook *et al.*, 2001). Services for child and adolescent emotional and behavioural problems, have been tackled by a multidisciplinary team offering preventative intervention, with positive results (Walker, 2003).

One of the greatest problems for team working in the NHS has been the constant effect of change brought about through a deluge of new policies: 'every time we settle down we are asked to change again' (O'Shea, 2004).

> We trained hard, but it seemed every time we were beginning to form up into teams, we would be reorganised. I was to learn later in life that we tend to meet any new situation by reorganising: and a wonderful method it can be for creating the illusion of progress while producing confusion, inefficiency and demoralisation (Petronius Arbiter, 210 BC; extract from O'Shea, 2004)

As mental health teams develop and become the norm for modern practice, in the midst of reorganisation and integration of mental health services, let us hope they can be left to spend time developing and maximising their potential.

Interprofessional education

Historically students in health and social care trained in silos. On qualification and entry into a registered profession or work stream, each profession was expected to know how to work together. Learning about each other's roles and responsibilities, service organisation and delivery began once qualified through reactions to patient/service user need. The vision for the modern NHS, as outlined in the NHS Plan (Department of Health, 2000a), focuses on care delivered through cooperation at all levels to ensure a seamless service in which patients are central. Emphasis was placed on new joint training models involving both multi- and interprofessional education to achieve this goal (Department of Health, 2000b). The government hoped this type of education would address historical and current problems of stereotyping and resistance to collaborate, often at the centre of NHS failures (Sainsbury Centre for Mental Health, 1998; Department of Health, 1974; Laming Report, 2003; Kennedy Inquiry, 2001; Department of Health, 1991).

Modern views of future health and social care education look likely to involve core profession-specific learning, complemented by *shared* or *multi-disciplinary learning* to underpin basic common theoretical/clinical needs and *interprofessional learning*. Shared or multidisciplinary learning will go some way to breaking down stereotypical views of each profession, while only inter-professional learning will ensure that students appreciate their collective skills to maximise service user well being. It seeks to achieve meaningful learning exchanges between the different professional groups to appreciate the nature of their interdependence. Core or uni-professional training will prepare learners for their one-to-one patient/service user profession-specific work. The future of health and social care, affected by demographic changes and advances in technology, requires greater cooperation between professions to maximise quality of life. This will be especially apparent in tackling poverty and deprivation, marginalised groups (e.g. homeless people, evacuees, refugees and travellers), and in addressing the needs of disabled people including those with mental health. Figure 5.1 shows the future model of education pre-registration.

The UK centre for the Advancement of Interprofessional education (CAIPE) has advocated the importance of interprofessional education for decades. As interprofessional education moves from peripheral thinking to centre stage, they provide clear directives for what constitutes quality education in which team working and collaborative practice are enhanced.

The underpinning theories for interprofessional education arise from adult learning theory in which learners are motivated, self-directed and able to reflect (Knowles, 1975). They frequently use learning models which allow for learning through experience, reflection and debate (Boud and Feletti, 1991; Kolb, 1984; Schön, 1983). The effect and rationale of different professions working together has its origins in psychological theories, especially Allport's 'contact hypothesis' where he explored the nature of prejudice (Allport, 1974). This was further developed by others and looks at the opportunity to develop new understandings of those we mistrust following positive contact (Tajfel, 1981). For many, the evidence base is currently being developed and new approaches are under development (Cooper *et al.*, 2001).

Types of interprofessional learning vary from action learning sets, through observation models, simulation in skills labs and practice, to university-based small group learning. Little didactic learning occurs. The Leicester model is one example of interprofessional learning based in CAIPE principles underpinned

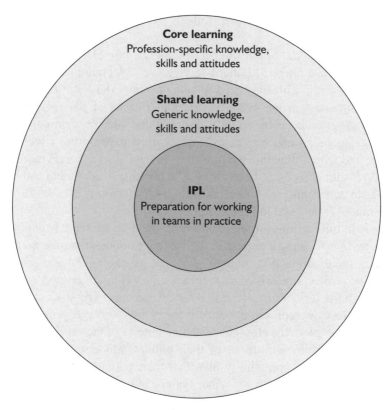

Figure 5.1: Future model of education pre-registration.

CAIPE: Principles for interprofessional education (Barr, 2002)
Puts service users at the centre
Promotes collaboration
Reconciles competing objectives
Reinforces collaborative competence
Relates collaboration in learning and practice within a coherent rationale
Incorporates interprofessional values
Complement common with comparative learning
Employs a repertoire of interactive learning methods
Counts towards qualifications
Evaluates programmes
Disseminates findings

by adult learning theory, in which students learn in practice settings (Lennox and Anderson, 2005).

The *Leicester Model of interprofessional education* offers students the ability to learn about a range of patient service users, including mental health. It emerged from work with medical students (Lennox abd Petersen, 1996). Students are immersed in the everyday life experiences of patients and service users. The programme is based on task-orientated and problem-solving methodology, designed around patient and service users case studies which span the age range and which illustrate the impact of financial, social and environmental factors on health choices and outcomes. The learning is adaptable and has been used in both community and hospital settings (Anderson *et al.*, 2003).

The model is outlined in Figure 5.2.

Step 1: In uni- or interprofessional groups of 3–5, students begin their programme by interviewing a patient in their home to understand the medical and social care issues impacting on their physical, psychological and social functioning. The patient's priorities and attitudes are explored alongside their relationship with the services involved in their current care. The student group then separately interview representatives of three or four services providing care to their patient to explore the strengths and deficiencies of the service, and to compare service priorities with those of their patient. Students additionally meet representatives of the community in which their patient lives (e.g. the police or tenants' association) to gain a wider understanding of the context of service provision.

Step 2: Facilitated by experienced clinical and academic tutors, the student group reflects on each interview. They relate service and theoretical perspectives and NHS policies to interpret the findings and prioritise the issues identi-

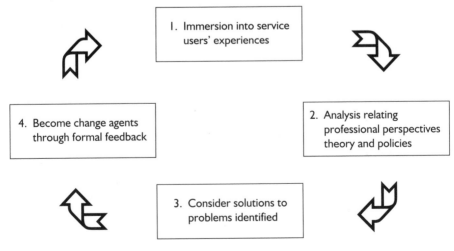

1. Immersion into service users' experiences

4. Become change agents through formal feedback

2. Analysis relating professional perspectives theory and policies

3. Consider solutions to problems identified

Figure 5.2: The Leicester Model of interprofessional education.

fied. In some programmes, this is supported by a range of experts (e.g. disability trainers or occupational psychologists).

Step 3: On the completion of interviews, the student group identifies practical multi-agency solutions to improve the patient's quality of life.

Step 4: The education cycle is completed with solutions formally presented to service representatives and managers in an interactive presentation, and as individual written feedback to the relevant service provider. Student assessment is aligned to the learning objectives and embedded within a uniprofessional curricular.

The Leicester Model includes learning from and with people with mental health problems. Other specific courses look promising, and for greatest impact need to consider partnerships with consumers of mental health services (Scheyett and Diehl, 2004).

The key to the success of interprofessional education is in the establishment of a learning situation which creates an ambience within which different value bases and ethical issues can be debated because difference is tolerated and respected (McMichael *et al.*, 1984). Indeed, the context and adequate preparation of learners for interprofessional education is frequently raised as vital to its success (Parsell *et al.*, 1998).

Progressing interprofessional education into the range of health and social care curricula remains the main task of Higher Education Institutions in partnership with health and social care organisations. Best opportunities will combine both classroom-based interaction and those in which students engage with the realities of service. The evidence for effective interprofessional education is growing (Koppel *et al.*, 2001; Freeth *et al.*, 2002). Some programmes for mental health have still to conclude that learners change their attitudes towards other professions through interprofessional education, although failures at post-qualified level may reflect that interprofessional education should begin at the level of pre-registration (Barnes *et al.*, 2000). Reports indicate there are few quality papers which cite the beneficial effects of interprofessional education in the field of mental health, especially the effect on patients and service organisation (Reeves, 2000). Nevertheless, there continues to be a strong belief that interprofessional education in mental health will achieve and promote effective team working (Sainsbury Centre for Mental Health, 1997; Department of Health, 2000a), despite different approaches to the care and treatment of users, accountability and responsibility of staff (Norman and Peck, 1999).

It is now evident, with a recent NHS project entitled 'Towards an Interprofessional Workforce', a three year programme funded by the Department of Health and hosted by the South West Peninsula Strategic Health Authority, to be delivered in partnership with CAIPE, that best practice for IPE will be outlined for the continuum of education from pre-registration through to post-registration and continual professional development and clearly set within achievable regulatory standards.

Conclusion

The direction for modern health and social care practice in mental health is coordinated interprofessional care in which the user is seen as expert and pivotal to the process. Policies advocate the bringing together of a range of professionals to work alongside each other in multidisciplinary teams.

As we have noted, team working is not easy, especially in mental health, where different approaches to care, and the complexity and difficulties of working with the person at the centre, can be challenging and frustrating. Where teams work well team members report increased job satisfaction, as attitudes towards group members improve (Carpenter and Hewstone, 1996), staff learn more about each others roles and responsibilities, develop team working skills (Virgin *et al.*, 1996), collaboration across boundaries is improved (Ridgely *et al.*, 1998), joint learning is valued (Cook *et al.*, 1995) and people's health needs are addressed (Davies, 2005). Partnership working is likely to have positive effects, if only in the re-consideration of best practice guidelines, colleague support and the work towards achieving patient-centred care.

The impact of newly developing interprofessional education curricula, at both the undergraduate and postgraduate level, on the nature of team working and its impact on service users, will emerge over the next five years as these new practitioners dissipate into the workforce, supported by a developing evidence base. Amidst the growth in team working and its potential power to improve service user care, we must not lose sight of the value and importance of the one-to-one care and responsibilities each profession holds.

References

Allport, G. W. (1974) The nature of prejudice. In: *Social Psychology*, 2nd edn (eds. P. F. Secord and C. W. Backman). New York: McGraw-Hill.

Anderson, E. S., Lennox, A. and Petersen, S. (2003) Learning from lives: a model for health and social care education in the wider community context. *Medical Education*, **37**, 59–68.

Barr, H. (2002) *Interprofessional Education. Today, Yesterday and Tomorrow.* Learning and Teaching Support Network (LTSN) Centre for Health Sciences and Practice. Occasional Paper 1.

Barnes, D., Carpenter, J. and Dickinson, C. (2000) Interprofessional education for community mental health: attitudes to community care and professional stereotypes. *Social Work Education*, **19**(6), 565–583.

Boud, D. and Feletti, G. (1991) *The Challenge of Problem Based Learning.* London: Kogan Page.

Carnwell, R. and Buchanan, J. (2005) *Effective Practice in Health and Social Care. A Partnership Approach.* Maidenhead: Open University Press.

CAIPE: http://www.caipe.org.uk/

Carpenter, J. and Hewstone, M. (1996) Shared learning for doctors and social workers. *British Journal of Social Work*, **26**, 239–257.

Cook, G., Gerrish, K. and Clarke, C. (2001) Decision-making in teams: issues arising from two UK evaluations. *Journal of Interprofessional Care*, **15**(2), 141–151.

Cook, J., Jonikas, J. and Razzano, L. (1995) A randomised evaluation of consumer vs. non-consumer training of state mental health service providers. *Community Mental Health Journal*, **31**, 229–237.

Cooper, H., Carlisle, C., Gibbs, T. and Watkins, C. (2001) Developing an evidence base for interdisciplinary learning: a systematic review. *Journal of Advanced Nursing*, **35**(2), 228–237.

Davies, T. (2005) *Team Work in Action – Views From Practice.* Institute of Psychiatry, Kings College London. North Lambeth Assessment and Treatment Team. Oral paper presented at the Royal Society of Medicine, 9 June 2005 – What Makes Team Tick? Interprofessional Working in Healthcare – Education and Practice.

Department of Health (1974) *Lost in care.* Report of the tribunal into the abuse of children in care in the former County Council Areas. London: HMSO.

Department of Health (1975) *Report of the Committee of Inquiry into the Care and Supervision in Relation to Maria Colwell.* London: HMSO.

Department of Health (1983) *Mental Health Act.* London: HMSO

Department of Health (1990) *NHS and Community Care Act.* London: HMSO.

Department of Health (1991) *Working Together to Safeguard Children: New Government Proposals for Interagency Co-operation Consultation Paper.* London: HMSO.

Department of Health (1995) *Building Bridges.* London: HMSO

Department of Health (1997a) *The New NHS: Modern, Dependable.* Cm 3807. London: Stationery Office

Department of Health (1997b) *Developing Partnerships in Mental Health.* London: Stationery Office.

Department of Health (1999a) *Effective Care Co-ordination in Mental Health Services. Modernising the Care Programme Approach.* London: HMSO.

Department of Health (1999b) *A National Service Framework for Mental Health,* London: HMSO.

Department of Health (2000a) *The NHS Plan: a Plan for Investment, A Plan for Reform*. Cmnd. 4880. London: HMSO.

Department of Health (2000b) *A Health Service of All the Talents: Developing the NHS Workforce*. London: Stationery Office

Department of Health (2001) *National Service Framework for Older People*. London: HMSO.

Department of Health and Social Services (1975) *Better Services for the Mentally Ill*. Cmnd. 6239. London: HMSO.

Druskat, V., Urch, S. B. and Wolff, S. B. (2001) Building emotional intelligence of groups. *Harvard Business Review*, March, 81–90.

Eaton, J. (1998) Arranged marriages. *Health Service Journal*, **108** (5627), 24–6.

Farrell, M., Schmitt, M. and Heinemann, G. (2001) Informal roles and the stakes of interdisciplinary team development. *Journal of Interprofessional Care*, **15**(30), 281–295.

Firth-Cozens, J. (1992) Building teams for effective audit. *Quality in Health Care*, **1**, 252–253.

Firth, M. T., Dyer, M., Marsden, H. and Savage, D. (2003) Developing a social perspective in mental health services in primary care. *Journal of Interprofessional Care*, **17**(3), 251–261.

Freeth, D., Reeves, S., Koppel, I., Hammick, M. and Barr, H. (2002) *A Critical Review of Evaluations of Interprofessional Education*. LTSN for Health Sciences and Practice. London.

Glasby, J. (2004) A healthy dose of partnership. *Community Care*, (1549), 56.

Glasby, J. and Lester, H. (2004) Cases for change in mental health: partnership working in mental health services. *Journal of Interprofessional Care*, **18**(1), 7–16.

Hannigan, B. (1999) Joint working in community mental health: prospects and challenges. *Health and Social Care in the Community*, **7**(1), 25–31.

Home Office (1990) *Probation circular 66/1990. Provision for mentally disordered offenders*. London: Home Office.

Hornby, S. and Atkins, J. (2000) *Collaborative Care – Interprofessional, Interagency and Interpersonal*, 2nd edn. Oxford: Blackwell Science.

Hudson, B. (1998) Prospects of partnership. *Health Service Journal*, **108**(5600), 26–27.

Kennedy Inquiry (2001) *Learning From Bristol: the Report of the Public Inquiry Into Children's Heart Surgery At the Bristol Royal Infirmary 1984–1995*. Command Paper: CM 5207. London: Stationery Office.

Kolb, D. A. (1984) *Experiential Learning: Experiences As the Source of Learning and Development.* New Jersey: Prentice Hall.

Koppel, I., Barr, H., Reeves, S., Freeth, D. and Hammick, M. (2001) Establishing a systematic approach to evaluation of the effectiveness of interprofessional education. *Issues in Interdisciplinary Care,* **3,** 41–49.

Knowles, M. S. (1975) *The Adult Learner: a Neglected Species,* 4th edn. Houston: Gulf.

Laming Report (2003) The Victoria Climbié Inquiry: http://www.victoria-climbie-inquiry.org.uk/.

Leathard, A. (2003) Models of interprofessional collaboration. In: *Interprofessional Collaboration. From Policy to Practice in Health and Social Care* (ed. A. Leathard), Chapter 7. London: Brunner-Routledge.

Lennox, A. and Anderson, E. (2005) *The Leicester Model of Education.* The University of Leicester.

Lennox, A. and Petersen, S. (1996) Development and evaluation of a community based, multiagency course for medical students: descriptive survey. *British Medical Journal,* **316,** 596–599.

McMichael, P., Irvine, R. and Gillora, A. (1984) *Pathways to the Professions: Research Report.* Edinburgh: Moray House College of Education.

Millar, P. and Rose, N. (1986) *The Power of Psychiatry.* Cambridge: Polity Press.

Norman, I. and Peck, E. (1999) Working together in adult community mental health services: exploring inter-professional role relations. *Journal of Mental Health,* **8,** 231–242.

O'Shea, T. (2004) Take your partners? A local authority perspective on reform, re-organisation and integration in mental health services. *Mental Health Review,* **9**(4), 19–24.

Parsell, G., Spalding, R. and Bligh, J. (1998) Shared goals, shared learning: evaluations of a multiprofessional course for undergraduate students. *Medical Education,* **32,** 204–311.

Payne, M. (2000) *Teamwork in Multiprofessional Care.* Basingstoke: Palgrave.

Reeves, S. (2000) A joint learning venture between new nurses and junior doctors. *Nursing Times,* **96**(38), 39–40.

Richards, M. and Vostanis, P. (2004) Interprofessional perspectives on transitional mental health services for young people aged 16–19 years. *Journal of Interprofessional Care,* **18**(2), 116–128.

Ridgely, M., Lambert, D., Goodman, A., Chichester, C. and Ralph, R. (1998) Interagency collaboration in services for people with co-occurring mental illness and substance use disorder. *Psychiatric Services,* **49,** 236–238.

Sainsbury Centre for Mental Health (1997) *Pulling Together: the Future Roles and Training of Mental Health Staff*. London: Sainsbury Centre for Mental Health.

Sainsbury Centre for Mental Health (1998) *Together We Stand – Effective Partnerships: Key Indicators for Joint Working in Mental Health*. London: Sainsbury Centre for Mental Health.

Sainsbury Centre for Mental Health (2000) *Taking Your Partner: Using Opportunities for Inter-agency Partnership in Mental Health*. London: Sainsbury Centre for Mental Health.

Scheyett, A. and Diehl, M. (2004) Walking our talk in social work education: partnering with consumers of mental Health Services. *Social Work Education*, **23**(4), 435–450.

Sheppard , M. (1990) Social work and community psychiatric nursing. In: *The Sociology of the Caring Professions* (eds. P. Abbott and C. Wallace), pp. 67–89. Basingstoke: Falmer Press.

Schön, D. (1983) *The Reflective Practitioner*. New York: Basic Books.

Tajfel, H. (1981) *Human Groups and Social Exchanges*. Cambridge: Cambridge University Press.

Virgin, S., Goodrow, B. and Duggins, B. (1996) Scavenger hunt: a community based learning experience. *Nurse Educator*, **21**, 32–34.

Walker, S. (2003) Interprofessional work in child and adolescent mental health services. *Emotional and Behavioural Difficulties*, **8**(3), 189–204.

CHAPTER 6

The GP and mental health

Jo Wright

There has long been a tension between primary and secondary care services. Both systems are under strain, with resources failing to match workload. There has been a lack of understanding of each other's skills and ways of working. Communication between services has all too often been woeful and the patient has been stuck in the middle.

There have been many exciting (and overdue) changes in recent years in the way mental health care is delivered. In general practice we have seen other areas of (physical) health care change and develop. However, until recently there has been little change in an archaic mental health system. In this chapter we will look at why GPs have the potential to be a pivotal part of these changes and at some of the initiatives that are already making a difference.

Why are GPs so important in the provision of good mental health care?

- Patients and carers want care to take place in the community whenever possible (Minghella *et al.*, 1998).
- The GP will frequently be the first professional a patient will turn to when they are unwell.
- The GP acts as a conduit to access other services.
- Up to 40% of patients attending their GP for any reason have a mental health problem (Kendrick *et al.*, 1991).
- In up to 25% of consultations a mental health problem will be the sole purpose of attending (Kendrick *et al.*, 1991).
- 90% of people with depression will be treated within primary care rather than by a psychiatrist (Goldberg and Huxley, 1992).
- 25% of people with a serious mental health problem (e.g. recurring psychotic illness) have no contact with secondary care (NICE, 2002).

- People with serious mental illness are more likely to have physical health problems (Harris and Barraclough, 1998).
- People with a serious physical health problem are more likely to have a mental health problem (Kisely and Goldberg, 1996).
- Patients *choose* when to see their GP rather than being *told* when to attend.
- Usually a patient will choose their GP, i.e. choose their practice or choose an individual within a group practice.
- The GP frequently will remain constant for many years, while other professionals change posts.
- The GP will frequently remain constant when a service user moves between teams, e.g. from acute care to 'Treatment and Recovery', or CAMHS to adult services.
- The GP will often have an understanding of a patient's family background and have experienced that individual when the person has been well.

What problems have prevented good care?

- Lack of interest amongst some GPs.
- GPs who believe that mental health is not really their job.
- The unempathic GP.
- Time – even for the most enthusiastic GPs it can be difficult to fit good mental health care into 10 minute consultation time slots.
- Poor training in mental health, e.g. poor detection rates for depression and inadequate knowledge of drug treatments.
- Lack of treatment options for common mental health problems.
- Access to a GP – many inner city practices have closed lists.
- Access to an appointment – even with 'advanced access' getting an appointment when you need one can be a struggle.
- Access to an emergency appointment – getting past the receptionist as gatekeeper.
- GPs who continue to practice using the medical model.
- Lack of awareness of cultural diversity (in its wider forms) amongst doctors.
- Poor communication with secondary care, social services and other agencies.
- Trust – the status of the medical profession has been declining, helped on by scandals such as that at Alder Hey Hospital and the Harold Shipman murders.

The drivers of change

Until recently there had been little change to the structure of mental health services. While service user groups had long been calling for improvement it wasn't until the government produced a new policy document that health services had to plan and implement change. The National Service Framework for Mental Health was launched in 1999 and was intended to set standards to improve services year on year for the following 10 years. At its heart was the principle that 'Individuals in need should be able to access services which are responsive, timely and effective'. It stressed that the voice of service users and careers should be heard in the development of new services and that all services should be sensitive to the cultural needs of the community. Carers' needs were put on the agenda for the first time. There was plenty for general practice and the primary care trusts to do as a result.

While some GPs will have little idea of the contents of the NSF, they will have been unable to ignore the second government initiative that has driven change in primary care mental health provision. The new General Medical Services contract (GMS2) has been in operation since 2004. It links practice income to performance in achieving quality indicators over key areas of health care. With regard to mental health the new contract only affects those with severe and enduring mental illness, in particular bipolar affective disorder and recurring or chronic psychotic disorders. Practices must compile a register of those with severe and enduring mental illness, and perform an annual physical health check and medication review. People taking the drug lithium (usually for bipolar affective disorder) also need to be on a register and the practice must show they are being correctly monitored.

Many are cynical about the new contract, feeling it is more about ticking boxes than caring for patients. Some service users are understandably unhappy with the idea of being on a register. While some feel that the new contract does not go far enough to encourage better standards of care, others feel that it is at least a good start.

Ultimately the drivers of change have not been government policy but service users and their carers. While individual voices have not been heard, people have felt passionately enough to organize into representative groups that have been able to lobby effectively for change.

New ways of working for GPs

For the 80% of people with mental health problems that are treated exclusively in primary care there has been a large gap in provision of services. Until recently, resources aimed at improving care had been aimed at secondary care services only. There has been little to offer other than a prescription and ten minute follow-up appointment in the middle of another busy surgery. GPs have felt frustrated by their limited therapeutic options in the face of such need. The following are some examples of local initiatives that have sought to fill the gap.

The Common Mental Health Problems Service (CMHPS)

This service was set up in Leicester in 2001 and is being used as a model for similar services in other areas of the country. The aim has been to put a Practice Therapist into every GP surgery. The therapists are experienced practitioners drawn from different professional backgrounds and trained in a range of psychological therapies (e.g. cognitive behavioural therapy, interpersonal therapy, solution focused therapy, anxiety management, and psychodynamic psychotherapy). They provide assessment, treatment and follow-up to patients with the 'common mental health problems' (mainly anxiety and depression) that are not severe enough to require referral to secondary care.

As the therapists usually have a good working knowledge of secondary care services, potential referrals can be screened and signposted to the appropriate service, thus fulfilling the role of Gateway Workers. Since the service has been in operation, referrals to Community Mental Health Teams (CMHT) have significantly reduced, giving them more time for people with more severe illnesses. Therapists have a role in developing the mental health skills of the primary care team and have provided clinical placements and training for Graduate Workers.

When the service was evaluated GPs expressed a high level of satisfaction. From my personal experience of working with a Practice Therapist it has given me a sense that I have a high-quality therapeutic alternative (or addition) to drug treatment. This is especially helpful when I am out of my depth or simply do not have the time that a patient needs. Through jointly managing patients and being able to consult/liaise with the therapist face to face, I have increased my confidence and skills.

Patients too have expressed a high level of satisfaction with the service. They appreciate being able to see someone in their own surgery (a place with which they are already familiar) and within a short period of time. Interestingly, some patients seem to find it helpful that they are being seen by a member of their practice team rather than an 'outsider'. This may be something to do with perceptions of trust and 'care' provided by the practice as well as avoiding the stigma of attending a psychiatry outpatient clinic.

Book prescription schemes and patient libraries

Many people are prepared to find out more about their problems and seek solutions for themselves without resorting to drug treatment. With this in mind a pioneering scheme in Cardiff sought to assist people with mild to moderate mental health problems by prescribing an appropriate self-help book (Dobson, 2003). A list of 35 books was compiled with the help of psychologists and counsellors working in primary care. The topics include anxiety, low self-esteem, depression, bereavement, surviving sexual abuse and eating disorders, amongst others. Many books take a step-by-step Cognitive Behavioural Therapy (CBT) approach, with exercises, self-assessments and diary sheets. The GP can write a prescription that is taken to the local library. All libraries have agreed to stock the books so that any GP in the city can take part. The scheme has attracted wide interest and other local councils have set up similar schemes. The National Institute for Clinical Excellence (NICE) has recommended this as an approach in mild depression.

In a variation of the book prescription scheme some surgeries have set up their own patient libraries, with books covering both mental and physical health problems. Patients are recommended a particular book or invited to browse.

Computerised CBT (CCBT)

With different psychological therapies available for anxiety and depression, the one that has the strongest evidence base for its effectiveness is Cognitive Behavioural Therapy (Roth and Fonagy, 1996). This aims to break the link between stressful situations and the negative habitual reactions to them. There are not the resources to refer all with mild depression and anxiety to Cognitive Behavioural Therapists, but using an interactive computer interface may provide the answer to the resource issue. Research suggests that CCBT is as effective as face-to-face therapy, but uses a fraction of the therapist hours (Marks, 2004; Proudfoot, 2004). However the drop out rate is significantly higher, reflecting the motivation needed to succeed with self-directed treatment. Guidelines on depression produced by NICE in December 2004 suggest that clinicians should consider the use of CCBT for those with mild depression.

Like the book prescription schemes, CCBT relies on the patient having a good working knowledge of English. Those of us working in the inner cities continue to struggle to find equity of treatment for our patients who are learning the language.

Further information on these topics may be found at http://www.ccbt. co.uk/ for the Institute of Psychiatry's 'Fear Fighter' system and at http://www. media-innovations.ltd.uk/ for the University of Leeds' 'Calipso' software.

Referral for exercise

There is good evidence for the benefits of regular structured exercise in the treatment of mild to moderate depression and anxiety. NICE guidelines (2004) recommend 'Patients of all ages with mild depression should be advised of the benefits of following a structured and supervised exercise program of typically up to three sessions per week of moderate duration (45 minutes to one hour) for between 10 and 12 weeks'.

I have seen many people groan at my suggestion that exercise will help them – it's the last thing you feel like doing when your mood is low. I feel that one needs a good therapeutic rapport before a patient will take this seriously and not feel fobbed off. However, it is a truly holistic treatment with widespread benefits for the body as well as mind (particularly for dealing with high blood pressure, diabetes and obesity and reducing the risks of stroke, heart attack and osteoporosis).

There are several reasons why it will benefit mental health. Firstly, on a biological level the release of endorphins produce a feeling of relaxation and wellbeing. Regular attendance at a gym or exercise class provides an opportunity to make social contacts and friends in an unpressured way. It provides distraction from negative thoughts and feelings and can create a sense of normality through participating in a 'healthy' activity.

Many GPs' practices have access to a referral scheme through collaboration between PCTs (Primary Care Trusts) and local council leisure services, where sessions are free or subsidized for those on a low income. They have been used widely for patients with physical health problems but less so for mental health problems. Usually patients attend a local gym for a first appointment with an instructor and an appropriate program of exercises or classes is devised for that individual.

Case history – Val

I had met Val, a 51-year-old woman, four months previously when she had consulted because of a mixture of non-specific physical symptoms and general lack of well-being. She appeared depressed and downtrodden by life. Her low self-esteem was particularly evident. In a long consultation she eventually disclosed a history of sexual abuse that she had kept hidden all her life. She declined referral to the practice therapist – she didn't feel she could go into what had happened. I had seen her once or twice subsequently just for a catch-up and support.

On this occasion she entered my consulting room with a spring in her step, her hair tied back and a sleeveless top on that revealed more of her body than I had seen before. She held herself differently and her voice was strong. She wanted a passport photo signing. I couldn't help saying to her 'Val, you look great... what's happened?'. She laughed and looked embarrassed. 'I've got a new friend. She's made me go to the gym with her – we go to aerobics and swimming.' 'Swimming!?' 'Yes, can you believe it. I looked at some of the other women in the pool and I thought if they can do it so can I. I've lost over a stone.'

'Why didn't I think of that?', I thought.

Prescriptions for healthy learning

Learning can be good for your mental health. In this local scheme, patients attending their GP for problems like anxiety and depression can be given a 'prescription' to see an advisor who helps find a course appropriate for that person's educational level and interests.

This can be a first step towards getting out of the house, making new friends, learning a new skill and finding a sense of achievement. For those recovering from a long-term illness the increase in self-confidence can be a major factor helping them return to the workplace.

Case history – Carol

Carol attended her GP with depression. She was 42, happily married and had three sons, all teenagers and living at home. She had spent most of her adult life being a homemaker and keeping her growing family well fed and looked after. She didn't know why she was depressed, but wondered if it was something to do with her boys not needing her in the way they used to. When I asked when she last did something just for herself she burst into tears and said she couldn't remember. She elected not to take a prescription for antidepressants, but was interested in seeing the education advisor.

I saw her two months later with another problem and she was clearly feeling much better. She was doing a landscape gardening course and was loving it. 'The family think I've gone mad', she added with a smile.

See http://www.nextstep-leics.org.uk/ for more information.

Crisis houses

Service users and carers have long been saying that they want care in a community setting whenever possible. In particular, inpatient services can be experienced as punitive and dehumanising. Crisis houses can provide emergency accommodation and a place of sanctuary for people experiencing a mental health crisis. Most are led by service user groups or have strong input from service users. They are usually modelled on a philosophy of 'recovery' and sometimes reject conventional psychiatric methods of treatment in a crisis. Guests can self refer and are encouraged to take responsibility for their recovery (which may mean making the decision to take medication or temporarily put their care in hands of another person). In a situation that would previously have led to hospital admission, this outcome can often be avoided.

Further information can be found in Sainsbury Centre for Mental Health (2002).

Community mental health websites

There is a wealth of services in the non-statutory and voluntary sector that are hugely valuable to the people who use them (sometimes making a bigger difference than the statutory agencies). As a GP I sometimes feel disconnected from these agencies and realise too late that I've missed an opportunity to signpost a patient to them. Top of my 'favourites' list on the computer in my consulting room is the local community mental health website. In my area this is run by a registered mental health charity called LAMP, and I would recommend their website as a good example of a local resource for professionals as well as users and carers (http://www.lampdirect.org.uk/). Their aim is to provide news about mental health issues and to offer a broad range of information about services, activities and support available within the local area. For me it is their directory of services (both statutory and non-statutory) that I most often refer to during a consultation – for example, signposting patients to where they can find help with advocacy, benefits or special interest services like those for domestic violence, drug problems or carer support.

Services to address special groups – the asylum seekers service

ASSIST is a pioneering service and one of the few services in the UK solely dedicated to the 'primary care' of asylum seekers. They are a disenfranchised, vulnerable and stigmatised group in our society. They arrive in the UK with complex physical and mental health needs. They have no initial understanding of the NHS and therefore cannot access services effectively.

ASSIST is a nurse-led service operating a flattened hierarchy between its clinicians – a nurse consultant, GPs, nurse practitioners and practice therapists. The team reflects the multiculturalism of the city and some of the staff have direct experience of the asylum system. As a brand new project, ASSIST was able to take an innovative approach to its service design based around its values of providing client-centred care with dignity and respect for people from all backgrounds and cultures. Particular attention was paid to the provision of language support. Clinical staff undertook training with the Medical Foundation for Victims of Torture. Strong links were made between statutory and non-statutory agencies in the city, in particular Refugee Action, the National Asylum Support Service, the Red Cross, housing providers and the city council.

From the service's conception there was an awareness of the massive and extraordinary need within this patient group for appropriate mental health care. Many patients have suffered extreme trauma in the form of war, imprisonment, rape and torture.

The foundation of good care begins with creating a safe place where people feel respected and believed. The act of bearing witness to the story of a victim of torture remains the simplest therapeutic tool that can be offered with limited resources. Over time these stories can change from those of anger, grief and bewilderment to stories of survival.

The Graduate Mental Health Worker set up a 'Signposting Service' to link people with local activities and groups, e.g. sports, language study, places to practice spiritual and religious beliefs, and places where newly arrived asylum seekers might meet people from their own countries or backgrounds. This project is thought to have had a significant impact on mental health problems and is an excellent example of mental health promotion.

Some patients require a greater level of expertise than the doctors and practice nurses can offer. These patients can be referred 'in house' to the practice therapists, one of whom is trained in 'Intercultural Therapy'. It is hoped that therapeutic group work will be undertaken shortly. It is believed that the service has reduced the number of referrals to secondary care by meeting the therapeutic needs of the client group in a specialist primary care environment.

All clinicians are provided with supervision in order to continue this demanding therapeutic work without putting their own well-being at risk.

GP training and mental health

I would argue that the stereotype of the powerful, arrogant (white, male?) GP who barely looks up from the computer before printing off a prescription is dying out and will soon be no longer relevant to general practice.

Traditional medical education produced doctors accomplished in diagnosis and treatment of physical problems framed on a medical model. That is, the problem is seen to lie within the patient, who consults an expert doctor who will make him or her better. Thinking is first order and positivist, with no account taken of uncertainty or diversity, and on no account are the feelings of the doctor reflected upon.

For some years the more forward-looking medical schools have given over time in an already packed curriculum to teach social sciences and communication skills, and the more traditional medical schools have followed suit. All too frequently these embryonic skills are metaphorically beaten out during the years of hospital practice, both as students and junior doctors. There is evidence that medical students become less person-centred as their training progresses (Barbee, 1970; Preven, 1986).

The GMC document *Tomorrow's Doctors* was published in 1993 and proposed fundamental changes to undergraduate medical education. It set down learning outcomes in particular relating to communication skills and the relationship that a new doctor should have with his or her patients and colleagues.

Junior hospital posts continue to provide a poor environment to build on these skills. Worse still, workload and fatigue while dealing with death and distress frequently result in doctors learning to cut themselves off from their emotions in order to 'get the job done'. When doctors with this background enter general practice training they are asked to start paying attention to these feelings. Some young doctors meet this challenge with resistance, while others are relieved to have the opportunity to practice in a more holistic way.

Current general practice training centres on the consultation. The GP registrar learns the importance of empathy and rapport, exploring the patient's ideas, concerns and expectations, making a bio-psycho-social diagnosis and negotiating a shared management plan. Emphasis is placed on the ability to explore and understand patients' 'lifeworlds' (Barry *et al.*, 2001), seeing them as unique individuals in the context of their families, work and relationships, and the impact this has on their health.

Rather than paying lip service, these values are enshrined in the criteria for selection of doctors on to General Practice Vocational Training Schemes, the qualifying assessment (Summative Assessment), and the Royal College of General Practitioners membership examination. Included in these exams are video or simulated patient assessments whereby the doctor must demonstrate their wider consultation skills.

A good deal of attention is focused on the interface between psychological and physical health and the different ways that problems with psychological well-being may present – for example, the presentation of anxiety or depression with physical symptoms, or the many different ways in which emotional distress may present. In order to develop these skills and understanding, the use of simulated patients is becoming more widespread in both the training and the assessment of GPs. Simulated patients are individuals trained to play the part of a patient in a consultation. Not only do they know the physical symptoms being experienced, but also their psychological and social circumstances. Therefore they can react to *any* question within role. The beauty of simulated patients lies in their ability to stop and rewind a consultation to try it in different ways. They are also able to debrief the doctor in or out of role when the consultation is finished.

Not only are the patient's thoughts and feelings focused on, but also the feelings that the doctor may have in response. Some GPs join a Balint Group (based on the work of psychoanalyst Michael Balint (1957)) in order to gain a better understanding of how those feelings can be helpful within the consultation.

The improvements in training of new GPs, particularly around using a biopsychosocial framework and encouraging a curiosity about how the context of a patient's life affects their well-being, are a sound foundation for improving the care of patients with mental health problems.

It can be argued that the traditional GP training of six-month attachments in hospital specialties is not an ideal way to train in mental health. The spectrum of problems and types of treatment on an acute inpatient unit does not reflect the work of a GP. With this in mind some vocational training schemes are moving to an innovative approach where the registrar receives training within a team that has more relevance to the challenges of general practice mental health work. Examples include placements with the Common Mental Health Problems Service (see before), Crisis Resolution Team and Liaison Psychiatry. This may involve having the training supervised by a mental health practitioner who is not a doctor – further underlining the fact that the traditional medical model is not useful in the general practice setting.

Patient, service user or client?

The rhetoric within general practice is that of *patients* rather than *service users* or *clients*. I notice I have used the terms interchangeably – no offence is intended if individuals prefer one name over another.

References

Balint, M. (1957) *The Doctor, His Patient and the Illness.* London: Pitman. (Millennium Edition, 2000. Edinburgh: Churchill Livingstone.)

Barbee, R. A. and Feldman, S. E. (1970) A three year longitudinal study of the medical interview and its relationship to student performance in clinical medicine. *Journal of Medical Education,* **45**, 770–776.

Barry, C. A., Stevenson, F. A., Britten, N., Barber, N. and Bradley, C. P. (2001) Giving voice to the lifeworld. More humane, more effective medical care? A qualitative study of doctor–patient communication in general practice. *Social Sciences and Medicine,* **53**, 487–505.

Department of Health (1999) *A National Service Framework for Mental Health.* London: HMSO.

Dobson, R. (2003) GPs prescribe self-help books for mental health problems. *British Medical Journal,* **326**, 1285.

General Medical Council (1993) *Tomorrow's Doctors.* London: General Medical Council.

Goldberg, D. and Huxley, P. (1992) *Common Mental Disorders. A Biosocial Model.* London: Routledge.

Harris, E. C. and Barraclough, B. (1998) Excess mortality of mental health disorder. *British Journal of Psychiatry,* **173**, 11–53.

Kendrick, T., Sibbald, B., Burns, T. and Freeling, P. (1991) Role of general practitioners in the care of long term mentally ill patients. *British Medical Journal,* **302**, 508–510.

Kisely, S. R. and Goldberg, D. (1996) Physical and psychiatric comorbidity in general practice. *British Journal of Psychiatry,* **169**, 236–242.

Marks, I., Kenwright, M., McDonough, M., Whittaker, M. and Matai, C. (2004) Saving clinicians' time by delegating routine aspects of therapy to a computer: a randomized controlled trial in phobia/panic disorder. *Psychological Medicine,* **34**, 9–17.

Minghella, E., Ford, R., Freeman, T., Hoult, J., McGlynn, P. and O'Halloran, P. (1998) *Open All Hours: 24-hour Response for People with Mental Health Emergencies.* London: Sainsbury Centre for Mental Health.

NICE (2002) *Schizophrenia: Core Interventions in the Treatment and Management of Schizophrenia in Primary and Secondary Care.* National Institute for Clinical Excellence clinical guideline. London: National Institute for Clinical Excellence.

Preven, D. W., Kachur, E. K., Kupfer, R. B. and Waters, J. A. (1986) Interviewing skills in first year medical students. *Journal of Medical Education,* **61**, 842–844.

Proudfoot, J., Ryden, C., Everitt, B., Shapiro, D., Goldberg, D., Mann, A., Tylee, A., Marks, I. and Gray, J. A. (2004) Clinical effectiveness of computerised cognitive behavioural therapy for anxiety and depression primary care. A randomized controlled trial. *British Journal of Psychiatry*, **185**, 46–54.

Sainsbury Centre for Mental Health (2002) *Being There in A Crisis. A Report of the Learning From Eight Mental Health Crisis Services.* London: Mental Health Foundation in association with the Sainsbury Centre for Mental Health.

CHAPTER 7

The mental health solicitor – an overview of our role and day to day work

Ranjit Thalliwal

Mental health solicitor – what's that?

In my attempt to try to provide an overview in relation to the work of a mental health solicitor, a useful starting point will be a discussion about the levels of understanding that exist in relation to the mental health law area generally. This is clearly intertwined with the conceptions that people have about the mental health system, which itself can be shrouded in mystery and sometimes misinformation. The range of services that solicitors can provide is well known to the general public, as they will use the conveyancing department when buying or selling a home, or the personal injury department if they are involved in a road traffic accident where they were not to blame and sustained injury; and so it goes on. So when it comes to the issue of legal advice the different areas of law that exists are generally well known to the public. This scenario does not necessarily apply to the area of mental health law, as my experience is that when people ask me what area I specialise in they will often struggle with the answer and then require further elaboration as to what this actually entails on a day-to-day basis. Clearly the reasons for this may be complicated and include the fact that they have had no contact in the past with the mental health system or understand the powers that exist within it.

Awareness in this area is growing, however, probably helped by the existence of specific support groups such as MIND as well as the fact that it is perhaps easier to access information, for example through the Internet.

In broad terms, though, the area itself remains to a degree insular, because in effect it serves a specific client base, namely those who are either in hospital or encountering difficulties with the mental health system generally in respect of their care, including any aftercare issues that arise.

My firm

My area of work concentrates solely on the mental health area of law, and therefore my firm services no other areas of law at all. This kind of specialism is more common in terms of subject areas now, as in previous times individual solicitors would deal with different areas of law. Although to a degree this still happens, the general move is towards specialism, with solicitors often dealing with a single subject area. The subject area that I deal with is clearly extremely specialised and in the legal market providers of advice and representation in relation to mental health law are relatively limited in number in comparison with other subject areas.

Representation through the area of mental health law is completed with the benefit of a Legal Services Commission (LSC) franchise, which in effect authorises my firm to provide advice and representation under the Legal Aid scheme and requires compliance with the regulations of the LSC. This involves periodic audits of our work as well as the examination of random files to ensure that quality standards are maintained. To this extent the firm is in effect sternly supervised on an ongoing basis via the LSC and independent scrutiny continues in this regard.

In terms of my own development I have become wholly immersed in the area of mental health law and have been able to develop certain additional areas which I feel complement my day-to-day work in this area. I am a member of the Diverse Minds National Advice Panel, which is a specialist sub-group of the National MIND organisation; involvement in this group is of particular interest to me as I am of Asian descent, being Punjabi, although I was born in Leicester. To that degree I have perhaps had the advantage of being able to converse with Asian clients in particular and overcome the language barrier which often exists in that regard.

In terms of our specialism to deal with Legal Aid, I am a member of the Law Society Mental Health Review Tribunal Panel, which again acts as another quality mark in that the panel membership is subject to periodic review and scrutinises your ability to deal with representation in this area. The panel membership therefore proceeds on an ongoing basis. As part of extending my personal experience and specialisms I have become involved in teaching at the local School of Nursing in relation to the area of mental health law, which again has acted as a very beneficial process for myself, and hopefully for the students, primarily to impart my knowledge and skills in terms of the Mental Health Tribunal procedure to nursing staff who will in effect be operating on the mental health wards in the future.

I hope the above provides an overview of the firm and its flavour and in particular my background. Over and above the usual CV-type details I think there are some core personal characteristics that are required for a person to be working in this area; these obviously come from my own personal experience and may not have general application. The ability to deal with individuals in distress in a calm and reassuring manner seems a central requirement for building trust so as to convey to those that you are assisting that you are advocating on their behalf. That they are the primary person that you are concerned with is also critical, and being a good listener and having patience plays a part in the instruction-taking process. In the appropriate circumstances, humour and the ability to have a laugh can also be a valuable way of taking tension out of the dialogue process. Being both flexible and open minded and not rigid in your approach would also seem to be helpful in this area.

The work, by its very nature, is extremely varied both in terms of the clients that you deal with and the establishments that you visit, and therefore an ability to be flexible and to be able to adapt to different circumstances is part of the day-to-day role.

How do we get our clients?

The issue of how clients approach you and make contact with the firm is both complex and varied. By being a specialist mental health law firm, franchised by the Legal Services Commission, you will form part of their official database and directory and this is accessible to the public through various routes, including publications and the Internet. This may be one way in which clients or their family and friends make contact with you.

The procedure in terms of the hospital wards themselves is varied, but details of the solicitors who provide representation in the mental health law area locally are normally available on each and every ward; for example in Leicester, where I practise, the details of myself and the firm are readily available to any patient who may request this on the ward itself. The procedures within hospitals for tribunals involve the Mental Health Act Office, which would carry the details of any local solicitors, and from time to time you may receive communication from them in relation to a client who seeks representation.

In terms of the general mental health area, support groups exist which from time to time have to provide information to their clients and signpost them to legal services; again, contact with the firm from these groups is sometimes received with regard to clients who, for example, have been admitted and have moved into a tribunal scenario.

The above factors would relate to how new clients could access details of our firm. Of course there is a large proportion of clients who may have used our services previously in terms of a previous admission or a difficulty with regard to the mental health law area. These individuals would already have our details, and to a degree they would return to us by way of follow-up. One example where this arises is the so-called 'revolving door patient', who may of course have previous admissions under the Mental Health Act, and therefore tribunals may arise on an ongoing basis from time to time.

It is interesting to draw comparison with other areas of law, as generally speaking we would not rely on any 'passing trade', and in fact the office itself retains a relatively low profile with regard to its signage; clients do not often visit the office itself. Therefore work from this source is clearly negligible. However, one similarity which does exist with other areas of law is word of mouth, which can still be a valuable tool as, with luck, the quality of service you provide to existing clients will be conveyed to potential new clients, who may then also instruct you in relation to mental health law matters. Clearly one circumstance in which this arises is with respect to patients on the wards themselves, as they form friendships and speak amongst each other, and cross-referral can arise as a consequence. A critical issue with regard to all mental health law clients is that they have complete and open freedom of choice to instruct who they choose, and in fact to change solicitors if they so wish.

This should provide a snapshot of the diverse sources from which clients can come, particularly with regard to tribunal work.

Seeing the client

Once initial contact has been made (which can happen in various forms, most commonly by way of a telephone call to us), follow-up is required to see that client. If the client is detained on a ward on Section, and is seeking a tribunal hearing, it is important that the visit takes place as soon as possible and that telephone communication is made almost immediately. The purpose of the initial telephone call will be to reassure the client about the broad procedure and to arrange a visit to allow detailed discussions to take place. In terms of the initial visit, prior arrangement will be made with the ward, usually by calling through to the ward staff themselves, and then also with the client. This is to ensure that the timing of the appointment is convenient both to the ward and to the client. The visit will usually take place on the ward in an appropriate private room.

The issue of privacy is critical, as it is not appropriate to be having dialogue in open or communal areas, as the information to be discussed is of a sensitive nature and the client should have full confidence to be able to speak openly and clearly about all matters. The initial attendance with the client is usually one in which a certain amount of fact finding has to take place, both in terms of the historical information leading up to admission, the admission scenario and the current situation. Any information taken from the client can be supplemented via dialogue with the staff team, and is often followed up by dialogue with the family if this is also appropriate. In terms of speaking to family members, the approval of the client clearly should be sought, as sometimes, particularly in the run-up to admission, tensions can arise between the client and next of kin (for example, family members are often seen as the instigators of the admission process). Therefore sensitivity on this issue is important.

It is important that the time-scale in responding to a client should be as short as possible after the initial phone call is received, as this is the point at which the client will often require the greatest amount of reassurance with regard to the role you can play and the procedures. Usually at the time of the first visit no written reports or information are to hand, and therefore the fact-finding process is clearly very important. As part of the initial attendance after detailed discussions and advice has been provided, completion of the relevant Tribunal Appeal Form will be finalised (if this has not already been done). This would normally be despatched via our office to the Tribunal Service. We would also seek access to the client's notes and a request in writing would be made to the Registered Medical Officer (RMO) to allow access to these notes to be facilitated in due course. All these factors are clearly part of the process of building up information and gleaning as much detail as possible. At the time of the initial visit, time-scales can vary in terms of each particular matter. In circumstances where the client is being seen on a Section 2 detention, time is of the essence, as a hearing will normally be fixed within seven days of the appeal itself being submitted, and therefore the work has to be completed within this time frame.

However, if the client is being seen in relation to a Section 3 detention or a Section 37/41 scenario the time-scales are much longer, ranging from four to six weeks and often up to three months or beyond in relation to tribunal hearings being set. Therefore the response is gauged in accordance with both the time-scale of the case and of course the needs of the individual client. After the conclusion of the initial visit the relevant documentation will be completed, which would include the above as well as Legal Aid documentation. This will be explained in detail to the client and reassurance will be provided that in effect no charges will be raised to the client in terms of the legal services provided. It is often important to communicate to the client that, after the initial visit, if any follow-up is required throughout the case they can call us at any point and appointments will be arranged on an ongoing basis as the case proceeds. The process of communication after the initial visit, including writing to the tribunal and accessing medical notes, in essence puts the firm on record as acting for that client if this had not already been done by a Tribunal Appeal previously submitted by the client. In essence, after the first visit matters are under way.

How a tribunal case proceeds

We now turn specifically to the scenario in which representation is provided in relation to a Mental Health Review Tribunal Hearing. We have explained that the time-scale from the point of initial contact and submitting the appeal to the Tribunal Service can vary from seven days in the case of a Section 2 to four to six weeks on a Section 3 and three months and beyond in the case of a 37/41 appeal. This sets the agenda in terms of the course of conduct, as ongoing visits will be arranged with the client to update matters, and these clearly are influenced by the needs of the client. For example, some clients will be more needy and will request visits on a more frequent basis. This may be due to developments in terms of their care situation (for example leave being blocked, or problems arising in the ward environment), and therefore the solicitor has to remain sensitive to acting on a case-by-case basis; to a degree no standard rule applies in this regard. Other clients will remain more reassured through the process. Telephone contact will cement this and visitation can sometimes be less frequent. One of the critical issues is the receipt of written reports for the tribunal itself, which would generally include a report from the RMO and ASW (Approved Social Worker) and in some circumstances a report from the Nursing Staff. The timing of these reports again varies depending on the type of case.

In respect of a Section 2 matter, as mentioned earlier, everything is done within a compressed time-scale and the reports are received usually on the day of the hearing itself which will usually be within seven days of the appeal being sent in. Therefore the preparation is influenced by this. In Section 2 cases the date of the hearing is one on which clients are extremely busy, as often they have to complete an attendance with the tribunal doctor, go through relevant reports with the solicitor and then sit through and give their evidence within the context of the tribunal hearing.

In relation to Section 3 and Section 37/41 applications the reports would be received much later. Again, upon receipt they will be discussed with the client. The reports are not always received at the same time, so for example an ASW report may be received first and then the RMO's report received later; appointments are usually arranged to discuss these as matters proceed.

Subject to the client's approval, part of the preparation process can include dialogue and visits with family members, who may of course attend the tribunal hearing itself. There may be certain historical information to be examined:

for example, the client may possess historical reports and/or past information which is of relevance and which the client wishes to share with us.

One of the preparatory steps which is available, again subject to treatment on a case-by-case basis, is that an independent report can be commissioned with an independent psychiatrist for the tribunal hearing. This is something which is examined during the context of the matter and can be influenced by varying factors, including when the report itself is received, as often it is received at a time close to the tribunal hearing itself; in those circumstances the option of seeking an adjournment is available if the time-scale does not allow an independent report to be prepared within that period. For an independent report to be prepared an authority for the expenditure in terms of the report must be sought from the Legal Services Commission; it has to satisfy various criteria and the process takes a few days to finalise, which has to be factored into the overall equation. However, this is an option which is available.

The other wider point to consider is that after the time at which the tribunal application is made by the client, his or her situation may well develop and improve in terms of detention on ward. For example, if an appeal is submitted three weeks after detention the client may well be enjoying leave sessions, which can then be increased to a stage where leave is quite extensive at the time of the hearing itself. Therefore the client's circumstances as they were at the time of the appeal, or even at the time the reports were written, can be outdated by the time the tribunal hearing itself occurs. If matters proceed progressively, the other scenario that can arise is that, at the time of the hearing itself or just before, the Section itself can be removed by the RMO due to the client's progression and the circumstances as they are at that particular juncture; if the Section is removed the tribunal itself is cancelled and in effect the client has what he or she wanted: namely to be taken off Section. This happens on many occasions, and tribunals can often be cancelled the day before the hearing or even on the day of the hearing itself.

It is important to repeat and reiterate the advice that is being given to the client in terms of the tribunal procedure, in particular in relation to how the hearing itself proceeds. It may be the first time that a client has been detained under Section and therefore it is a completely new experience as far as he or she is concerned. An important piece of information to discuss is the role of the tribunal doctor, who will complete a visit prior to the tribunal hearing itself. This often takes place on the date of the hearing, and the doctor is obviously one of the three decision makers in terms of the tribunal, although the doctor will be independent of the hospital and would have a one-to-one dialogue with the client prior to the hearing. It is therefore vital to discuss the doctor's role with the client in order that the client is clear about it and ultimately provides cooperation, as this is an avenue for the client's perspective of the situation to be conveyed.

As can be seen from the above, the steps in preparing for a tribunal are varied. The intensity depends on the nature of each individual case and the circumstances that arise.

Reports for the tribunal can vary from a few pages up to a relatively bulky document, and clearly the time that will be taken to analyse the documents will vary accordingly. Flexibility in the approach to the run-up to the tribunal is required.

The tribunal hearing

In the run-up to the tribunal, the client should have received information on more than one occasion regarding the procedure at the hearing. On the day of the hearing the advice is reiterated and repeated in order that the client is clear as to the form and conduct of the hearing. In essence, a Mental Health Review Tribunal hearing comes to the client, in that the hearing takes place in a room often proximate to the ward itself. The layout of the hearing usually sees the three panel members seated behind one table, while the other participants, including the client and myself, as well as the RMO, ASW, Named Nurse member and often the Tribunal Clerk, sit opposite. In addition, there may be some other members of the team who sometimes attend to give evidence as relevant. The other significant additions are observers who are come to gain experience, and permission is required from the client and the tribunal for these to sit in the hearing. Therefore in some circumstances the meeting room itself can be quite full. This in itself can unintentionally act as an intimidating factor; therefore reassurance to the client is required in the run-up to the meeting and through the meeting itself.

The solicitor would normally sit next to the client in order to allow dialogue to proceed through the hearing as relevant in terms of any developments that arise.

In terms of discussions prior to the hearing itself, one of the important points to emphasise to the client is that the meeting allows every participant to speak in turn. Generally interruptions are not allowed, and therefore patience must be shown by the client to allow others to speak until it is their turn. This issue is very difficult to maintain in practice, as if a client is listening to the RMO saying a number of things which are potentially negative with regard to past conduct and about which the client disagrees, the natural response is often to interrupt. This would not go down well with the Tribunal Panel and obviously would interrupt the flow of the meeting. It is at this stage that the client has to remember the point in question and provide a riposte at the time when it is his or her turn to give evidence.

In the normal course of events the Tribunal usually hears from the clinical team first, and therefore the order of evidence would normally involve these parties giving evidence first.

Once all parties are in the room, introductions by the Chairperson are made in terms of all panel members and all parties in attendance will normally provide introductions in respect of their attendance. At this stage the tribunal doctor will then provide an brief summary of the discussion with the patient prior to the hearing. This is given as a preliminary prior to the evidence taken in the hearing.

After confirmation of the written reports that have been submitted has been made, the normal course of evidence is that initial evidence is provided by the RMO and then evidence is given by the ASW, Named Nurse member and any other parties related to the clinical team.

It is after the team has given its evidence that the client will normally go through his or her evidence and will be allowed to ask some questions to take the tribunal through the salient points that the client wishes to raise.

With regard to any evidence given by the team, the solicitor would have the opportunity to, in effect, cross examine any points of contention or disagreement, and the panel also will ask any questions that may arise, as they will do with the client. The tribunal will normally raise questions with each individual and then allow the solicitor to ask about any points that arise. Clearly this is an important phase of the tribunal as it allows the solicitor to raise any issues which are contested and inaccurate from the client's perspective, and also to put alternative submissions to them in terms of the next phase. Questions may be of a very challenging or contentious nature, but would always be put forward in a cordial and appropriate manner. A balance has to be drawn, and clearly the priority and the duty are to the client. Therefore these issues have to be raised robustly to relevant members of the team, whether that be the doctor or the ASW. As an aside, most professionals will take no umbrage at this process, as it is a typical part of the tribunal procedure and by asking for a tribunal the patient is merely exercising a legal right that is available to him in law.

In reality, the solicitor will often be challenging the same doctors and social workers through various tribunals, and by and large professional relationships are maintained on good terms as each party takes its respective position. Ironically, referral of patients to you can even occur from a members of the professional team, such as the RMO or ASW, from time to time. No doubt this is supportive of the view that good relations can be maintained. If on occasion a professional member becomes 'frosty' post-hearing, that is an unfortunate by-product of our role and the duty remains clear that we have to advocate on behalf of the client. Fortunately this is a very rare scenario, as all professionals generally remain on appropriate terms.

The order of evidence can vary, and in certain circumstances the client may wish to give evidence earlier or at the beginning; for example if you feel that the client may not be able to refrain from interrupting the other parties. In those circumstances you may choose to ask for the client's evidence to be taken first on the basis that he or she can say their piece without interruption and then listen patiently when other parties are speaking. The client may also then be given a brief opportunity at the end of the tribunal to come back on any fresh issues which came out during the course of evidence.

Once all parties have spoken, closing submissions are normally allowed by the solicitor in terms of submissions that are sought in terms of a discharge and formal recommendations. The tribunal hearing can vary in length, and obviously this depends on the length of reports and detail to be covered, the number of parties in attendance and the presence of any interpreters, as this will often lengthen the hearing considerably: they will need to interpret what is being said both during the hearing and during the process of the client giving evidence to the panel.

Typically, hearings can range from an hour up to two or three hours and even beyond, depending on the breadth of evidence to be taken.

It is no doubt easy to understand that the day of the tribunal will be a challenging one for the client, as it will involve a lot of concentration and attention as well as the stress that will often be involved in the run-up to the hearing itself. For example, some clients will have their sleep affected the night before because they will be nervous and concerned about the hearing.

Reassuring the client about the process and during the process is clearly a critical factor through to the conclusion of the tribunal hearing. Depending on the length of the hearing, on occasion the tribunal will provide a short break if requested by the client or if they feel that it is appropriate. This may last for 10 or 15 minutes as relevant.

Once the tribunal proceedings have concluded the panel will send all parties out and then deliberate on their decision in private. The period of deliberation again can vary and once the panel has decided (normally on the day of the hearing itself), it will call all parties back and provide a verbal decision. If the decision is one for immediate discharge it obviously comes into effect at that point; other options can include a deferred discharge, which may take effect at a later point, or an adjournment of the case for some specific reason, whereupon it may reconvene at a future point.

By and large the tribunal will provide a verbal decision on the day of the hearing itself, and therefore the client will be clear as to the decision. The procedure is that the written decision is then sent out in due course, but the period of time that it takes for this to be received can vary, as it often comes via the Tribunal Service in London and can in theory take two to three weeks to arrive. The written decision does not, however, affect the practical result of the hearing coming into force immediately; namely, if a discharge is ordered it is in effect from that time. Usually after the hearing there will be a brief discussion with the client on a one-to-one basis to explain the decision in broad terms.

Clients' responses to hearing results may vary, and if a positive decision is reached the response is usually an affirmative one. In reality, when a negative decision is received at the end of the hearing – for example a decision not to discharge – the vast majority of clients take the decision relatively well, and therefore the natural response that you might anticipate, namely one of anger, disappointment, frustration and the like, is not as prevalent as one might expect. In the most extreme scenario a negative result may prompt anger to the extent that physical or verbal acts take place, but my experience this is very much the exception. The post-result discussion is also important. Certain reassurances may be given within the context of the hearing (for example the Section may be removed on the basis that the client will remain on the ward on a voluntary basis for a few days), and in these circumstances the post-hearing discussion will be critical in emphasising and re-emphasising this to the client, as although they have their liberty back (the Section has been removed) it will be important to remind them of what they said in the hearing about remaining and discussing pre-discharge planning with the staff as relevant.

The post-hearing discussion would then normally bring the tribunal day to a close.

After the completion of the tribunal hearing there will normally be follow-up visits, depending on the client's instructions, as there may be post-hearing matters that would have to be addressed and discussed. This can be particularly important: for example, if a deferred discharge is made with the discharge taking place in 21 days' time, there may be preparatory steps required to be completed as part of the pre-discharge scenario; follow-up with the client will have to be undertaken to ensure that the discharge is effected smoothly. This is the point at which further contact will be required with the client pending his or her discharge from hospital. The follow-up after the hearing will have to be reappraised depending on the client concerned and his or her individual needs.

Other mental health law issues

Representing individuals on Section is not the only area in which advice and assistance is required, as some clients may be in the mental health system on an informal basis but have valid and real issues to raise about which they require advice in relation to their situation within the system generally. The subject matters which are discussed can be varied and depend on the individual client's needs. The other area where a need for advice can arise is in relation to post-discharge matters in terms of aftercare provisions: both post-discharge planning and the support that is provided to an individual, often in the home environment, such as ASW, CPN and general follow-up.

It will be noted that there is also the forensic sector, where individuals can be detained on Home Office Orders on a restricted basis; in the early stages of such detention, although discharge is not necessarily the objective there may be other issues which arise and are pertinent, for example the extension of a person's leave or a transfer into lower secure accommodation. Therefore it is important to note, over and above the main tribunal scenario, that other matters can arise which fall within our remit for advice, assistance and support to individuals.

The learning process continues for all of us and new and novel situations can arise from time to time, upon which external sources may have to be approached for additional information. To this end formal dialogue with other colleagues in the mental health area can be of assistance. Additionally, MIND and its legal unit are of great assistance in terms of specific advice lines that they provide, in addition to other sources of information, including the Internet and reference texts. In relation to unusual scenarios advice from Counsel may be taken if there is a potential cause of action on a specific issue arising from the mental health law area. Chambers are quite helpful in providing informal advice as matters arise before the matter becomes formalised.

Conclusion

The above has provided an overview of the day-to-day work in which I am involved as a mental health law solicitor. The views come from an experienced-based perspective in terms of the experience that my firm has in terms of the representation of our client base. The area itself is a niche, and to a degree we operate in a bubble from the point of view of our client base and other work areas. The circumstances in which our clients find themselves is often both very distressing and challenging, and they need to feel that they have an ally whose role is to advocate on their behalf in an unequivocal fashion. It is important that detailed explanations are provided to them, as the information process itself provides some relief and clarity about the next phase, particularly when it is the first time they have been brought into the mental health system.

The experiences I have conveyed are wholly personal and clearly others in my position may have views and experiences that differ. I find it important to retain contact with external agencies and groups and to expand my personal profile so as to remain connected to external sources and to retain a balanced perspective, as working in this very narrow field can sometimes be isolating. It is almost, to draw a very rough analogy, sometimes like the legal equivalent of being in quasi-seclusion. Thus networking and cross-referencing with other parties is vital to keep a broader picture in the context with clients. On the reverse side it is an extremely rewarding area, as you feel you are providing a service to your client which alleviates their distress, helps to clarify their position and provides assistance to them in working towards a goal, which is often to seek a discharge. Even if a discharge is not secured, the tribunal process itself is often valuable in clarifying what the plan of action is for the next phase. Clients who are not discharged after a tribunal often still feel more positive about the situation because of the clarity and the support that they have received. Therefore, despite its challenges, the job satisfaction that it provides is excellent.

CHAPTER 8

The role that counselling psychology plays in the evolution of working in mental health services

Sarah Supple

When I was asked to write this chapter I thought it might encourage me to sit and seriously try to answer some of the questions that had been lurking in the corners of my mind since I began my training as a Counselling Psychologist. Originally I, as many do, took the field of clinical psychology as the obvious place to start looking for postgraduate training in order to be a practitioner in the field of psychology. However, I discovered a course in counselling psychology which took me down a road which is different, in ways that I feel are subtle but important, from the one I would have taken as a clinical psychologist. In this chapter I will give a brief sense of the evolution of counselling psychology as a discipline, moving on to consider what a Counselling Psychologist does. I will then give an idea of the mode of therapeutic work that counselling psychology has allowed me to develop thus far and illustrate this with some clinical examples, considering how counselling psychology, as a branch of psychology, can contribute to finding new ways of working within mental health services.

The origins of counselling psychology

Woolfe and Dryden (1996) give an historical overview of the beginnings of counselling psychology. They suggest that this is a necessary starting point when understanding this area. They report that the British Psychological Society (BPS) set up a Counselling Psychology section in 1982 and at the end of that year it had 225 members (British Psychological Society, 1993). By 1989 this had become a special section of the society with 1,208 members, making it the third largest section, after clinical and occupational psychology. Full professional status was achieved in 1994, by which time diplomas and courses had been developed to achieve chartered status. Wolfe and Dryden (1996, pp. 3–4) conclude that 'it could be said that in the space of 12 years a new profession had been established'. Although there is an institutional focus to the overview that Woolfe and Dryden provide, they also assert that 'it is necessary to move beyond this in order to understand what counselling psychology represents, in terms of its knowledge base, practises and last but not least its philosophical orientation' (Woolfe and Dryden, 1996, p. 4). They assert that it is in the last domain that the identity of counselling psychology is to be found. Although they define it as 'the application of scientific knowledge to the practise of counselling' (Woolfe and Dryden, 1996, p. 4), they also go on to discuss how a focus on value systems is needed rather than focusing on contexts or approaches.

As I understand it, part of the motivation for developing counselling psychology as a discipline was to provide an alternative to clinical training, one that was not paid for by and thus produced for the NHS. Thus, it could be argued that counselling psychology is indicative of the ongoing evolution of psychology, a new branch or sub-species of the psychological family tree. The BPS's website states:

Historically, Counselling Psychology has developed as a branch of professional psychological practice strongly influenced by human science research as well as principal psychotherapeutic traditions. Its relationship with mainstream academic psychology has been mutually challenging because Counselling Psychology has drawn upon and developed phenomenological models of practice and enquiry which have been at odds with the dominant conceptions of scientific psychology. Fruitful relationships have also been established with other counselling and psychotherapeutic practices which have evolved outside the framework of academic psychology.

Part of the problem in defining this new branch is that at the time of writing there still seems to be a lack of consensus regarding what counselling psychology is and how it should be treated in relation to other psychological approaches. I think this problem is being perpetuated by the fact that there are many varied roots to becoming a Counselling Psychologist, some entailing doctorates, some diplomas or masters, some following an independent route, and some full-time courses. In this chapter I will be referring mainly to my own training, which was a three-year full-time doctoral course at the University of Surrey. However, I would ask the reader to hold in mind that although I will be making generalisations of course, clinical and counselling training will differ significantly, as well as the fact that individual practitioners will have their own idiosyncrasies.

I felt that the course that I undertook relished the independence it had from more traditional training programmes. As a result I felt that throughout we were encouraged to critique established presumptions and norms: that is, reflecting on and eventually questioning or disagreeing with some of the historical assumptions inherent to the field of psychology. Psychology has always been the child of the medical model, yet it seems to me it has not always been free to explore, away from its parent, or free to question what it had always been told. I felt my training allowed me to do this by not just teaching me facts but allowing me to question how those facts were decided upon and who decided upon them, and enabling me to reflect on whether I also wanted to accept those facts.

What is counselling psychology?

The British Psychological Society's website currently states that:

> Chartered Counselling Psychologists work therapeutically with clients with a variety of problems (for example, the effects of childhood sexual abuse, relationship breakdown, domestic violence, major trauma) and/or symptoms of psychological disorder (such as anxiety, depression, eating disorders, post-traumatic stress disorder, and psychosis). They offer an active collaborative relationship which can both facilitate the exploration of underlying issues and can empower people to confront change.

The site goes on to give a lengthy list of what kind of settings Counselling Psychologists may work in and gives some basic information on what working in specific areas, e.g. adult mental health, may entail. However, it struck me that such a description only gives brief details regarding what Counselling Psychologists do, offering little insight into what counselling psychology is. Perhaps this is an ongoing problem, as it is very hard and even a contentious issue at times to try and define what counselling psychology is, and even if you could it is probably always in flux. In answer to such ambiguity I shall tell you something of what I understand counselling psychology to be.

I have concluded that there are three concepts that are core to my identity as a Counselling Psychologist. Firstly, as the name implies, counselling skills are integral to my therapeutic work: that is, the ability to listen in a non-judgemental way. The fact that my training begins with a year focused on humanistic or client-centred ways of working seems indicative of the fact that a humanistic way of working is integral to counselling psychology (McLeod, 1993). Such an approach focuses on the therapeutic relationship and relationships in their broader sense and promotes respect for the client and their perspectives. The humanistic paradigm places great value on the 'human capacities and potentialities' (McLeod, 1993), and views the person as a contextualised and complex whole. It requires a clinician to develop some core conditions, for example, empathy, congruence and unconditional positive regard. It also promotes the importance of self-acceptance by client and therapist (Rogers, 1957) and supports the notion that clients have the potential for positive growth and change (Kirschenbaum and Henderson, 1990). This at time seems to conflict with the more traditional approach to the science-based medical model which underpins psychology. Such a traditional stance perceives the client as sick and in need of being cured. In such a paradigm 'One party is seen as powerful and active, doing something to another party who is essentially a passive object' (Woolfe and Dryden, 1996, p. 8). To adopt a more contextualised focus, based on a mutual and respectful therapeutic relationship, allows the client and their problems to be viewed in different, more collaborative and empowering ways.

Once this foundation to therapeutic work has been established it is built on, drawing upon different therapeutic and theoretical perspectives to develop what I feel is the second core feature of counselling psychology: that is, an integrative way of working. I feel that the fact that counselling psychologists are trained in a variety of therapeutic orientations provides flexibility and creativity. My course split its placements and thus its training into three broad sections. The first year's teaching and placement focused on a client-centred way of working, consolidating counselling skills and the ability to formulate psychologically. The second year involved a psychodynamic approach (and compulsory personal therapy to facilitate use of self- and reflective practice) and the third introduced us to a cognitive behavioural approach whilst also working towards combining these different aspects to create an integrative way of working. Such an eclectic approach enabled me to enjoy an epistemological and clinical freedom that allowed me to work creatively and flexibly, tailoring my therapeutic work to individual clients' needs rather than being tempted to use more formulaic approaches.

However, a central part of what defines counselling psychology is not just what theoretical orientations are combined in clinical work but the perspective that underlies this.

That is, the third area I feel is of saliency is the attention that counselling psychology gives to reflective practice, not just drawing upon the relationship between therapist and client but also being aware of the process of therapy and how the therapist's use of self may impact upon this. These concepts are further expanded upon later in this chapter when discussing therapeutic work, as I feel it is easier to explain this way of working when it is contextualised.

However, an approach based on relationship, integration and reflection is not always unproblematic, particularly when considering clinical context. The NHS is a service under immense pressure, mental health services particularly so. From my experiences of working in the NHS I have seen first hand the massive waiting lists that can accrue. In this environment the pressure on resources means that financial and time efficiency become paramount, and thus often short-term work becomes the preference. Such demands do not always fit easily with some of the central aspects of a counselling psychology approach. The BPS website states:

> Counselling psychology claims its place within mainstream professional psychological practice. It continues to develop models of practice and research, which marry the scientific demand for rigorous empirical enquiry with a firm value base grounded in the primacy of the counselling/psychotherapeutic relationship.

However, such an emphasis on the therapeutic relationship and use of self as well as attending to the therapeutic process and working reflectively does not easily fit into such a pressured environment, where efficiency is key. Despite this I would assert that counselling psychology can make a positive contribution to the culture of psychological work within the NHS because it brings a perspective and emphasis that I would argue links together more traditional areas of clinical psychology, psychotherapy and counselling in a way which facilitates new ways of working. That is not to say that I think we should disregard what has come before, but rather that we should all work in collaboration to help evolve the systems we work in that deliver support and care to those people who come into mental health services. Also, I feel this is where the strength of working integratively shows itself. That is, although counselling psychology draws from ideas traditionally used in longer term therapy it also draws upon newer, more short-term/focused approaches and thus can integrate these together to develop novel ways of working in systems that enforce time restrictions whilst also being able to attend to the difficulties of working with complex cases.

Therapeutic work

It seems that now would be a good point to move on to a consideration of what this all actually means for therapeutic practice. The considerations so far have clarified to me that one of the characteristics central to counselling psychology is the fact it seems to hold as salient the therapeutic relationship, not just as something necessary to build rapport, but as central to therapeutic work as a vessel for change. I suggest that this brings a therapeutic focus which differs from that traditionally focused upon. As already mentioned, historically psychology has conceptualised the psychologist as a objective, detached observer, rather than as in collaborative relationship with the client. This perhaps is reflected in the focus on technique and bias towards theoretical certainty and diagnosis that seems to exist in the NHS and in psychological institutions more generally, who seem to strive to emulate scientific models of knowledge and thus therapy. As I understand it, contemporary training in clinical psychology tends to focus on cognitive approaches to psychological therapy. Again, I feel the need to emphasise that I am sure that this is not true of all clinical training, but on the whole this seems to be the case. However, this is only indicative of the wider institutional bias towards such an approach. For example the National Institute for Clinical Excellence (2001) publishes guidelines regarding best practice in a wide range of health services, including psychological and mental health services. This advocates the use of computerised cognitive behavioural therapy (CCBT) in the treatment of depression and anxiety. Also, it gives guidance on how best to treat certain presenting problems, i.e. generalised anxiety disorder/panic disorder, depression, post-traumatic stress disorder, schizophrenia and self-harm. In all of these areas it recommends a mixture of drug treatment in combination with cognitive behavioural therapy. It does mention that counselling may also be an option with mild to moderate depression, but actively discourages psychotherapeutic approaches with the treatment of schizophrenia. Certainly there is a bias towards CBT as the approach that should be adopted. Similarly, the NHS website on treatment choice in psychological therapies seems to have a central theme of CBT, although in fairness it does mention other approaches, i.e. counselling and psychotherapy. For example it recommends in the 'Principal recommendations' section that

> Post-traumatic stress symptoms may be helped by psychological therapy, with most evidence for cognitive behavioural methods

and

> Depression may be treated effectively with cognitive therapy

but does also mention interpersonal therapy and focused brief psychotherapy. It goes on to say that

> Anxiety disorders with marked symptomatic anxiety (panic disorder, agoraphobia, social phobia, obsessive compulsive disorders, generalized anxiety disorders) are likely to benefit from cognitive behaviour therapy

and

> Psychological intervention should be considered for somatic complaints with a psychological component with most evidence for CBT in the treatment of chronic pain and chronic fatigue.

Cognitive therapy is based on the principle that our thoughts have a profound impact upon our emotions, behaviours and physiology (Gilbert, 2000). Thus our thinking styles can affect how we interpret the world. These biases in how we perceive the world can in turn mean that we perpetuate and maintain our problematic ways of behaving in everyday life. Therefore, in its simplest form, cognitive therapy is based on identifying and changing these problematic thinking patterns. It is understandable that, within the NHS, cognitive therapy has gained much support due to the plethora of research undertaken pertaining to its effectiveness (although some fundamental concerns have been raised about the validity of this research but this debate is for another time). It lends itself well to such research, as it is based on clear techniques and protocols which also make it ideal for planning short-term very structured therapy. In part due to this, the therapeutic relationship has been less associated with the cognitive approach than with other approaches (Frank, 2002). However, as the collaborative nature of cognitive therapy is central, the relationship must also be a key concern. The therapeutic relationship has traditionally been more associated with a client-centred or psychodynamic approach than a cognitive one. However, Frank (2002) feels that on closer inspection the relationship needs to be just as central to cognitive work and Woolfe and Dryden (1996) suggest it has only been overlooked because it was always presumed to be necessary. However, perhaps counselling psychology's focus on the relationship is indicative of a broader shift. Waddington (2002) asserts that cognitive therapists have been encouraged to give more attention to the relational aspect of the therapy because research from other therapeutic approaches has shown that the relationship has an impact on therapeutic outcome, independent of technical interventions. Frank (2002) asserts the need to find a way of incorporating more of a focus upon the relationship into a cognitive approach by integrating it with other approaches, such as a psychodynamic one. This is where I feel counselling psychology lends itself to the evolution of therapeutic work. It seems well positioned to explore how to integrate different approaches because, as I have mentioned, Counselling Psychologists are trained in a variety of therapeutic orientations and my course specifically culminated in an integrative year. A quote I used to exemplify my integrative stance in an essay I wrote whilst training still summarises my position well: 'Effective therapists are also flexible. That is, they are not tied to a single ideology or methodology that they use for all clients. Flexible counsellors adapt methods and technologies to clients, rather than pushing clients and their problems to fit the use of a particular orientation or strategy.' (Cormier and Sherilyn, 1991, p. 17). However, such integration or eclecticism can be approached with suspicion or uncertainty regarding its validity. That is, some (such as Joiner and Rudd, 1997) feel that more current ideas, such as the cognitive approach, do not easily incorporate the more traditional ways of conceptualising the relational aspects of therapy. Such concerns seem appropriate when looking at integrating any therapeutic approaches and care should be taken not to assume that therapists can just pick and choose parts of different approaches without being accountable for why they have made such choices and without spending time on reflecting and appraising what has therapeutic value and what may not.

This highlights another consideration, which I think the stance inherent to the perspective of counselling psychology can help to address. A clinician working in an integrative and creative way therapeutically needs to consider more than just what theoretical approaches are being used, as often different approaches have different assumptions underlying them regarding epistemology, how to perceive psychological problems and even regarding reality and how we are in the world. I would argue that attending to the relational aspect of the work and reflecting on the process of therapy, i.e. how it is to be in therapy and what else is going on besides the overt dialogue and conscious focus of the work, also requires a greater 'use of self' by the therapist. Frank (2002) asserts that therapy, as a discipline, has come to realise that the therapist has no choice but to be in relationship with the client and thus the relationship's influence on the therapy must be considered. This is a focus integral to most therapeutic approaches; for example, a psychodynamic approach will talk about transference and counter-transference, whilst therapy based on cognitive ideas may refer to interpersonal schemas or reciprocal roles and interpersonal interactions will be reflected upon in a humanistic approach.

It seems to me that counselling psychology has devoted much energy to developing this side of the work. My particular course required me to submit process reports, i.e. transcripts of therapy sessions accompanied by a written reflective narrative. We also had to undergo our own therapy, at least a year's worth, although many trainees chose to continue this for the duration of the training and beyond. Also, we had group supervision as well as the individual supervision stipulated by the BPS. In addition, we attended an experiential group, which allowed us to explore how we are with groups and how we are in the world more generally. This was in addition to the psychodynamic teaching and practice we undertook, as well as a variety of course work which focused on reflective practise.

Implications for practice

Thus I would argue that the approach adopted by counselling psychology embraces and expands the shift within psychology from the more traditional psychological approach of the psychologist as a detached clinician expert 'doing to' the client. It moves towards a position of being in relationship with the client and using oneself and the therapeutic relationship as a tool of therapy, as well as reflecting all the time on the process of therapy and any assumptions inherent to it.

An example of how I feel this benefits my therapeutic work is the way in which it enables me to integrate in a way that enriches my therapeutic work. One benefit of this is that when working in the NHS it enables me to adapt cognitive ideas to ensure that they are meaningful for specific clients. Cognitive therapy aims to access a client's beliefs on three levels, i.e. automatic thoughts, underlying assumptions and core beliefs (or schema). It also tends to focus on the here and now and to identify and focus on specific goals to achieve in therapy, which is obviously attractive to a system such as the NHS, which is overstretched and thus looking for short-term therapeutic work. The therapeutic relationship, being the most present thing in a session, is an ideal place for testing out any assumptions distorted by a client's core beliefs (or schemas). That is, a client will perceive their daily interactions, in this case the therapeutic relationship, according to their core beliefs (prescribed by their schema). This may manifest itself as a distorted or exaggerated perception of what a therapist says or does. Thus, such a reaction can be used to explore the underlying beliefs that clients hold about themselves, others and the world in general, and I would argue that being trained in psychodynamic ideas helps to reflect on such relational dynamics in therapy.

For example, I worked with a client who was very engaged in therapy, motivated and keen. However, one session she mentioned that she had done the homework task (which is often a part of a cognitive approach, in this case relaxation) the evening before because she knew she was seeing me the following day. This elicited a discussion about what motivated her to be so engaged in the therapy. We explored her automatic thoughts and underlying assumptions regarding therapy, which related to how I viewed her. That is, she was doing the tasks for me, in order to be a good client and in her own words 'sparkle' for me. When we unravelled this further, it came to light that the client felt that she had to always be interesting and successful in order that people would love her. This enabled us to explore some possible core beliefs or maladaptive schemas, which involved her deepest fear, i.e. that she was unlovable. This is a particularly complicated scenario, as the problem in our relationship was that it was too good: that is, she was too compliant and willing to please me. This was not immediately obvious, as I would leave the session feeling we had done some good work. However, underlying this was the fact that she was unable to 'do' for herself out of a fear of being rejected. Thus I had to draw upon how I was feeling in relation to this woman and be able to reflect on the fact that I was feeling too good about this work and realise that this was an indication that the client was putting my needs as the therapist before her own.

However, in order to reflect on such relational dynamics mental space needs to be made so as to be able to stop and reflect on such process issues. I do not feel that this is as easy as I make it sound, as I feel that working in pressured environments such as the NHS can put a strain on the therapeutic work, as well as on therapists themselves. For example, I worked with a client who struggled to be assertive. She felt pushed about and under pressure from others. I felt that we were working well together and I was keen to keep moving forward with the work. We had identified her automatic thoughts and started to challenge them. However, as the sessions passed she seemed to become more depressed and less engaged in therapy. When I commented on this we reflected on our relationship and it became apparent that she felt under pressure from me. Therefore, although we had identified her passive victim role in her everyday life, we had not identified it in the session or my reciprocal, assertive dictating role. When we reflected on this we negotiated a new way of working together whereby the client was able to disagree with me and assert herself in the session. However, in order to give clients a sense of autonomy or control regarding the agenda for therapy there needs to be flexibility in the frequency and duration of the therapeutic work to some extent, which is also not an unproblematic area.

I also feel that the freedom that a more flexible reflective style of therapy, such as the one that counselling psychology facilitates, allows the therapist to attend not just to what they are doing as a therapist but to how it is to be in the therapy. I agree with the assertion made by Woolfe (2002, p. 169) that 'the most crucial factor in healing is not what we counselling psychologists do with clients but how we are with them'. An example of this can be seen in some work I undertook with a client who I shall call Ms Grange. She had been referred for some support with a difficult relationship break-up. Ms Grange seemed to find it hard to speak about her emotions, reporting that this was not what she was used to, as her mother and father were not emotionally expressive. We spent twelve sessions exploring the changes that she wanted to make, but she still described feeling 'stuck'. I struggled at this point, feeling inadequate and unsure. However, after discussion in supervision I decided that I should offer Ms Grange some extra sessions, making explicit that I was going to stay with her in her 'stuckness'. This 'being with' Ms Grange seemed to enable her to feel safe enough to reflect on some of the ways in which her own anxieties may have been preventing her from making the changes she wanted. This seemed to emancipate her, enabling Ms Grange to move on, both practically and emotionally. However, 'being with' does not mean overlooking the other aspects of therapy. Counselling psychologists are trained in a range of theory, research and practice and may draw upon implicit and explicit psychological theory (Wilkinson and Campbell, 1997). Thus, different approaches, or different aspects of psychological knowledge can be drawn upon according to the specific needs of each client.

An example of how different approaches can be useful within one piece of work is the therapy I undertook with a student, who I shall call Miss Ashford. She was in her final year and came to therapy because she was finding it hard to cope. Much of the work we did at this point was concentrating on her sense of self-worth and looking at her anxieties about being able to cope in the world after graduation. She had repeatedly been in relationships where she was dominated. Much of our work looked at her relationships and her feelings of ambivalence towards others because of feeling dependent yet resentful. Although I used some psychodynamic theory to conceptualise this work (Winnicott, 1960) I also relied heavily upon humanistic ideas. This allowed me to support Miss Ashford in finding her own sense of self, whereas a more traditionally psychodynamic method may have repeated the pattern of power imbalance. However, I came to realise that some practical cognitive techniques would be helpful in order to provide her with new ways of asserting herself and coping with academic pressure as an addition to the empowering and insight-based work we were doing.

Thus I have come to develop a therapeutic style which integrates different approaches into my therapeutic work in order to adapt to the individual needs of each client, listening on multiple levels; that is, using a client-led approach to ensure that I listened to the client's perspective on their experiences, using psychodynamic ideas to help me listen for any transferential or unconscious material whilst drawing on cognitive ideas in order to identify any problematic cognitions or beliefs and to use problem-solving to facilitate change. An example of this was when I worked with a lady who I will call Mrs Huesdon. She was referred for help with her depression. We used cognitive techniques to identify some of her problematic ways of interpreting. This enabled us to identify, challenge and find alternatives for her problematic patterns of thinking that seemed to contribute to lowered mood and thus to depressed episodes. However, in addition, I adopted a more humanistic approach to consider with Mrs Huesdon how some of her beliefs might be effecting how she related to others, and to ensure that she had an opportunity to address what was concerning her at this time. This led to us thinking about her sense of self: what it meant to be a woman, a mother, a daughter and a wife. This allowed us to look at how her past had contributed to her belief that she must be 'perfect' for others and how this meant overlooking her own needs. We used issues of transference to reflect on how this was being replayed in the session by her striving to be the 'perfect client' for me. Finally, cognitive behavioural techniques allowed us to find ways in which Mrs Huesdon could challenge her thoughts and beliefs about herself and put into practice new ways of behaving that allowed her to act on these.

Summary

At the end of this chapter I feel I can summarise by concluding that counselling psychology provides a way in which to continue evolving and moving psychology forwards, in large part because of the importance it gives to the relational aspect of therapy and because of the value it places upon integration and reflective practise. I hope I have made it clear that I do not suggest that we override or forget the psychological perspectives that came before, as counselling psychology itself draws upon much of this knowledge. However, I do feel that the counselling psychology approach can breathe new life into the discipline, allowing flexibility, creativity and a chance to question what has come before and to see where psychology's blind spots may have been. I feel that being a Counselling Psychologist allows me to step away from the idea of the clinician as the objective observer, as a knowledgeable expert armed with technique and theory. Instead, I can become another human being who needs to attend to my emotions and subjective experiences of the therapy alongside the client. This shift seems to bring much-needed humanity to the process of therapy.

I think the question of how to move forwards in psychology as well as in counselling psychology needs to continue to be thought about. I like the framework described by Norcross and Goldfried (1992). They assert that a therapist can work integratively using a theory of therapy practice. This includes assessment, therapeutic contract, a working alliance, generic and specific therapeutic skills and interventions, the therapeutic relationship, personal awareness, social and organisational context, theoretical understanding and the application of relevant professional ethical codes. Also, Clarkson (1995) suggests that the therapeutic relationship can be used as an integrative framework. She suggests that the work of therapy lives in the creative space between the client and the therapist: 'the relationship seemed to me to be the factor that was vivid and obvious as the substructure on which most psychotherapies find their being'. (Clarkson, 1995, p. viii).

Thus I feel that the strength of counselling psychology is not just that it draws on the relational perspectives, but that it seeks to use this reflective stance within the context of integrative practise. The exact nature of therapy will vary from client to client and moment to moment and thus I believe that an integrative style of working enables the therapist to adapt to each scenario. Fear and Woolfe (2000) describe the process of integration as a journey in which the practitioner's personal and professional selves move into some sort of harmony and congruence. Thus, I am drawn to therapeutic ideas that embrace issues of relationship, meaning and context, whilst still allowing me to incorporate the multitude of psychological theory and technique that is essential to my therapeutic work. I hope that these kinds of perspectives will add to the already complex mix of perspectives and skills within the field of mental health to add a new voice to the narrative of therapy.

References

British Psychological Society website: http://www.bps.org.uk/.

British Psychological Society (1993) *Annual Report*, p. 128. Leicester: British Psychological Society.

Cormier, W. and Sherilyn, L. (1991) *Interviewing Strategies for Helpers. Fundamental Skills and Cognitive Behavioural Interventions*. California: Brookes/ Cole.

Clarkson, P. (1995) *The Therapeutic Relationship*. London: Routledge.

Fear, R. and Woolfe, R. (2000) The personal, the professional and the basis of integrative practice. In *Integrative and Eclectic Counselling and Psychotherapy* (eds. S. Palmer and R. Woolfe). London: Sage Publications.

Frank, K. (2002) The 'ins and outs' of enactment: a relational bridge for psychotherapy integration. *Journal of Psychotherapy Integration*, **12**(3), 267–286.

Gilbert, P. (2000) *Overcoming Depression*. London: Robinson.

Joiner, T. and Rudd, M. (1997) Countertransference and the therapeutic relationship: a cognitive perspective. *Journal of Cognitive Psychotherapy: An International Quarterly*, **11**(4), 231–250.

Kirschenbaum, H. and Henderson, V. (1990) *The Carl Rogers Reader*. London: Constable.

McLeod, J. (1993) *An Introduction to Counselling*. Buckingham: Open University Press.

Norcross, J. and Goldfried, M. (1992) *Handbook of Psychotherapy Integration*. New York: Basic Books.

National Institute for Clinical Excellence (2001) *Treatment Choice in Psychological Therapies and Counselling: Evidence Based Clinical Practise Guidelines*. Department of Health.

Rogers, C. (1957) The necessary and sufficient conditions of therapeutic personality change. *Journal of Consulting Psychology*, **21**, 95–103.

Waddington, L. (2002) The therapy relationship in cognitive therapy: a review. *Behavioural and Cognitive Psychotherapy*, **30**, 179–191.

Wilkinson, J. and Campbell, E. (1997) *Psychology in Counselling and Psychotherapeutic Practice*. Chichester: Wiley.

Winnicott, D. (1960) Ego distortion in terms of true and false self. In Winnicott, D. (1965) *The Maturational Processes and the Facilitating Environment*. London: The Hogarth Press.

Woolfe, R. (2002). 'That's what gets results'. Letter in *The Psychologist*, **15**(4), 169.

Woolfe, R. and Dryden, W. (1996). *Handbook of Counselling Psychology*. London: Sage.

CHAPTER 9

New ways of working in mental health: psychological services

Aftab Laher

Introduction

In some respects, many of my colleagues in clinical psychology will be justi-
fied in arguing that finding 'new ways of working in mental health' has been
an ongoing concern for psychologists in the UK ever since psychology as a
health profession was first formally recognised in the 1940s. As such, there has
clearly been much change and diversification of the role of psychologists in
mental health work in the past few decades. Also, over the years, a number of
psychologists have moved from their posts in the National Health Service to private practice – so going independent is not in itself a new phenomenon amongst
professional psychologists.

On the other hand, the faster pace of change in recent years within
mental health care generally, driven largely by a vigorous government health
agenda, has given psychologists newer challenges which, arguably, will
require more radical ways of working both within the NHS and external to it
(Department of Health, 1999). In this chapter I explore some of the exciting
possibilities for new ways of working in mental health through drawing on
my experience of developing an independent 'portfolio' psychology service. My transition from working as a full-time NHS clinical psychologist to
working as a fully independent practitioner running a reasonably successful
psychological consultancy since autumn 2003 has generated a mixture of
feelings in myself and in others. On the whole it has been immensely exciting and I feel that I made the right decision for me. However, it has also been
(and remains to some extent) a hazardous and worrisome journey with much
uncertainty and many potential pitfalls.

This chapter is not intended to be a recipe for creating and running an independent psychological consultancy, and indeed it is doubtful whether there can be one rigid formula for such a complex undertaking. Rather, the aim is to give the reader a flavour of some of the issues to consider and the opportunities that exist. I also examine the challenges that lie ahead for psychologists as they move away from some of the traditional ways of working.

To gain a fuller perspective on these current and possible future developments it seems important to consider briefly the current mainstream profile of applied psychology in the mental health arena and to outline the historical context of how the role of psychology has evolved within mental health work. I use the word 'mainstream' tentatively, as I believe that this is subject to interpretation of the wider context of mental health services and how one sees change.

Current profile of mainstream psychology in mental health

Currently, most applied psychologists involved in some mental health work belong to, or are eligible as practitioners within, one or more of the professional groupings or Divisions recognised by the British Psychological Society (BPS). Namely, these are the Divisions of Clinical Psychology (by far the most established and largest group), Educational and Child Psychology, Health Psychology, Forensic Psychology, Neuropsychology and Counselling Psychology. In addition, some psychologists who belong to the Division of Occupational Psychology can be considered as being involved with mental health issues pertaining to the workplace.

Each Division has its own specific membership criteria and training requirements based on what is deemed to be the core purpose and philosophy of the profession that it represents. However, all of the professional Divisions require, for full practitioner status, an approved first degree in psychology followed by successful completion of a programme of postgraduate professional training combining academic learning and supervised practice lasting at least three years. Increasingly, the trend in recent years has been for such training to be in the form of an applied psychology doctorate (e.g. DClinPsy – Doctor of Clinical Psychology). The respective professional practice guidelines also stipulate a programme of continuing professional development (CPD) and ongoing supervision as essential aspects of post-qualification practice.

Full practitioner status also confers eligibility to register for the legally protected title of Chartered Psychologist with the British Psychological Society. Currently this is a voluntary register, but over the last couple of decades there has been a strengthening lobby from within the professional psychology community for the statutory registration of psychologists. At the time of writing, the government has opened a pathway for statutory registration to become a reality and it seems that statutory registration is imminent. However, some crucial issues remain unresolved. There is much debate between the BPS, the government and other health professional bodies about whether it should be the BPS that is given legal powers to operate a statutory registration of psychologists or whether such registration should come under the jurisdiction of a wider body representing an alliance of health professions, such as the recently formed Health Professionals Council.

In looking at the evolving role of psychology as a profession within the mental health field, one relatively undisputed observation needs to be considered – that is the ascendancy of clinical psychology from amongst the different applied branches of applied psychology. While we have seen that there now exist many professional branches of applied psychology, historically in the UK developments in psychological approaches to mental health have been dominated by the evolution of clinical psychology as a profession within the NHS.

Clinical psychology is the systematic application of psychological knowledge gained from theory, scientific evidence and clinical practice to reduce psychological distress and promote psychological well-being in individuals, families and communities. While many health disciplines use some psychological knowledge in their practice, clinical psychologists are expected to have a greater depth and breadth of psychological knowledge and skills on which they could draw. Thus, clinical psychologists work at a number of different levels in the health care system. Their range of work includes:

- Psychological assessment, formulation and treatment.
- Evaluation and audit of psychological and wider health services.
- Planning, organising and developing wider health programmes and services.
- Providing support, supervision, consultancy and training to other staff on all psychological aspects of health care.
- Developing new systems and procedures and/or informing clinical practice through research activity.
- Administrative and managerial responsibilities.

Currently the vast majority of clinical psychologists are employed in the NHS and typically work as part of multidisciplinary teams in one of the following specialities:

- Adult Mental Health
- Psychosocial Rehabilitation
- Child and Adolescent Mental Health
- Learning Disabilities

- Older Adults
- Primary Care
- Health Psychology/Physical Disabilities
- Neuropsychology
- Substance Abuse
- Forensic
- Genito-urinary medicine/HIV/Aids

It is not uncommon for clinical psychologists to work across specialities, especially in the first few years after training and particularly where there are obvious links in clinical problems (e.g. neuropsychology and physical disabilities). However, most psychologists tend to specialise as their career progresses and may even specialise in specific areas within the main speciality (e.g. pain management within health psychology services).

With regard to career progression, the situation up until October 2004 was that, typically, the first two years after professional training ware deemed to be a period of 'newly qualified' status and the clinical psychologist received closer supervision as well as having more restricted responsibilities than senior colleagues. After a minimum of six years post-qualification (often much longer in practice) the clinical psychologist became eligible to apply for a senior post as Consultant Clinical Psychologist if such a post was available. This was usually the career limit for most NHS clinical psychologists. Some consultant-grade psychologists could choose to move on to senior managerial positions, which at the lower end of the scale involved heading a psychology speciality and, at the higher end of the scale, entailed managing a wider group of psychologists and even other mental health staff in some cases.

After October 2004, the Department of Health's Agenda for Change initiative to create an integrated pay structure for all NHS staff has had some major implications with regard to clinical psychologists' job descriptions, pay structure and career progression. The main feature of Agenda for Change is the grading of posts in bands according to a competency framework of knowledge and skills. It is too early to evaluate the full impact of this development but currently it seems that the previously established guidelines about career progression still largely apply in practice.

Moving beyond the traditional NHS way of working: a historical critique

In many respects, the varied role of clinical psychologists and the wide range of clinical areas in which psychologists now work, as described earlier, appear to be a strong testament to the notion of a continually evolving way of working. This is particularly apparent when we consider that clinical psychology has its roots in a highly restricted supporting role to psychiatrists – acting as psychometric technicians and applying a narrow range of psychological techniques to help traumatised soldiers during the Second World War at the Mill Hill Emergency Hospital (Napier, 1995). Therefore by referring to the 'traditional way of working' I am not implying that clinical psychology is a static, unchanging profession. Rather, I am referring to the fact that clinical psychologists have never really developed a strong identity beyond the context of working in NHS mental health services.

The NHS has itself undergone many changes since its inception in 1948 and this has had a major bearing on clinical psychology. In fact, the inauguration of clinical psychology as a profession was in the same year as the formation of the NHS and it seems that much of the history of the former has been tied up with the ebb and flow of political and organisational changes concerning the latter.

Going independent: the example of Laher Human Solutions Ltd

In this section, I explore some of the salient issues as a psychology practitioner moves away from mainstream NHS mental health services into the independent sector. I draw on my experience of setting up and running an independent psychological Consultancy (LHS Ltd) which consists of a portfolio of services and which is based in the East Midlands but offers services across the UK. The theme is very much of the recognition of the following three sets of factors that are in continual interplay: *personal, professional* and *business.*

I first briefly outline my journey towards setting up an independent psychological consultancy. Next I describe some of the work that my psychological consultancy is involved with. This then leads on to a discussion of some of the key points that I wish to highlight in terms of personal, professional and business issues.

The initial journey

Following a career as a clinical psychologist in the NHS and as a lecturer in clinical psychology in the university sector for a sum total of ten years, I decided to pursue my ambitions for developing an independent psychological consultancy in 2003. Like many psychologists, I had toyed with the idea of some independent work for a number of years, but the thought of leaving a secure and largely satisfying career seemed somewhat frightening. However, from a personal, professional and business perspective the time seemed to be right for me to seriously consider independent work. I had also spent considerable time in the previous couple of years to prepare myself and to calculate, as far as I could, the relative risk of independent work. This involved talking to colleagues, reading, researching the market, drawing up initial plans and opening the whole Pandora's Box of creating and running an independent business. This latter involved a steep learning curve in respect of practical, legislative, economic and motivational aspects of setting-up and running one's own business.

As mentioned earlier, this chapter is not intended to be a complete 'how-to' of setting up and running an independent psychological consultancy, but I will briefly outline some of the pertinent issues that need to be taken in consideration. For a more detailed discussion specifically about independent psychological/counselling work in the UK, the reader is referred to the useful texts by Kasperczyk and Francis (2001) and Clark (2002). With regard to more general advice about setting up and running a business, there are numerous web resources and books readily available and it would be futile even to select a few of these here.

The current portfolio of services offered by LHS Ltd

The psychological consultancy was set up as a company in September 2003. The current portfolio of services and activity is listed in Table 9.1. In line with the broad business plans for the consultancy and current ongoing developments, it is forecast that, in the next two years, the percentage of time devoted to, and income generated by, *Training Delivery* and *Partnership Work with Occupational Psychology Firms* is likely to rise significantly. Accordingly, activity relating to direct clinical work and medico-legal work will be reduced.

Clinical work consists of assessment and treatment of individuals and couples presenting with the following clinical difficulties: anxiety, depression, PTSD, adjustment disorders, work-related stress, psychosexual dysfunction and chronic pain or other non-malignant medical illness that requires some psychological input. Most clients are insured and are referred by their GPs or hospital specialists. A small number of clients self-refer after consulting my listing on various professional registers. A further group of clients are referred to me by 'treatment agencies' or by other consultancies. I draw mainly on a cognitive behavioural framework complemented by aspects of client-centred counselling and motivational interviewing approaches. The clients are seen in various private treatment facilities where I rent clinic space on an hourly basis (e.g. BUPA Hospital, Nuffield Hospital, Harley Street). I do not see any clients in my own home although I use this as a business administration base.

Table 9.1: Breakdown of service portfolio according to time devoted and income generated for LHS Ltd.

Activity/service	% of time devoted	% of income generated
Condition management programme	30	45
Clinical work	20	25
Medico-legal work	10	15
Training delivery	5	5
Partnership work with occupational psychology firms	5	5
General consultancy	5	5
Research	5	0
Professional development	10	0
Administration and business development	10	0

Medico-legal work typically consists of instructions to prepare court reports for personal injury clients. Most of my referrals come directly from firms of solicitors with whom I have built up a working relationship or who have seen my listing on various expert witness databases.

The *Condition Management Programme* is part of the Government's Pathways to Work initiative and is a partnership between Jobcentre Plus and the NHS. It aims to give people with long-term health conditions who are on incapacity benefit the knowledge, skills and confidence to manage their health condition, so they can return to work. Currently, there are around eight pilot projects around the UK. My company is contracted, through the commissioning Primary Care Trust (Central Derby PCT), to offer a number of sessions of psychological input per week to the Condition Management Programme. There are a number of other providers and health professionals involved and the overall programme is managed by a Project Manager from the NHS. In line with service needs, most of the psychological input is geared towards planning, running and evaluating pain management programmes for clients with chronic pain conditions who are referred by their Personal Advisor from within their local Jobcentre Plus. My work on this project also includes contributing to the strategic plans, supervision and support of other staff (primarily physiotherapists) and training.

Training delivery currently takes up a relatively small amount of the overall activity of my consultancy. However, training is something which I personally find stimulating and I am hoping to develop this aspect of my work on a much larger scale. At present, through subcontracting with a small network of psychologists who allow me to broaden the expertise pool, my consultancy is able to offer a portfolio of training workshops mainly for health professionals.

Partnership work with occupational psychologists fits in with my interests in workplace issues and, in particular, psychological well-being at work. Currently, I have worked on an experimental basis with a number of occupational psychology colleagues on areas of mutual interest and where there is some overlap in our work (e.g. stress awareness training for companies), but where our respective expertise complements each other. The indications are that this type of joint working is very attractive in the corporate arena and it is likely that I will be developing and strengthening partnership arrangements with occupational psychologists.

General consultancy covers a miscellaneous range of activities where clients or companies have sought some advice on psychological matters and where the range of knowledge and skills offered by my consultancy is relevant. For example, I have acted as a consultant advisor to a private consortium of health professionals who are planning to develop a privately run pain management programme.

Reflecting on my experience

General issues

In developing my independent consultancy I have focused initially on my own specialist areas and competencies in Adult Mental Health and Health Psychology. This is of course an important ethical requirement in respect of expected standards of professional practice and conduct as detailed in the various documents prepared by the professional psychology community (these are listed later). However, focusing on my expertise has also made good sense from a business viewpoint in that I have minimised risk through harnessing skills, knowledge and professional networks that are very familiar to me. At a personal level, there have been a number of motivational reasons which propelled me to explore the possibility of setting up an independent consultancy and these are discussed later.

The portfolio approach also fits in with my personal ambition to develop a varied range of psychological services beyond my own expertise through partnership arrangements and by drawing on the expertise of a network of psychologists. This diversity approach has the potential to be quite stimulating from a professional perspective whilst also being robust from a business viewpoint as 'not all eggs are in the same basket' and a menu of options rather than just one or two narrow services may be more attractive to potential clients, whether they happen to be individuals or organisations. On the other hand, I am aware that the portfolio of services needs to be reasonably balanced and contained, as otherwise one could be pulled in too many different directions. This could be quite stressful at a personal level, prove to be disastrous from a business viewpoint and lead to a significant loss of credibility from a professional perspective.

Personal issues

At a personal level, two broad and related considerations in going independent are *motivation* and *impact*.

With regard to *motivation*, the prospective independent practitioner needs to reflect on the reasons he or she wishes to pursue the independent route and whether the reasons are compelling enough to turn the initial thoughts into action. It is likely that motivation for pursuing independent practice comprises of a gradual build-up of *pull* and *push* factors over a number of years rather than a sudden dramatic realisation that one wants to practice independently.

Pull factors are those things which attract the individual to the relevant option while push factors are those things which deter the individual. Clearly what are deemed to be pull and push factors are subject to individual interpretation and may not necessarily be borne out by the objective reality. The decision to go independent or stay within the NHS is unlikely to be clear-cut as there are advantages and disadvantages on both sides. Table 9.2 summarises some of the possible perceptions of pull and push factors. This is obviously not an exhaustive list, but can be seen as a starting point when reflecting on the factors which need to be taken into consideration.

In my own case, my ambition to develop an independent practice grew over a number of years. I was motivated far more by the attractions of working independently rather than by any significant disillusionment with my NHS career.

Working as an independent practitioner can *impact* at a number of different levels on the individual and their family and some of the impact factors are briefly mentioned in Table 9.2. The immediate negative impact I felt for the first several months was a financial one as I had given up very good salary and I forecast that I would not reach this salary level until my third year of trading. However, by being very realistic and accepting some degree of risk in respect of my initial financial targets I was able to maintain my psychological motivation. Furthermore, I chose to go fully independent only when I was sure that I could maintain at least a base regular income through contracting back some sessions to the NHS on an independent basis.

While a stepwise progression towards independent work seems to be a sensible approach, there is also a possibility that this could become protracted as the psychologist fears completely leaving his or her NHS job. This may then lead to a 'half-baked' approach to developing independent work such that the

Table 9.2: Some pull and push factors for independent and NHS work.

	Perceived pull factors	Perceived push factors
Independent consultancy	■ Greater independence ■ Possibility of better financial rewards ■ Greater degree of choice with regard to job conditions (e.g. hours worked) and the area of clinical practice to focus on	■ Greater uncertainty ■ May require major learning with regard to business practice ■ Juggling of professional, business and personal/family needs ■ Isolation ■ May take years to establish
NHS	■ Job security and benefits (e.g. pension etc.) ■ Familiarity ■ Existing network of professional contacts and support	■ Lack of further job development opportunities ■ Feeling overwhelmed by job demands with little sense of control ■ General sense of disillusionment with local and national NHS culture

full possibilities are never explored and the independent side of the work chugs along in fits and starts. Making a very clear commitment may help overcome some of these barriers and naturally motivate the independent practitioner to face up to and successfully manage the inevitable risks and fears.

Some sense of loneliness and isolation is also likely as one breaks away from the relative familiarity of an NHS department. Therefore, the type of person who opts for the full independent option is likely to be someone who is not easily fazed by some isolation and is prepared to venture into the wilderness. Over the longer term, proactive networking and developing professional relationships with colleagues, some of whom may be business competitors, becomes imperative if one is to survive in the independent wilderness. This issue is discussed further in the section on professional issues.

The impact on home and family life also needs to be considered when looking at options for independent working as a psychologist. For many individuals who opt to work for themselves, in any field, one of the motivations and fantasies is that they will be in much more control of their time and they will be able to make better choices regarding time spent with family or away from work. This fantasy is often quickly shattered as the self-employed find themselves working harder and spending more and more hours on all aspects of their business. This is particularly stressful if the business is based at home and thus the boundaries between home and work life easily become blurred.

However, my own view is that while in the first several months or so it is likely that the business becomes quite consuming as you are trying to get things off the ground, it is possible, with an appropriate mix of professional support, good planning and personal determination, to strike a reasonable work–life balance. It is a discipline to restrict the number of hours spent on the consultancy and to block off days and weeks well ahead of time.

Professional issues

Clinical psychologists are required to adhere to strict standards of professional conduct laid out in general guidelines produced by the British Psychological Society and specific guidelines for clinical psychologists produced by the BPS Division of Clinical Psychology (DCP). Some of the key documents are as follows:

- *Code of Conduct, Ethical Principles and Guidelines* (British Psychological Society, 2000)
- *The Core Purpose and Philosophy of the Profession* (Division of Clinical Psychology, 2001)
- *Guidelines for Clinical Psychology Services* (Division of Clinical Psychology, 1998)
- *Professional Practice Guidelines* (Division of Clinical Psychology, 1995)
- CPD Homepage (British Psychological Society, 2005)

It goes without saying that the standards of professional conduct set out in the above documents apply to all psychologists regardless of whether they are working in the private or public sectors. In some respects, it can be argued that it is even more imperative in the independent sector to uphold the standards of professional conduct. This is because moving away from the NHS often means losing the formal and informal structures for supervision, support and professional scrutiny that are in place at a local, regional and national level. However, my own experience is that as long as one prioritises these important concerns and adopts a proactive stance towards such things as supervision and continuing professional development then there is little danger of losing sight of ethical and best practice standards.

Apart from regular informal contact with NHS and independent colleagues, I have found it helpful to put in place three types of supervision, each of which happens on a monthly basis. Firstly, I meet with a senior NHS psychologist on a one-to-one basis to discuss general professional issues such as service standards. Secondly, I am part of a peer supervision group to specifically explore clinical issues and discuss case material. Thirdly, I am part of a small group of practitioners who meet to specifically discuss issues and case material around medico-legal work.

With regard to CPD, I feel that one of the biggest benefits of running my own consultancy is that I have been able to prioritise funds for a greater range of CPD resources than would have been the case with a finite departmental budget in the NHS. For example, in the past two years I have been able to attend many workshops and conferences at an annual cost of around £4000. Most NHS psychology departments would struggle to meet even a tenth of this figure per year per psychologist. I have also spent considerably more on books and other resources than would have been the case if I was working in the NHS. Obviously, there is no such thing as unlimited funds, but running even a reasonably successful independent consultancy does allow you to alter the budgeting priorities in favour of CPD and general professional development.

Business issues

As mentioned earlier, there are numerous books and resources on all aspects of setting up and running a business which the interested reader should consult. Here, due to the limited space, I will highlight just some of the key issues.

Firstly, it should be said that while professional and clinical competence needs to be at the core of running an independent consultancy, this does not guarantee business success. It is therefore vitally important to embrace the language and culture of business. However, herein there lies a potential dilemma: the culture of professional psychology may, in some respects sit uneasily, with the culture of business. How do we reconcile these apparently different ways of working? My own view is that as long as one adheres to the professional and ethical codes of psychological practice mentioned earlier there need not be any major dilemma in practice. In fact there is a good deal of rapprochement between ethical standards in general business and the professional codes of conduct and practice.

Secondly, the prospective independent practitioner should consider what type of legal business structure should be adopted. The three main structures relevant to psychologists seem to be Sole Trader, Partnership and Limited Company. All of these have well-known advantages and disadvantages depending on what your attitude to business is. I opted to form a Limited Company as it fitted in with my long-term ambition of developing a wider portfolio of psychological services that could be credible in the eyes of clients at a corporate level.

Thirdly, it is essential to seek not just the advice of professional psychology colleagues but to also have in place a network of professional business advisors. Obviously, professional business services come at a cost so it may be important to prioritise, especially in the setting up stages. For example, while web designers may not be a vital requirement early on, a good accountant is a must. Organisations such as Business Link and all of the main banks also offer comprehensive business advice backed up by very useful web resources.

Fourthly, having a reasonably clear and well-prepared business plan is likely to lead to much better chance of surviving in the crucial early years and flourishing thereafter. Key components of the plan are: the range of services to be offered; the fees/prices to be charged; the potential clients; marketing strategy and market opportunities; setup costs; forecast of income and expenditure; and contracting arrangements.

My own consultancy initially developed from my existing network of contacts, so I did not immediately find the need to market or advertise widely. My strategy has been to ensure that about 50% of my income is based on reasonably secure long-term contracts lasting at least 18 months. This allows me to take some calculated risks in trying to develop other aspects of my service portfolio.

Conclusions and future directions

In this chapter, through drawing on my experience of running an independent portfolio of psychology services, I have attempted to give the reader some flavour of how psychologists can operate beyond the confines of traditional NHS mental health services. I have tried to highlight some of the key issues as they appear to me in the context of the interplay between three broad areas: personal, professional and business. The transition to working in this independent way is by no means easy and there are many important considerations particularly about maintaining ethical standards of professional conduct and practice. However, I have given the reader a glimpse of how such a way of working can be rewarding and stimulating and can usefully play a significant role not only in complementing traditional mental health services but by forging new working relationships with a range of stakeholders.

With regard to how these new ways of working might develop in the future, I think that we cannot explore this without a historical context. Much scientific and professional debate continues about the history of clinical psychology and about its future. In the limited space available here it is not possible to do justice to the many complex viewpoints in this debate or even to present a detailed history. However, it is useful in the current discussion to present a summary of two contrasting interpretations of developments within psychology as applied to the NHS mental health arena: *a positive–optimistic* position and a *negative–pessimistic* position. It is likely that most psychologists will fall somewhere between these two positions, which are described below.

Within the positive–optimistic position one interpretation of the history of psychological approaches to mental health care in the UK is of a dynamic, evolving process of establishing professional legitimacy that has been inextricably linked to wider theoretical, scientific, socio-economic and political developments. As well as responding to changes in the mental health field, it can be argued that psychologists have helped to shape much of the agenda within mental health work in the UK. It is argued that it is this dynamism and readiness to push political, scientific and clinical frontiers that has given rise to a rich tapestry of psychological applications in mental health care (Division of Clinical Psychology, 2001).

If, on the other hand, we were to adopt a more critical stance about the history of psychological applications in mental health work in the UK then alternative interpretations come to the fore. One such interpretation is that far from being a dynamic, progressive contributor to the mental health field, professional psychologists have been resistant or slow to change and they have been too preoccupied by issues such as protecting what they perceive to be their professional territories. A related argument is that the early struggle to pull away from the shackles of the psychiatric profession has engendered in the clinical psychology profession a certain defensiveness which has continued to haunt the profession over the years. Thus, it is argued, that psychologists have struggled to really define who they are and they have toiled in the process of trying to establish their credibility in respect of the unique contribution they can purportedly make vis-à-vis other mental health disciplines (Cheshire and Pilgrim, 2004). This sums up a negative–pessimistic position.

It is important to note here that I am not arguing that going down the independent practice route somehow completely resolves, in a simplistic way, the supposed negative aspects of the history of clinical psychology, which *de facto* is the history of NHS clinical psychology for reasons that I have already explained. What I do feel, however, is that considering the independent practice option leads psychologists into an arena that has many different challenges from working in the NHS and which might force us, through brutal economic necessity if nothing else, to move on with greater urgency from some of the more stagnant discussions that have characterised our NHS history. I am not, however, claiming that greater urgency of discussion in the private sector will necessarily lead to better or quicker solutions. For this reason, I feel that it is important, when considering the options for independent practice, to bear in mind aspects of both the positive and negative interpretations of NHS clinical psychology discussed earlier.

References

British Psychological Society (1995) *Professional Psychology Handbook.* Leicester: British Psychological Society.

British Psychological Society (2000) *Code of Conduct, Ethical Principles and Guidelines*. Leicester: British Psychological Society.

British Psychological Society (2005) CPD Homepage. Retrieved 5 September 2005 from `http://www.bps.org.uk/professional-development/cpd/cpd_index.cfm`.

Cheshire, K. and Pilgrim, D. (2004). *A Short Introduction to Clinical Psychology*. London: Sage.

Clark, J. (ed.) (2002) *Freelance Counselling and Psychotherapy: Competition and Collaboration*. Brunner-Routledge: Hove.

Department of Health (1999) *The National Service Framework for Mental Health*. London: HMSO.

Division of Clinical Psychology (1995) *Professional Practice Guidelines*. Leicester: British Psychological Society.

Division of Clinical Psychology (1998) *Guidelines for Clinical Psychology Services*. Leicester: British Psychological Society.

Division of Clinical Psychology (2001) *The Core Purpose and Philosophy of the Profession*. Leicester: British Psychological Society.

Kasperczyk, R. T. and Francis, R. D. (2001) *Private Practice Psychology: A Handbook*. Leicester: British Psychological Society.

Napier, B. (1995) Clinical psychology. In: *British Psychological Society, Professional Psychology Handbook*, pp. 2–8. Leicester: British Psychological Society.

CHAPTER 10

The role and function of crisis resolution services: a model

Tim Davis

Background context

The National Service Framework (NSF) for Mental Health (Department of Health, 1999) established standards for mental health promotion, primary care and access, severe and enduring mental health problems, meeting the needs of informal carers and reducing the suicide rate. Subsequently, the NHS Plan (Department of Health, 2000) extended the specification of national standard models of care. Following the NHS Plan all areas of the country are to have Assertive Outreach Teams (220 in total) and Crisis Resolution Teams (335 in total) by 2004. These developments are supported by the service specifications outlined in the Mental Health Policy Implementation Guide (Department of Health, 2001). By 2008 every client who requires it should have access to comprehensive community, hospital and primary mental health services with round the clock crisis resolution and assertive outreach services. The Leicestershire Partnership Trust is committed to the development of these new services that can meet local priorities and delivery plans in conjunction with the aforementioned national targets and integrate health and social care (Leicestershire, Northamptonshire and Rutland Strategic Health Authority, 2003).

This model focuses on the development of Crisis Resolution and Home Treatment Services (Crisis Resolution and Home Treatment Team) for the county. The service should be aimed at adults (16–65) who are experiencing a severe mental health problem with an acute crisis of such severity, that without the involvement of a crisis resolution/home treatment team, hospitalisation would be necessary (Department of Health, 2001). There may be a breakdown in normal coping mechanisms, an increase in symptoms, and deterioration in social performance and increasing concern from others. Such a crisis may be developmental, situational or as a result of severe trauma (Sainsbury Centre for Mental Health, 2001). There may be significant risk factors for the client themselves or others, which would warrant the client being seen within 24 hours (Northern Centre for Mental Health, 2003). Crisis Resolution and Home Treatment Teams can provide rapid assessment and a range of psychotherapeutic interventions as an alternative to inpatient care.

The themes and values which underpin this model of service delivery follow the concept of the Integrated Care Pathway and the provision of emergency response as part of an integrated range of local services has substantial advantages in terms of continuity of care and service accessibility (Burns *et al.*, 1993). Discrete crisis services should be regarded as specific elements of a system-wide approach to crisis rather than the sole specialised response (Ryan *et al.*, 2001), with collaborative working, clear lines of communication and service user involvement. This requires a change of culture and working practices with a bottom up approach rather than top down being locally determined and accessible (Sainsbury Centre for Mental Health, 2003).

The client must be seen independently of their illness. To promote a positive approach focusing on health/coping strategies, not just illness (Leicestershire Partnership NHS Trust, 2003), and the approach should be proactive, not just reactive, encouraging self-empowerment and self-management in the client – evidence suggests that where crisis teams attempt to work with people in the community and maintain them in their home, this promotes higher levels of user satisfaction than with traditional services (Muijen *et al.*, 1992). In short, this is a whole systems approach (Rae, 2003), which is preventative and has an explicit crisis avoidance agenda rather than retrospective resolution.

Crisis resolution model: what is needed? Aims and objectives

- Community-based, not hospital-based, model.
- 24 hour per day, 365 days per year, assessment and home treatment for clients presenting with psychiatric crisis (Johnson and Thornicroft, 1995).
- For this treatment/support to be provided in the least restrictive environment with minimum disruption to the client's life (Department of Health, 2001).
- For the team to remain involved with the client until the crisis has resolved and other further support networks are identified.
- Intensive intervention and support in the early stages of the crisis – crisis intervention is characterised by a rapid response and short-term work in the 'here and now' (Waldron, 1984).

- Rapid response following referral (Department of Health, 2001).
- Screening admissions.
- Involvement in discharge planning.
- Multidisciplinary team involvement to reflect a broad range of skills, experience and interventions.
- Access to a range of local mental health care services.
- Collaborative working with other service providers, statutory and non-statutory. Particular attention to be paid to the assessment and inclusion of the needs of service users and carers in the ongoing development of crisis resolution services. Other established Crisis Resolution and Home Treatment Teams reiterate the early and ongoing involvement of users and carers in the service model and a whole systems-based coordinated approach is highlighted in the Policy Implementation Guidance (Department of Health, 2001).
- Access to an alternative bed/place of treatment rather than just hospital admission (NSF, Standard 5, Department of Health, 1999).
- An economically viable model (Minghella *et al.*, 1998).

The model

This model proposes that members of the Crisis Resolution and Home Treatment Teams be dispersed across county localities aligned with PCT boundaries and work alongside the Community Mental Health Teams. This model promotes collaborative 'on site' working with other teams through dispersion, whilst adhering to the Department of Health policy guidance that: Crisis Resolution and Home Treatment Team teams are discrete specialist teams whose sole remit and responsibility is the management of clients with severe mental health problems in crisis (Department of Health, 2001).

It is recommended that Crisis Resolution and Home Treatment Team workers be also based in CMHT bases. However, limited room occupancy may not practically enable this to be a workable option. If the dispersed model is to work effectively, these bases should be solely operational sites with the majority of clinical activity taking place in the community. Imperative to the success of this model is the accessibility of Crisis Resolution and Home Treatment Team workers, irrespective of location, if a crisis call/referral is received. Each PCT and CMHT base therefore benefits from having accessible and designated crisis resolution team members covering the geographical area they serve.

It is important that the aims and objectives of the Crisis Resolution and Home Treatment Service can be met with specific reference to the availability of the service 24 hours per day, 7 days a week, and the policy guidance that a minimum of two trained case workers be available at all times (Department of Health, 2001). Quicker response times to urgent referrals can be met if team members are operating alongside Community Mental Health Teams (Sainsbury Centre for Mental Health, 2003). More time can therefore be spent on therapeutic interventions rather than just assessment only. The workers' knowledge of the local area and services is an essential prerequisite so that clients are informed of additional support networks and referrers can be redirected to more appropriate agencies if the referral is inappropriate, rather than merely being refused a service (Brimblecome, 2001). This dispersed model promotes wider multidisciplinary team involvement with Care Programme Approach reviews, care planning, admission/discharge planning and ward rounds. The model should also aid collaborative working with other locally based mental health services, thereby affording greater continuity in the client's care (Johnson and Thornicroft, 1995; Sainsbury Centre for Mental Health, 2003).

The teams (staffing)

With case loads of 20–30 clients (Department of Health, 2001), Minghella *et al.* (1998) suggested that 14 staff per 150,000 population for 24 hour cover is appropriate, and that the overall service costs for a 14 staff crisis service would be in the region of £481,000 in 1997, including overheads and costings. Clearly, over the last eight years costs have risen and the implementation of the Agenda for Change pay scales will have an impact upon these estimates. In this example the population served by the four PCTs is 614,060, and following the aforementioned policy implementation guidance of 14 staff per 150,000 population a minimum staffing requirement could be as follows:

Ratio of designated workers to population is 1 per 10,714
County PCT population of 614,060 ÷ 10,714 = 57.31 (rounded up to 58)
Therefore total team size = 58 designated workers

The team should be multidisciplinary as this promotes an holistic and eclectic approach to clients who are in a crisis. It is suggested that teams should essentially incorporate the following:

Team Manager
Team Administrator
Service User Development Workers
Support, Time and Recovery Workers (Department of Health, 2003)
Team Coordinators Nurse/equivalent OT

Mental Health Practitioners 'senior'/equivalent OT
Mental Health Practitioners 'junior' Nurse/equivalent OT (including Link workers)
Senior Nurse Practitioner (SNP)
Team Secretaries
Medical Secretary
Consultant Psychiatrist
Staff Grade Psychiatrists
Approved Social Workers

Prior to recruitment of staff, the initial appointment of senior team members (Team Manager, Senior Nurse Practitioner, Team Administrator for example) should enable the mapping current mental health service provision and care pathways and establish networks and liaise with all agencies, statutory and non-statutory, in respect of each county locality. The results of this should contribute to an operational policy and specific team configuration.

Although teams may vary in size, it is essential that there is uniformity in each of the team's structures to enable:

■ Clear lines of managerial accountability
■ Effective leadership at a local level
■ Team support and supervision
■ Appropriate experience and skill mix
■ Clear roles and responsibilities

Roles and responsibilities

Link workers

Approval has been be given to the development of Crisis Resolution and Home Treatment Team 'Link workers' as potentially new posts to support integration and collaborative working between the Crisis Resolution and Home Treatment Team service and inpatient areas. The specific remit of these posts should be to support the client in crisis in the community and then, if hospitalisation is warranted, to continue to support the client in the inpatient area. Supporting this transition from community to hospital enables the client to retain the same key worker and thereby promote continuity of care that is client-led not systems-led. These potential posts should in effect be split between the community and the wards and would therefore require flexibility in their capacity to follow the client from crisis, to the ward and then back into the community again. Such posts would not negate the need to have dedicated Crisis Resolution and Home Treatment Team workers offering a discrete crisis resolution service, but would be an additional resource to complement both services and be paradigmatic of a whole systems approach.

Consultant Psychiatrist

The Consultant should have overall clinical responsibilities for those people that are accepted by the Crisis Resolution and Home Treatment Team. All such cases should be discussed with the Consultant at the earliest opportunity. The need and process of medical assessment and prescribing should reside with the Consultant. The Consultant should work within multidisciplinary colleagues in all aspects of developing and implementing the Crisis Service and establish links with other service providers. Outside of normal working hours the 'on-call' Senior Registrar or Consultant should be contacted with due regard given to the east/west division.

Responsibility for people referred into the Crisis Service and receiving home treatment should often be shared between the Crisis Resolution and Home Treatment Team Consultant and the locality Responsible Medical Officer, but would usually pass completely to the Crisis Resolution and Home Treatment Team Consultant. The Consultant should be supported by an Associate Specialist or Staff Grade doctor.

Team Manager

The Team Manager should have responsibility for the recruitment, supervision, leadership and development of the crisis resolution teams in providing an effective, efficient, quality service. This should be subject to ongoing research and review. The Team Manager should also have a significant role in providing training/education to the teams and promoting the Service, though liaison both locally and nationally, to other service providers.

Team Administrator

The Team Administrator should manage and supervise all the administrative support staff attached to the Crisis Resolution and Home Treatment Team, and be responsible for the administrative support. The Team Administrator should in addition control/authorise all site and non-pay budget expenditure. All site management issues, including Estates and Supply Services as well as Health and Safety matters, should reside with the Team Administrator. This role should be supported by Team/Medical Secretaries.

Service User Development Workers

These workers should be actively involved in the assessment and home treatment of those people referred to the Crisis Resolution and Home Treatment Team and the role should be aligned to that of the support worker but with the additional perspective of a service user.

They should also be responsible for establishing links with other service user groups, examining specific service user issues as a means of contributing towards the Crisis Resolution and Home Treatment Team service improvement.

Team Coordinators or Mental Health Practitioners (MHPs)

The Team Coordinators (G Grade level or equivalent Approved Social Worker/ Occupational Therapist) should play a key role in the development and running of the team. They should be responsible for the duty system, the daily allocation of assessments and home intervention, and should review priorities in relation to all work demands, taking into account the urgency of the crisis. Both the Team Coordinators and the MHPs should be responsible for coordinating and delivering the process of assessment, planning, intervention and resolution for all those referred to the service as appropriate. In the absence of the Team Coordinator the MHP should coordinate the duty workers' responsibilities.

Approved Social Workers (ASW)

The Approved Social Workers in the team should be Team Coordinators, and as such should fulfil the same duties as those outlined with other workers. They should also contribute to the development of the Crisis Resolution and Home Treatment Team service, advising on social care and approved social work issues in the team.

Senior Nurse Practitioner (SNP)

The Senior Nurse Practitioner should contribute to the development and promotion of the Crisis Resolution and Home Treatment Team Service, advising on health care and nursing issues in the team and promoting the professional development of registered Mental Health nurses, Support Time Recovery Workers and Nursing Students. The Senior Nurse Practitioner should manage a limited caseload and provide supervision to healthcare staff under the direction of the Team Manager.

Support, Time and Recovery (STR) Workers

The Support, Time and Recovery Workers provide support and give time to those people referred and accepted to the Crisis Resolution and Home Treatment Team, promote their recovery and maintain them in their community environment. The Support, Time and Recovery Workers also assist the Team Coordinators and Mental Health Practitioners in the assessment, planning, implementation and evaluation of crisis care plans and contribute to the development and promotion of the Crisis Resolution and Home Treatment Team Service. There is an expectation that all Support, Time and Recovery Workers should be at or work towards NVQ level 2/3, as the main remit of their work is community-based as opposed to site-based.

Referrals

The referral pathway is shown in Figure 10.1.

- The Community Mental Health Team can refer urgent cases to the Crisis Resolution and Home Treatment Team Service.
- Additional team bases for Crisis Resolution and Home Treatment Team.
- Link workers for Crisis Resolution and Home Treatment Team
- Those individuals that can 'fast track' to the ward and have already been seen by the Crisis Team are able to contact the Crisis Service directly, out of hours.

The Policy guidance stipulates that the Crisis Resolution and Home Treatment Team Service is aimed at 'Adults (16–65) with severe mental illness with an acute psychiatric crisis of such severity that, without involvement of a crisis resolution/home treatment team, hospitalisation would be necessary' (Department of Health, 2001).

Consensual agreement from all parties regarding what constitutes a 'crisis' is problematic, partly in respect of the subjective evaluations by both client

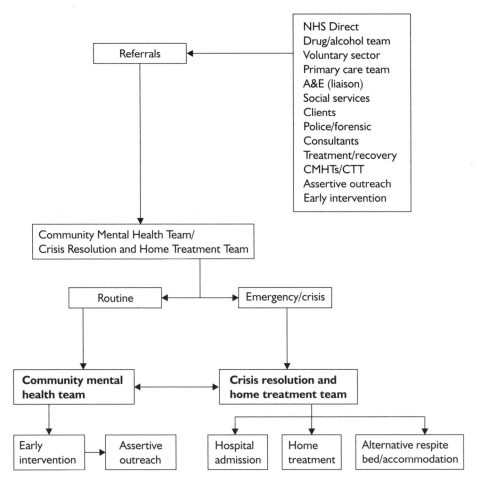

Figure 10.1: The referral pathway.

and referrer of what a crisis is and potential disagreement between both. This reinforces the legitimate need for crisis prevention work once a client is known to the service, so that the Crisis Resolution and Home Treatment Team can become involved and implement the 'early warning signs/relapse prevention plan' before a crisis occurs.

For clients newly referred to the service the essential component is the 'Assessment' in determining suitability and appropriateness issues.

Exclusion criteria:

■ The client is under 16 years of age.
■ The client is of no fixed abode, does not reside in the county of Leicester and/or is not registered with a county GP.
■ The client is over 65 years of age and new to psychiatric services.

- The client has a learning disability to a moderate/severe level and is known to the Learning Disabilities Service.

  Clinical exclusion criteria:

- There is a high level of aggression/violence that will put Crisis Resolution and Home Treatment Team workers at risk.
- The client's presenting problem is one of mild anxiety.
- The client's presenting problem is the result of brain damage or other organic disorder including dementia.
- Primary diagnosis of alcohol or substance abuse.

As previously mentioned, the exclusion criteria, particularly the clinical criteria, can only be accurately established once an assessment has taken place. The first part of this process is eliciting information from the client themselves, by telephone, to determine whether a visit is warranted. Other Crisis Resolution and Home Treatment Team teams testify to many referrals being successfully dealt with by telephone.

Gathering collateral information about the client from other agencies and significant others, as part of the assessment process, might be conclusive enough to point towards the exclusion criteria. In this event, the referrer can be notified of these findings and redirected to a more appropriate service. If ambiguity remains about a client's suitability for the Crisis Resolution and Home Treatment Service then a face-to-face assessment should take place and that assessment then discussed with the rest of the team.

Further aspects pertaining to assessment and treatment protocols and other associated policies are discussed and developed in the Crisis Resolution and Home Treatment Team's Operational Policy.

Screening admissions

The 'screening' role is an integral part of the Crisis Resolution and Home Treatment Team service, rapidly assessing clients with acute mental health problems and referring them to the most appropriate service (Department of Health, 2001).

If, following a referral, admission to inpatient facilities is indicated then the Crisis Resolution and Home Treatment Team contacts the relevant parts of the service to arrange this. If not, a home treatment plan is offered, incorporating other locally based services/multi-agency involvement if appropriate.

In some situations the referrer, particularly Consultant Psychiatrists and other Community Mental Health Team members, should have personal and considerable historical background information about the client that should enable the referrer to be wholly cognizant of whether the client warrants admission or home treatment. Such a 'working' knowledge of a client's difficulties informs professional decision making. In this event the referrer should quite legitimately arrange admission directly without referral to the Crisis Resolution and Home Treatment Team service, as home treatment should not be a viable option. If a client's mental health is deteriorating then involvement of the Crisis Resolution and Home Treatment Service can support that client and other potential members of the team in trying to prevent an admission. Whoever knows the client best should be in the best position to make a clinically appropriate decision about whether to refer to the Team.

Likewise, if a client previously known to the Crisis Resolution and Home Treatment Service is referred, then the member of the Team that knows the client best should be the most appropriate team member to get re-involved to promote continuity and a therapeutic rapport.

The important aspect of the Crisis Resolution and Home Treatment Team service is that it offers a viable alternative to hospitalisation, where the client can receive intensive support at home until the crisis has been resolved.

The assessment/screening scenarios are as follows:

(a) The Crisis Resolution and Home Treatment Team worker receiving the referral assesses from the information given that Crisis Resolution and Home Treatment Team involvement is not appropriate and that admission is required. The Crisis Resolution and Home Treatment Team worker should advise and assist the referrer to access inpatient services.

(b) The Crisis Resolution and Home Treatment Team worker accepts a referral and, following assessment, finds the client suitable for home treatment. The referrer should then be informed of the subsequent care plan. If the client who is receiving support from the Crisis Resolution and Home Treatment Team does deteriorate to the extent that admission is indicated then the Crisis Resolution and Home Treatment Team worker should contact the Crisis Resolution and Home Treatment Team Consultant Psychiatrist in order to facilitate this process.

(c) Following referral the client is assessed as not being suitable for mental health services involvement. The referrer should then be informed of alternative services more appropriate to the client's needs.

The assessment/screening pathway is shown in Figure 10.2.

Referrals should be accepted on a 24 hour, 7 days a week basis and should be screened by the duty Team Coordinator/Mental Health Practitioner. This may be a duty worker who should prioritise and allocate all crisis referrals amongst the respective teams. A second duty worker may also be nominated for each shift to respond to calls specifically from Casualty Departments/Liaison Serv-

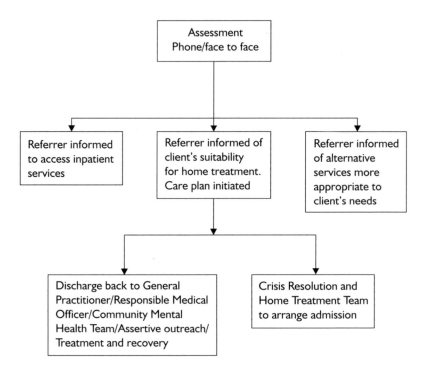

Figure 10.2: The assessment/screening pathway.

ices. Where the Responsible Medical Officer and/or member of the Community Mental Health Team/Community Treatment Team has assessed someone as requiring inpatient care, i.e. through the outpatient clinic, then the Crisis Resolution and Home Treatment Team can quite legitimately be bypassed and admission arranged directly, as home treatment will not be viable.

In the case of a referral where someone has taken an overdose or suspected overdose, the Crisis Resolution and Home Treatment Team should request a medical assessment, prior to acceptance, to ensure that they are medically fit. Those referrals that are deemed inappropriate should be offered alternative suggestions if available. The referrer should be offered an explanation as to why such a decision was taken. Any unresolved issues relating to the appropriateness of referrals should be directed to the Team Manager. In practice, however, the essential component is the assessment in determining suitability and appropriateness issues.

The assessment/screening role is an integral part of this type of service, rapidly assessing people with acute mental health problems who are in crisis and/or where admission is being considered. All such potential admissions should need to be screened to see if home treatment can be offered as a viable alternative. Such a screening (triage) role has been shown to offer a greater flexibility of response to urgent referrals whilst encouraging continuity of patient care (Morrison *et al.*, 2000).

There should also be a nominated Accident and Emergency Liaison Worker on each shift whose primary responsibility should be to respond to referrals from casualty departments following screening from the Duty Team Coordinator.

The assessment may be conducted by a Team Coordinator/Mental Health Practitioner working with another colleague whenever possible. If somebody is already known to the service, a joint assessment with their Key Worker/Care Coordinator is preferable. The assessment should take place in the person's home unless there is a request made for another area or there are concerns over worker safety. The assessment should be holistic in approach and take into account the person's strengths; past and current problems; the nature and development of the crisis; mental, social and environmental factors; and a comprehensive risk assessment. The planning of care should be discussed and negotiated with the full participation and agreement of the person and their carer/family, who should produce their own care plan.

Intervention

The aim of Crisis Resolution and Home Treatment Teams is to provide safe, appropriate and effective community support in the least restrictive environment with the minimum of disruption to the person's life. The person assessed by the service is to be seen independently of their illness and is encouraged to focus on his or her health and coping strategies. The intervention offered by the team will be intensive and comparatively short term, not normally lasting beyond six weeks and in the majority of cases less than one week. Interventions focus on the safety, empowerment and wellbeing of the person referred and their family/carers during the period of mental health crisis.

Someone on enhanced care programme approach (CPA), who can currently fast-track to a ward out of hours and has been through the Crisis Team, should be able to contact the Crisis Service out of hours. During working hours the Key Worker/Care Coordinator should refer to the Crisis Service. In the event that the person experiencing the mental health crisis contacts the ward directly, requesting admission, the ward staff should then refer that person to the Crisis Service for assessment.

Intervention might require negotiating the need for admission where appropriate. Where home treatment is viable, information (verbal and written) should be given to enable the person to understand how the crisis presented itself, prerequisites to its presentation, signs and symptoms of relapse and most importantly the person's own perception of the crisis and what has or has not helped in the past. (Bridgett and Polak, 2003). Intervention should assist the person in developing understanding, skills and abilities to work through the crisis towards resolution and/or management. Intervention should include liaison with other professionals involved in the patient's care and also include family and other social support networks in education regarding the nature of the crisis and the proposed interventions (Rosen, 1997). Intervention should also focus on the longer term crisis prevention/avoidance strategies and should be coordinated with other services. Like assessment, it should be jointly facilitated for people already known to the service.

Discharge

The person should be discharged from the Crisis Resolution and Home Treat-ment Service following cessation of the mental health crisis. Some degree of management and/or resolution would have been achieved. The person may be kept on the Crisis Service's books for a further two weeks, as an open con-tact, following cessation of the crisis in the event that further crisis could occur during this period.

The person is discharged from the crisis service by nature of the team arrang-ing admission, as home treatment should no longer be viable, and all necessary services, family/carers should be informed of the decision to discharge or refer to the other services.

Carer support

The role of carers is crucial to maintaining the person in crisis in the commu-nity. Crisis Resolution and Home Treatment Team workers must identify all sig-nificant carers and actively seek out their wishes and needs as an integral part of the assessment, planning, implementation and resolution of the crisis. Liaison with carers' support agencies, where indicated, is imperative in this respect.

Reviews

Reviews should be conducted at each handover for every person receiving sup-port from the Crisis Resolution and Home Treatment Service. Additional review processes must also be established for those individuals who are difficult to engage and/or present with a high level of risk, and whose psychiatric crisis is increasingly difficult to manage. In this situation it is essential that:

- Such additional reviews are conveyed at the earliest opportunity.
- If other service providers are involved in the person's case, they are then fully informed and inclusive of that review/planning process.

All reviews should consider the assessment, interventions and ongoing needs of those individuals and their families/carers in order to determine the level and appropriateness of the interventions offered and longer term identifiable needs after discharge.

Service development

It is anticipated that Crisis Resolution and Home Treatment Teams should maintain collaborative working relationships with all other service providers, both statutory and non-statutory. The Team Manager, in collaboration with senior team members, should be responsible for Personal Development Plans and Annual Development Reviews, together with the organisation and implementation of supervision. This could be achieved through the establishment of a monthly Clinical Governance Forum, whereby members of the Crisis Service can discuss articles/reviews/topics relevant to their profession and/or related to crisis resolution.

All team members should be encouraged to attend their own respective progressional forums and to feed back any relevant clinical governance/service development issues into the Clinical Governance Forum meeting to explore operational aspects of service delivery, policy formation and review, service development and quality improvement initiatives.

Worker safety

All Crisis Resolution and Home Treatment staff should receive training in the identification and management of risk related to clinical work. Those staff that have not received 'Breakaway Training' should be offered this at the earliest opportunity, in line with Prevention and Management of Aggression Department recommendations. It is suggested that if staff experience threatened or actual violence on an assessment/visit, then the police should be contacted via a team-owned mobile phone.

Each Crisis Resolution and Home Treatment Team worker carrying out assessments/home treatment should notify the Duty Worker of their itinerary prior to visiting and should contact the Duty Worker following the assessment/ visit to affirm their safety. If the Duty Worker, after a reasonable period of time has elapsed, has not heard from the Crisis Resolution and Home Treatment Team worker, then they should make contact with the specific worker to seek affirmation of their safety.

Assessments conducted by Crisis Resolution and Home Treatment Team workers should always have two staff present. The exception to this is where the environment is considered to be relatively safe, such as inpatient unit, casualty department, Community Mental Health Team base, police presence, etc.

The Duty Worker should be responsible for ascertaining aspects of potential and/or realised risk at the point of referral, including:

■ Physical, psychiatric, social and forensic history
■ Level of agitation
■ Explicit threats/acts of violence
■ History of violence
■ Person's perception of referral
■ Use of alcohol/illicit drugs
■ Environment

Where the suggestion of risk is apparent, the person referred should be asked to make their way to an appropriate base for the assessment to be carried out. Out of hours this should be the appropriate inpatient unit, and the Duty Worker for the Crisis Service should contact the Duty Coordinator at the respective site to make arrangements. If the out-of-hours General Practitioner Service has made the referral then this service may arrange transport for the person to be assessed at the appropriate inpatient unit.

Supervision

The role of the Team Coordinators and Mental Health Practitioners may be to offer supervision and debriefing as and when required to all crisis workers who request this following an assessment/visit. In a stressful, difficult and often demanding area it is imperative that this type of *ad hoc* supervision is offered in addition to more structured and scheduled supervision. All staff will need to be made explicitly aware of this from the outset as well as new staff joining the team at a later date. Following handover, the crisis workers that have been on duty should meet to discuss the shift and any particular issues that have arisen.

Conclusion

The model incorporates the recommendations made in the Policy Implementation Guide that crisis teams have the following essential operational elements:

- To be community-based in providing assessment and home treatment for patients experiencing psychiatric crisis where hospitalisation is being considered.
- For the team to be multidisciplinary in providing support in the least restrictive environment with the minimum of disruption to the patient's life.
- For the team to offer intensive intervention and support in the early stages of the crisis and to remain involved until the crisis has resolved and other support networks identified.
- To offer a rapid response, following referral, 24 hours per day, 365 days per year (Department of Health, 2001).

The team went operational on 30 December 2004 and in its first three months of operation had received 563 referrals, of which 77 were screened as inappropriate. Whilst Crisis Services cannot negate the need for inpatient care, they nevertheless offer a viable alternative to hospitalisation, where patients are encouraged to contribute to their own recovery through taking ownership of their own care plan. This principle of self-empowerment can contribute to the development of the patient's own resources and coping strategies for future management of crisis.

The challenge that remains for this team, and many others, is to work collaboratively with other service providers in a whole systems approach, that is multi-agency rather than just multidisciplinary. Ongoing discussion and elucidation of roles and responsibilities is imperative if crisis services are to be truly integrated into their service provision.

References

Bridgett, C. and Polak, P. (2003) Social systems intervention and crisis resolution. Part 2: Intervention. *Advances in Psychiatric Treatment*, **9**, 432–438.

Brimblecome, N. (ed.) (2001) *Acute Mental Health Care in the Community. Intensive Home Treatment*. London: Whurr.

Burns, T., Beardsmore, A., Bhat, A. V., Oliver, A. and Mathers, C. (1993) A controlled trial of home based acute psychiatric services. 1. Clinical and social outcome. *British Journal of Psychiatry*, **163**, 49–54.

Department of Health (1999) *The National Service Framework for Mental Health*. London: HMSO.

Department of Health (2000) *The NHS Plan. A plan for Investment, A Plan for Reform*. London: HMSO.

Department of Health (2001) *The Mental Health Policy Implementation Guide. Crisis Resolution/Home Treatment*. London: HMSO.

Department of Health (2002) *Delivering the NHS Plan. Next Steps on Investment, Next Steps on Reform*. London: HMSO.

Department of Health (2003) *Mental Health Policy Implementation Guide, Support, Time and Recovery (STR) Workers*. London: HMSO.

Health Informatics Services (2003) Leicestershire Partnership NHS Trust.

Johnson, S. and Thornicroft, S. (1995) Emergency Psychiatric Services in England and Wales. *British Medical Journal*, **311**, 287–288.

Leicestershire, Northamptonshire and Rutland Strategic Health Authority (2003). *Towards Better Health. A Strategic Framework for the Improvement and Development of Health Services Across Leicester*. Leicestershire, Northamptonshire and Rutland Strategic Health Authority.

Leicestershire Partnership NHS Trust (2003) *Making Sense of the Future for Mental Health and Learning Disabilities Services*. Conference Report.

Minghella, E., Ford, R., Freeman, T., Hoult, J., McGlynn, P. and O'Halloran, P. (1998) *Open All Hours: 24-hour Response for People with Mental Health Emergencies*. London: Sainsbury Centre for Mental Health.

Morrison, A., Hull, A. and Shephard, B. (2000) Triage in emergency psychiatry. *Psychiatric Bulletin*, **24**, 261–264.

Muijen, M., Marks, I. M., Connolly, J. and Audini, B. (1992) Home based care for patients with severe mental illness: a randomised controlled trial. *British Medical Journal*, **304**, 479–754.

Northern Centre for Mental Health (2003) *More Than the Sum of All the Parts. Improving the Whole System with Crisis Resolution and Home Treatment*. Durham: Northern Centre for Mental Health.

Rae, M. (2003) *Launch of Home Treatment/Crisis Resolution and Acute In-Patient Services Network*. East Midlands Conference. Conference Notes.

Rosen, A. (1997) Crisis management in the community. *Medical Journal of Australia*, **167**, 633–638.

Ryan, T., Newbigging, K. and Pidd, F. Developing 24 hour services. *The Mental Health Review*, **6**(1), 6–10.

Sainsbury Centre for Mental Health (2003) *Leicestershire Partnership NHS Trust. Future Bed Requirements Report* (D. Seward and A. Barnes). London: Sainsbury Centre for Mental Health.

Sainsbury Centre for Mental Health (2001) *Mental Health Topics. Crisis Resolutions*. London: Sainsbury Centre for Mental Health.

Waldron, J. (1984) Crisis intervention. *British Journal of Hospital Medicine*, **31**, 4283–4287.

Warner, L. (2002) *Being There in a Crisis*. Mental Health Foundation.

CHAPTER 11

Primary care mental health services: models of clinical delivery for common mental health problems

Introducing the role and function of the Graduate Mental Health Worker and alternative new ways of working

Dave Kingdon

Primary care has received renewed energy and interest in mental health since the advent of the NSF in 1999 and the NHS Plan in 2000. This chapter reports on national developing trends and guidance in primary care mental health delivery, as well as describing local implementation within Leicester and Leicestershire.

The chapter pays particular attention to the conception, introduction and development of the new professional role known as the Graduate Mental Health Worker (GMHW) (Department of Health, 2000). It highlights the role as it has been configured and developed nationally, as well as reporting on the Leicestershire implementation model, in which the role of the GMHW is considered within the context of a comprehensive primary care mental health service.

By the end of the chapter, the reader will have an understanding of:

- The background and key features of the GMHW role and its functions
- The National Service Framework and primary care mental health
- The development of psychological therapies in primary care
- Key aspects of the GMHW role and function
- The primary care implementation model within Leicester and Leicestershire
- Ethical and clinical governance considerations
- The discussion around role, function and career pathways

Introduction

1000 new graduate primary care mental health workers, trained in brief therapy techniques of proven effectiveness, will be employed to help GPs manage and treat common mental health problems in all age groups, including children.... By 2004 more than 300 000 people will receive help from new primary care mental health workers (Department of Health, 2000).

I remember working in a psychological therapy unit in 1999, where there were psychologists, psychiatrists and a variety of psychotherapists from different backgrounds. When we heard this statement it caused a range of reactions amongst the team. On the one hand, the government seemed to be recognising that psychological distress is widespread and that resources should be directed to primary care; was this yet another government target that would not materialise? Furthermore, there was a sense of astonishment that there could be a group of new practitioners employed with little clinical training or NHS background, and thrown into a complex clinical setting such as primary care. We all wondered what pitfalls might arise.

There continues to be a range of opinions about this new role amongst mental health practitioners, GPs and commissioners, which stimulate the debate about mental health care delivery in primary care, as well as considering the skills which should be utilised therein. By December 2004 nearly 1000 graduates had been recruited into the NHS (Department of Health, 2004) and it is worth at this stage considering the range of different applications and working practices of this role, its effect and its future.

Implementation guidance has been available through NIMHE NW, as well as a small number of pilot sites (Northumbria, Manchester etc.). Seventeen higher education institutions have developed the Postgraduate Certificate in mental health or similar, and been involved in recruitment and selection alongside service staff and commissioners. There were staggering numbers of applicants (mainly psychology graduates) for these new posts; indeed locally there were over 90 applicants for 20 posts. These workers have now been employed across a number of PCTs on a range of contracts ranging from one to three years. As yet there is no defined career pathway. Many PCTs have elected not to adopt this model of mental health delivery and there are only a few intakes to these training posts anticipated.

Across the country, there are differences in the models of service provision for mental health in primary care. These may have evolved as a result of opportunist funding, strong specialist leads and other historical factors, such as voluntary sector services, secondary care facilities or psychological therapy departments. As such, whilst there is increasing guidance regarding psychological treatments and services, there are differing preferences towards how such guidance is best followed. Some of the features behind implementation are discussed.

The NSF and primary care mental health

The National Service Framework for Mental Health (Department of Health, 1999) is to be loudly applauded. It recognises a broad approach to mental health as a concept, highlighting mental health promotion and well being, as well as paying attention to serious long-term illnesses and their impact on carers. Furthermore, it pays overdue attention to a major group of mental health sufferers such as those presenting with 'common mental health problems'.

This is significant, because for the previous 20 years mainstream mental health services had been forced to direct all their attention towards long-term mental illnesses, such as schizophrenia, manic depression, psychosis and chronic depression, and those seen as at risk of suicide etc.

As a result, the burden of managing what is now noted as 95% of mental health problems has fallen on the primary care health team and significantly the GP (Goldberg and Gournay, 1997; Jenkins, 1999; Elder and Holmes, 2002). The NSF and subsequent implementation advice have now begun to attend to this volume of clinical need with a mental health component where there is significant distress and unremitting symptomology. There is recognition of a global burden of disease relating to these conditions (Dawson and Tylee, 2001) and long-term pharmacological implications, as well as the complexity of managing the range of psychosocial features that are now increasingly acknowledged.

The term 'common mental health problems' is a misleading one. It could be construed to mean simple, easy to treat or routine. Yet the range of difficulties presented under this heading is far from straightforward. Within this umbrella term, we can include many distinct diagnostic categories and a range of co-morbid factors. Table 11.1 shows some of the main clinical presentations within primary care settings.

As such, the NSF for Mental Health 1999 provided the backdrop and stimulation for much overdue attention to this field. It began to recognise the significant amount of mental health issues within contemporary society and took heed of WHO recognition of the prevalence of common mental health problems (Dawson and Tylee, 2001). Not only did this note the high incidence of conditions such as depression and anxiety, but also their impact on areas such as absenteeism in the workplace as well as high consultation rates for GPs with such problems.

Table 11.1   Clinical presentations within primary care settings.

Anxiety	Panic disorder	Phobias	PTSD
Psychosomatic complaints	Bereavement	Marital and family problems	Sexual abuse issues
Alcohol and drug problems	Depression	Stress	Problems with work or job security
Sleep disturbance	Self-esteem and confidence	Emotional abuse in childhood	Early childhood loss

It reported that up to 40% of GP consultations involved a psychological component, and that many conditions were stress related. Some 95% of mental health management was recognised as occurring in primary care. Overburdened GPs with little time or expertise to address such features, and frustrated about lengthy waiting lists within secondary and other psychological therapy departments have resulted in an increasing recognition that such forms of mental distress could not be overlooked anymore.

Table 11.2 highlights the extent of mental health problems in primary health care.

Table 11.2: Mental health problems in primary health care. (Taken from Thompson, K., Strathdee, G. and Woods, A. (eds.) (1997) *Mental Health Services Development Skills Workbook*. London: Sainsbury Centre for Mental Health.)

Diagnosis	Rates per population per year	Rates per single GP caseload ($n = 2010$) per year
Schizophrenia	2–6	4–12
Affective psychosis	3	6–7
Organic dementia	2.2	4–5
Depression	30–50	60–100
Anxiety and other neurosis	35.7	70–80
Situational disturbances	26.7	50–60
Drugs/alcohol	2.7	5–6
Personality disorder	1.1	2–3

The provision of psychological services in primary care

Historically, there has been *ad hoc* attention paid to the needs of 'worried well' in primary care (Burton, 1998; Elder and Holmes, 2002). Some more progressive practices elected to employ forms of psychological help, with services ranging from relaxation therapy to bereavement counselling. These were often provided by volunteers, practitioners in training and even receptionists or the GP's wife! Little attention had been paid to working conditions, terms of employment, let alone training, clinical standards or governance issues. Other disciplines, from hypnotherapists to yoga instructors, may have been recruited to address this task; however, the overall picture was inconsistent. With the advent of GP fund-holding in the 1980s some GP practices formed contracts with counselling services, and to varying degrees found this satisfactory.

As the evidence base for psychological approaches has become stronger (Roth and Fonargy, 1996) and talking therapies are now noted as more acceptable to patients (Department of Health, 1999, 2002), psychological therapies have begun to receive their proper recognition in the role of treating common mental health problems.

Their applicability beyond secondary and specialist care environments, where most have been trialled, is now being understood and generalised, albeit at a stage of infancy. The Department of Health subsequently provided a substantial report into treatment choice for psychological problems (Department of Health, 2002), which built on an earlier, and well constructed, report into 'psychotherapies within the NHS' (Department of Health, 1996). This finally meant that recognition of depression and anxiety, as well as other common mental health problems, could benefit from specific skilled attention and this has led to the increasing ability for commissioners and purchasers to understand what standards they could begin to expect from practitioners. Furthermore, the increasing evidence base has also placed the emphasis on commissioners to introduce and provide such clinically indicated services (Department of Health, 2004).

The themes highlighted within the NSF 1999 placed Primary Care at the forefront of service delivery, raising the profile of mental health and proposing to address them. It viewed primary care, not only as the arena where many common mental health problems were brought, but also where patients could now be assessed for access to speciality psychological services and indeed provided with some forms of psychological help at their local surgery (Department of Health, 1999, Standard 2). The National Development Centre for Primary Care (Bower *et al.*, 2001; Gask *et al.*, 2003) provided clear guidance to commissioners and PCTs to begin to develop appropriate services, both in terms of implementing psychological services in primary care, as well as providing guidance on quality indicators to the implementation of the NSF (Department of Health, 1999).

The stepped model of service delivery

The 'stepped' or tiered model of care and service delivery (Figure 11.1) has been recently developed by NIMHE NW in their guidance on 'Enhanced Services for Depression' (NIMHE, 2004; Department of Health, 1999; Paxton *et al.*, 2000), and has also been incorporated into NICE's guidelines for depression and anxiety (NICE, 2004a,b). The model is adapted from that used by GPs as pathways for dealing with physical illness. Treatment commences gently and at an appropriate level in accordance with the complaint and treatment NES guidelines. When initial interventions do not yield remission, an enhanced intervention is sought or delivered. Applied to mental health, this process makes sense when we consider the amount of mental health presentations in primary care and the variety of levels of distress or dysfunction associated with a significant number of clinical problems.

The model begins to assist us in thinking about the variety of presentations within primary care, and can begin to be applied beyond simple medical descriptions such as anxiety and depression. It begins to identify and allocate appropri-

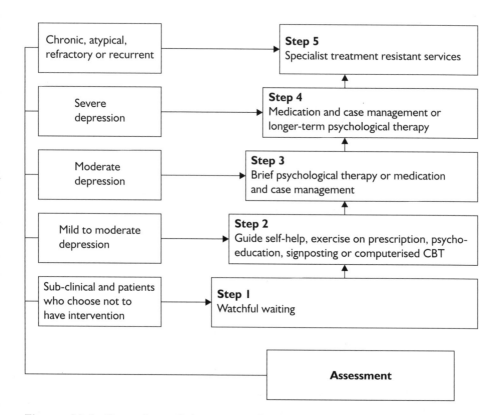

Figure 11.1: Overview of the stepped care system in the NES model.

ate levels of skills and resources towards each category. Step 2 has been seen as the most relevant level for the role of the GMHW, allowing for interventions such as guided self-help, book prescription schemes and signposting, amongst others, and this will be demonstrated subsequently in the Leicestershire model of implementation.

Debate continues around Step 1, which remains undoubtedly the cornerstone of assessing for suitable indications for the application of each relevant tier. The author proposes that qualified mental health professionals should be involved particularly at Step 1 and indeed at each 'gateway' along the steps. Indeed, in routine practice, the author has found that GPs do not discern the levels of intervention required and will therefore refer for an opinion as to what intervention is required. The author proposes that referrals should be screened by a suitably trained and experienced professional operating as a 'gateway' (Department of Health, 2003) in order to spot early signs of more complex states. In doing so the case scenario of Mrs A, highlighted in Department of Health (2004, p. 7), 'Organising and Delivering Psychological Therapies', is mitigated.

The author also proposes that Step 2 presentations are more in the minority, and that the majority of mental health work referred within GP practices is often complex. There are usually co-morbid factors, or evidence of latent developmental issues, which are compounding the remission of presenting axis 1 symptoms (Kingdon, 2004).

Key aspects of the GMHW role

The job role for these workers has been focused on functional tasks. These have been discussed elsewhere (Richardson, 2002; Crossland *et al.*, 2002) and the areas prescribed contain three broad remits. On examination of a range of developing job descriptions, these have remained consistent across the national picture:

1. Health promotion
2. Clinical audit and governance related activity
3. Brief clinical interventions

Mental health promotion

NSF Standard 1 provides directives regarding mental health promotion. It recognised the role of health information and the destigmatisation of mental health through providing relevant information. With this in mind, GMHWs have been involved in a high amount of activity relating to this.

Within Leicester, for example, each GP practice and PHCT now has web addresses and a directory of mental health support agencies as well as fact sheets to educate the public on a wide range of mental health information. Furthermore, specific vulnerable groups have been selected, including the deaf community, traveller communities, asylum-seeker populations and some sixth formers with exam stress. It is noted that the impact of such an increase in profile in health promotion is always difficult to measure, and indeed more avenues could be developed, including further visits into schools and other community groups. However, members of the public can now visit their GP practice and be able to walk away with mental health advice should they request it. Variations on implementation across earlier sites have also been recorded (Department of Health, 1999; Gask *et al.*, 2003; Crossland *et al.*, 2002).

Clinical audit and governance activity

Across the country, this aspect of the job role is being interpreted in a variety of ways. At the time of the introduction of the NSF, and coinciding with the New GP Contract (British Medical Association, 2003), practices were being directed to develop and maintain mental health registers for those patients with clinical depression, manic depression (the lithium register) and long-term mental illness. It was seen that GMHWs could assist in this role, both in developing and providing monitoring. Furthermore, GMHWs could be used as a link between primary and secondary care, in order to assist with a variety of interface issues.

Brief clinical interventions

The third component of the proposed role involved the GMHW seeing patients referred by the GP for brief (evidence-based) clinical interventions. This area gave some concern to many mental health clinicians who have been involved with the GMHW developments, including also GPs, PHCT members and clinical mentors. This centred on issues of accountability, patient selection and levels of clinical supervision, and will be discussed within the conclusion.

In order to provide an evidenced-based approach, the practitioner must have been trained to a suitable degree. The evidence base frequently states Cognitive Behavioural Therapy (CBT) as the indicated treatment for many common mental health problems such as anxiety disorders or clinical depression. Whilst current popular views indicating CBT as the treatment of choice are seen almost as a panacea for all common mental health problems in the NHS these days, the author is concerned that relational aspects of psychotherapeutic interventions are also recognised (Kingdon, 2004).

Nonetheless, CBT has formed a reasonable place to begin assisting GMHWs' skills development, as well as paying attention to other features of psychological approaches.

Nationally, in working practice, this has been adapted to involving GMHWs in 'facilitated self-help', or brief manualised approaches such as Padesky's Mind over Mood (1995) and similar. Other forms of intervention include the 'Book Prescription Scheme'; a new spin on advising patients to read certain self-help texts (Frude, 2004a,b).

Some self-help groups or workshops have been developed utilising these approaches to varying degrees of success, and this all adds to making this level of psychological help more available than it has been before.

The Leicestershire model of implementation

In 2001, Leicester and Leicestershire's PCTs and Mental Health Partnership Trust made their own response to the NSF, which varied in a number of ways from specific parts of the guidance which later emerged from NIMHE. In conjunction with GPs, psychotherapy departments, service user representatives and managerial leads, large funding was secured to develop the Common Mental Health Problems Service (CMHPS).

This huge undertaking aimed to place a suitably qualified mental health therapist in each GP surgery to take and manage direct referrals. Initially, four PCTs commissioned the service, with a steady 'roll out' phased over three years. Mental health practitioners were recruited from a variety of specialist mental health services, CMHTs and other psychological therapy departments to achieve what can now be considered as a 'managed psychological service' (Department of Health, 2004). Around 35 advanced mental health practitioners, employed as Practice Therapists, now fulfil this role.

Following a large audit by the Sainsbury Centre for Mental Health (SCMH) in 2004, the final roll out into two further PCTs was achieved. The service was seen as a robust response to the NSF, not only providing the primary health care team with direct access to an experienced mental health practitioner for advice and consultation, but also offering access to practitioners who could manage the diversity and texture of primary care mental health presentations with confidence. The service has been able to operate beyond tiers 1 and 2, offering expert assessment at the primary care 'gateway', as well as more advanced (enhanced) or complex treatment (levels 3 and 4).

The report by SCMH was favourable towards the model of implementation, and whilst the service had already met many of the functions of the proposed GMHW roles, it was noted that their could be further benefits in assisting the CMHPS to meet targets in areas such as health promotion, group work and developing audit activity etc.

PCTs, De Montfort University (DMU) and the Trent Workforce Development Confederation (WDC) were keen to capitalise on available funding for GMHWs. The CMHPS was seen as an ideal host service for GMHWs.

As recurrent funding had already been committed to the development of the CMHPS, this meant that GMHWs could only be funded for one year. The Sainsbury Report recommended that (p. 68):

> ... the 12 month period during which GMHWs are in place provides a unique opportunity to develop work streams that meet the requirements of the NSF and increase longer term adherence to the Graduate and Gateway guidance. E.g. development work around audit, information and care pathways etc. Much of this work is 'resource-hungry' in early stages of set-up, and therefore advantage can be taken of the additional resource (GMHW). Subsequent work in audit is not so resource-intensive, and therefore following the departure of GMHWs (on completion of their training) this work would be maintained by the CMHPS.

GMHWs in Leicester and Leicestershire

Eighteen GMHWs were recruited to Leicester to work across seven PCTs for a one-year contract whilst they were receiving training towards the Postgraduate Certificate in Primary Care Mental Health. It was agreed that they would be hosted by the LPT and placed within the CMHPS, including a special arrangement to place two workers within inpatient and personality disorder services.

This afforded PCTs an indirect relationship to each of their GMHWs via the management, mentorship, clinical supervision and governance of the CMHPS. There were obvious benefits to both parties as a result of this arrangement, noting the CMHPS as a 'managed psychological service' commissioned by the PCT over the preceding 2–4 years to provide a service directly within primary care.

Two to four GMHWs were placed within each PCT and operated under the direction of Practice Therapists and CMHPS teams, in accordance with local needs and diversities. A Lecturer Practitioner post was developed to provide a valuable task in assisting in the development and activity of each GMHW, ensuring progress towards academic targets, clinical experience, and adoption into the CMHPS.

Initially, PCTs were disenfranchised from this process, except for electing to embark on GMHW implementation and tendering the contract over to the CMHP service and DMU. They were naturally regularly informed of progress, as were commissioners.

The benefits of the CMHPS's ability to host and provide relevant introduction of the GMHW meant that PCTs could be satisfied that the new workers could be suitably orientated and led. Indeed, this had been highlighted by the implementation site (Crossland *et al.*, 2002) who maintained (p. 12):

> ... to avoid the GMHWs from being subject to ambiguous or intractable PCT difficulties, workers may best be linked with existing areas of good practice within the PCT. This would allow those who have developed these areas the space and time and energy to develop other areas of practice. It could also ensure that GMHWs have positive role models.

Around 12 CMHPS mentors were required to attend 'mentor workshops' as well as meeting with the GMHW for over one hour per week, orchestrating and provide governance for a variety of clinical initiatives locally within the time frame. GMHWs were accepted into other forums such as team meetings, group supervision and a variety of continuous professional development sessions within the CMHPS. Teams taking on 2–4 new workers were required to make significant provision in order to line manage, supervise, teach, model and assess competence.

The key role components provided a reasonable structure to work within, and forged the identity and purpose of the role within the initial three months. It provided a structure for both the CMHPS team manager and each GMHW mentor. It was also matched by 'front-loading' the first training module, which aimed to begin to orientate and introduce GMHW to the envisaged aspects of the role.

Table 11.3 highlights GMHW activities developed within each domain within a one year period.

Work in progress; the map is not the same as the territory

It must be noted that introducing 18 young and keen, yet novice graduates into a direct health care setting, where there is some role ambiguity, where impressions on PHCT staff are important and where there are a variety of boundaries and work settings to contemplate, is a huge challenge. Indeed, the CMHPS, still in its infancy, had found it difficult to find its own place in primary care initially.

Table 11.1: GMHW activities developed within a one year period.

Health promotion	Clinical activity	Audit, governance or practice development
Local services directory developed: each GP surgery in receipt	Social support for women GP work (10 sessions in health and social center)	Audit into clinical pathways in primary care
Providing direct advice to PHCT regarding all aspects of MH; sources of referral, literature, knowledge of care pathways etc.	Stress and anxiety management group – voluntary centres, e.g. MIND, health centres	A depression audit\An audit into applying IPT within primary care
Direct health promotion activities such as asylum signposts, traveller community, work with deaf community	Stress, anxiety and depression consultation – signposting	A cost–benefit analysis into CCBT
Exam stress sessions in education	Joint session with GPs and PHCT	An audit into clinical care pathways from A&E to primary care
MH leaflets distributed to all practices	Joint consultations with psychological therapists/ mentors/clinical supervisors	Patient Satisfaction Questionnaire and analysis to CMHPS
	Benzodiazepine withdrawal psychoeducation group (6 sessions)	A benefits analysis into implementing the CORE system for research and governance activity
	Social skills group in voluntary setting (6 sessions)	Audit into service provision for the deaf community
	Signposting for asylum seeker service	Collecting data on BME access to new MH provision
	1:1 counselling	

These new workers were looked on with confusion. Whilst the CMHPS had paved the way for introductions and a variety of induction experiences for the GMHW, they nonetheless felt unclear initially, as well as highly anxious (see also Bower (2004) for useful discussion).

Naturally they could not shadow Practice Therapist clinics consistently, because this would be inappropriate for patients already engaged in some forms of psychological treatment. Assessment interviews were haphazard in terms of patients consenting to two practitioners being involved, and this led to GMHWs often being asked to wait outside the room for periods of the day. Not all GMHWs felt confident enough to engage with GP practices at this early stage, and there were periods of demoralisation. Two GMHWs elected to resign.

There were two PCTs where the CMHPS had yet to be implemented at the time of the GMHW start, and these areas proved more difficult to initiate. Some practices declined the offer of a new staff member who could help them with their mental health targets in return for hosting the training placement. PCTs seemed powerless to influence this, and significant time within the contract was lost, to the detriment of a few GMHWs until finally placements could be agreed.

There were many other hitches and glitches, which cannot be covered here; however, towards the mid-point in the contract we began to feel that GMHWs were beginning to be assimilated into Primary Care and the CMHPS, with sufficient purpose and clarity to develop the activities listed above.

A wide variety of clinical education was provided between the DMU, CMHPS and other specialists brought in (see the DMU course handbook) and approved by Manchester University. Specialists with a variety of psychological, primary care or psychiatry expertise were coordinated to provide workshops and lectures in all aspects of mental health care delivery.

Evaluation and discussion: integration and skill mix

Crossland *et al.* (2002, p. 10) wrote:

> ... graduates can not be seen as a cheap alternative and issues of capacity to manage and supervise, along with considerations of safety and local governance arrangements will undoubtedly influence the extent to which PCTs as employing agencies are prepared to support graduates in working in a range of activities with clients.

In considering the effect of the GMHWs in Leicestershire, we are naturally considering their influence within the context of a broad and comprehensive existing primary care mental health service. Indeed, at the time of writing, the Workforce Development Confederation is expressing concern about the difficulties in retaining these workers when funding is already accounted for through the CMHPS.

This might have been best considered by commissioners and planners at the outset (see Appleby (2004) for comments about commissioners), and it is unfortunate for a small number of keen individual GMHWs who have shown promise that some of these tensions surfaced throughout the year. In the author's opinion, additional funding would indeed be welcomed, and would provide the best model for the deployment of GMHWs. Attempting to introduce an alternative skill mix into primary care *instead* of more experienced staff, however, needs careful consideration.

Areas nationally, without a CMHPS, are probably finding some benefit to the new workers, because they have been starved of resources previously. Nonetheless, attention to level 3 and 4 (enhanced) interventions will need to be addressed in due course by their respective commissioners.

The efficacy of increased health promotion, advice about treatment pathways and evidence-based treatments provided to surgeries and the general public by GMHWs should, not surprisingly, have the effect of increasing referrals to expert psychological help – something which specialist and secondary departments will be unable to meet without further planning and investment.

The challenge of mobilising 18 new workers into meaningful and necessary clinical activity within a short period of time, across a range of untrodden clinical, geographical and departmental boundaries, and with often novice and inexperienced workers, cannot be understated. Small pockets of clinical work were identified for the level of training that GMHWs had received, under the direction of experienced teams and mentors. Audit was forged into the identification of salient, manageable areas for analysis within the time frame and where there was cooperation from various stakeholders (when this was not forthcoming, additional challenges were created).

It is notable that, in many cases, GP practices had begun to maintain both serious mental illness registers and lithium registers, as well as having undergone a depression audit within the recent two years. As such there was mutual recognition by practices, PCTs and the CMHPS that there could be other audit initiatives open to the GMHW. Most of these were adapted from the Sainsbury report, and this provided a fresh and direct lead. Each audit was approved via the relevant audit group and stakeholders, especially at practice level and within the CMHPS. GMHWs therefore provided a beneficial arm to the CMHPS in beginning to initiate what the Sainsbury Report referred to as 'resource-hungry tasks'. The same could be said of mental health promotion activities (see Table 11.3).

At a glance, GMHW activity appeared impressive and relevant in relation to GMHW targets. Caution needs to be applied, however, when we examine the broad spread of workers across a large county with six PCTs. Activities can be best seen to occur in pockets, and where there was sufficient cooperation amongst relevant parties. To achieve many of these initiatives equitably, and to a consistent level to make a significant impact, would take many years.

Of note, for example, is that developing group work activity appeared exciting, but preliminary evaluations revealed that it was labour-intensive and we were unsure of its full therapeutic efficacy. Furthermore, the effects of the role of 'signposting' are difficult to measure, and appeared to have little impact on CMHPS referral trends, where this was implemented. Work with GP practice teams was also patchy, and depended on the confidence of the GMHW to assert their role as 'mini experts' in mental health, which is quite difficult when beginning to find their own feet.

Overall GMHW activity represents only a small proportion of outcomes relating to the key targets, whilst much of this is taken on by the CMHPS in routine practice. Furthermore, activity was happening in pockets and was not consistent across each PCT for many reasons, including skill development, variation in confidence of the GMHW and numerous housekeeping matters. Of course, it is possible to assume that much of this would improve over a further term of employment and that a one-year contract involving training and induction into PCTs would never yield its greatest benefits consistently across the full period.

It is important to recognise that the Leicester and Leicestershire model is fortunate in comparison with that of many parts of the national picture, and that the CMHPS had arrived in primary care in the preceding years. They were already meeting the burden of primary care mental health needs in a comprehensive way. This had both advantages and disadvantages in analysing the overall impact of the GMHWs in Leicester. Whilst this provided useful hosting and mentoring, it meant that many of the NSF targets were well under way.

We should briefly summarise this section by examining GMHWs as an alternative source of NHS recruitment to provide appropriate therapeutic help to patients and GPs seeking mental health expertise.

Firstly, if we consider the volume and range of clinical work which would be directed towards the GMHW by GP practices for their employment to be beneficial to the PHCT, we could imagine that GPs will be referring at the rate at which the CMHPS in Leicester has received referrals (Durcan and Knowles, 2004, unpublished).

Of course it could be argued that GPs will follow different referral trends when faced with a less experienced worker; however, in my experience, not all mental health issues are suitably graded by GPs in their referrals, especially when various protocols dictate a procedure (see any protocol for depression). Furthermore, in order to be of significant benefit to both the GP and patient group, the GMHWs will be asked to see a wide range of personalities. This raises huge questions about governance, and also about the capacity of second-ary or specialist departments to be accessible to work that is generated.

If we consider an average clinical session (3½ hours), once weekly in a small GP practice, a practitioner will provide 6 × ½ hour consultation sessions. These would be occupied by approximately three follow-up appointments and three new assessments. Over a few months this becomes a staggering clinical weight, and of course is replicated in up to seven clinics a week across several practices.

The number of GMHWs proposed within the original reports (i.e. 2–3 per PCT) would be untenable if it were to provide an equitable distribution of any-thing like the ranges of some of the activities proposed and achieve a significant impact.

Providing both a helpful and meaningful contact at every stage of the clini-cal encounter is a prerequisite in any profession's conduct, and there should be caution regarding the capacity of the GMHW initially. As a result, we can imag-ine that over a period of years the GMHW could quite well develop keen and cute enough skills to manage this. However, in the meantime such high levels of clinical activity would need expert clinical supervision to support both the patient and the GMHW.

There are subtleties which should be attended to within mental health work, and these include the effect of practitioners' constant exposure to mental health issues on their well being. When these factors are taken into account, it is impor-tant to recognise the limitations on the role.

From this point of view, the GMHW needs to be integrated into a robust and managed primary care mental health service, which is equally connected to the GMHWs specific area of practice, and also operating as an integral part of primary care. Indeed, Northumbria was familiar enough with the demands of primary care to note:

> ... if these workers are to be effective in supporting primary care practi-tioners in meeting targets for the NSF, they are going to have to hit the ground running.

Whilst this is an accurate reflection of the pace in primary care, it none-theless raises ethical concerns: placing such workers at the forefront of mental health care delivery to the general population needs careful atten-tion. Indeed, I recently heard of a GMHW elsewhere in the country who had seen 22 patients in one day, on 15 minute appointments. Indeed, it transpired that she was working with minimal supervision and was exposed to a large GP practice who were undiscerning in their referral trends. This indicates that new practitioners need significant support and structure to avoid a range of well-known factors including burn out, therapeutic omnipotence and pro-tection of patients.

Career pathways

When the NHS Plan announced the introduction of GMHWs, the agenda appeared to be two-fold. Firstly, it was recognising the difficulties that psychology graduates were having in accessing clinical psychology training, and secondly that the NHS needed to encourage people with such interests and skills into mental health as part of recruitment initiatives.

An 'organised and managed psychological (*primary care*) service' (Department of Health, 2004) provides suitable governance, line accountability and clinical supervision, which can also provide a cohesive and integrated approach to complete mental health delivery in primary care. In this way, GMHWs can be directed towards strategic and well-defined matters such as practice team work and clinical audit, as well as being supervised and supported with key clinical tasks. It may also provide a care pathway.

It is unclear as to how many further intakes of GMHWs will occur now that the targets have been met by PCTs and commissioners. Indeed, NIMHE will now be turning its attention towards the matter of enhanced clinical services.

Higher education departments are developing further postgraduate training in mental health, but it is unclear whether a professional discipline of GMHW will be sustained. Moreover, the roles and functions of GMHWs as well as other mental health care delivery in primary care, may be adopted by a range of different disciplines depending on the model of implementation. Indeed, practice nurses and health care assistants could be suitably trained in some of the tasks outlined above.

Within the Leicester cohort, over half of the GMHW intake have secured further employment (often within mental health or social care roles), two have been accepted into clinical psychology training and two others will pursue further postgraduate training. They all maintain that these opportunities would not have been available to them without the one-year training and work experience.

Conclusion

Due to the significant incidence of mental health problems and the recognised role of mental health in physical problems, work absenteeism and of course suicide, primary care is now experiencing a period of renewed interest. Creative ways are being sought, at local levels, between PCTs and commissioners to meet the demands of patients and their GPs. As society becomes more versed in its ability to choose and request reliable and consistent responses to mental health matters, psychological interventions require specific expertise at all levels of consideration and application.

Professional career pathways and the retention of a skilled workforce in the NHS should be seen as an attempt to achieve high quality for the public at all levels. The GMHW is probably best placed within the model of primary mental health care delivery provided in Leicester and Leicestershire (or similar), for the reasons highlighted. It also begins to provide a career pathway for the GMHW to progress to the level of Practice Therapist and subsequently Senior Practice Therapist over an eight-year period, with training. Such an initiative should be highly commended, supported and nurtured over a reasonable period of time by key stakeholders, commissioners and professional bodies alike.

The stepped model of care delivery outlined is helpful in offering a structure for the level of mental health disturbance and indicated treatment interventions. It is also recognised that where the GMHW is employed, the role is best applied at level 2 and supported by experienced mental health workers and therapists. It can also be noted that delivering level 3 and 4 treatments are also achievable in primary care under this model with Practice and Senior Practice Therapists. Such experienced staff also undertake all gateway (Department of Health, 2003) functions for adults.

Managers and commissioners must not be shy in acknowledging that there is sufficient volume of clinical need to be addressed by such a range of workers. This is demonstrated anecdotally, through local routine clinical data statistics, and within the public domain, and demand will still continue to outstrip supply.

The overall benefits of introducing a comprehensive and skilled mental health workforce into primary care are not only demonstrated in reduced referrals to secondary mental health services, but more immediately in clinically therapeutic responses to brief and medium psychological consultations across broad populations, including earlier returning to work and the potential to reduce relapse when clinical states are addressed properly. If the NHS is going to continue to be serious in acknowledging the impact of mental health on a broad range of societal matters, including domestic violence, work absenteeism, bullying, drug abuse, family breakdown and many other areas of personal misery, then continued developments and attention will be essential.

Attention to this field has been welcomed, as it has brought new investment and begun the process of raising the profile of all aspects of mental health within a much more visible public domain. That members of the public can now walk into their GP surgery and receive a range of mental health advice and access to help is a huge departure from the days of outpatient settings in remote psychiatric hospitals which carried so much stigma that the majority of people would avoid acknowledging any personal mental health difficulty, which would thus remain unattended to.

New ways of working in primary care are developing rapidly, and will continue as PCTs are driven by targeting a range of mental health issues from 'lithium registers' to reducing benzodiazepine prescribing. Potent psychological interventions need to be skilfully and sensitively applied to seize this opportunity to impact on significant numbers of people referred for help, in order that the massive gains to them are achieved. Furthermore, this needs to be demonstrated systematically and transparently to contribute to the growing evidence base and to ensure sustained commitment and investment in this field.

References

Appleby, L. (2004) The National Service Framework for Mental Health – Five Years On. London: HMSO.

Bower, P., Foster, J. and Mellor Clark, J. (2001) *Quality in Counselling in Primary Care: a Guide for Effective Commissioning and Clinical Governance.* University of Manchester: National Primary Research and Development Centre.

Bower, P., Jerrim, S. and Gask, L. (2004) Primary care mental health workers: role expectations, conflict and ambiguity. *Health and Social Care in the Community,* **12**(4), 336–345. Oxford: Blackwell.

British Medical Association (2003) *Investing in General Practice. The New General Medical Services Contract.* London: British Medical Association.

Burton, M. (1998) *Counselling and Psychotherapy in Primary Care.* London: Wiley.

Crossland, A., Tomson, D. and Freer, M. (2002) *Primary Care Mental Health Graduate Workers; Issues of Content, Delivery and Implementation of A Programme of Training.* Northumbria University.

Dawson, A. and Tylee, A. (eds.) (2001) *Depression: Social and Economic Time Bomb,* pp. 31–54. London: BMJ Books.

Department of Health (1996) *NHS Psychotherapy Services in England: Review of Strategic Policy.* London: HMSO.

Department of Health (1999) *The National Service Framework for Mental Health.* London: HMSO.

Department of Health (2000) *The NHS Plan. A plan for Investment, A Plan for Reform.* London: HMSO.

Department of Health (2001) *Treatment Choice in Psychological Therapies and Counselling. Evidence Based Practice Guidelines.* London: HMSO.

Department of Health (2003) *Fast Forwarding Primary Care Mental Health: Gateway Workers.* London: HMSO.

Department of Health (2004) *Organising and Delivering Psychological Therapies*. London: HMSO.

Durcan, G. and Knowles, K. (2004) *Audit of Primary Mental Health Care in Leicester, Leicestershire and Rutland*. Sainsbury Centre for Mental Health. Unpublished.

Elder, A. and Holmes, J. (2002) *Mental Health in Primary Care*. Oxford: Oxford University Press.

Frude, N. (2004a) Bibliotherapy as a means of delivering psychological therapy. *Clinical Psychology*, **39**, 8–10.

Frude, N. (2004b) A book prescription scheme in primary care. *Clinical Psychology*, **39**, 11–14.

Gask, L., Rogers, A., Roland, M., Bower, P. and Morris, D. (2003) *Improving Quality in Primary Care: a Practical Guide to the National Service Framework for Mental Health*. University of Manchester: National Primary Care Research and Development Centre.

Goldberg, D. and Gournay, K. (1997) *The General Practitioner, the Psychiatrist and the Burden of Mental Health Care*. Maudsley Hospital: Institute of Psychiatry

Jenkins. R (1999) The Contribution of David Goldberg; A British Perspective p. xvi-xxi, in Common Mental Disorders in Primary Care, Ed Tansella M and Thornicroft G 1999, Routledge

Kingdon, D. (2004) An introduction to psychotherapeutic perspectives in primary care: a qualitative and subjective observation on underlying clinical trends in common mental health problems. *Journal of Primary Care Mental Health*, **2**(3–4), 157–164.

NICE (2004a) *Anxiety: Management of Anxiety in Adults in Primary, Secondary and Community Care*. Clinical Guidelines 22. London: National Institute for Clinical Excellence.

NICE (2004b) *Depression: Management of Depression in Primary and Secondary Care*. Clinical Guidelines 23. London: National Institute for Clinical Excellence.

NIMHE (2004) *Enhanced Services Specification for Depression under the New GP Contract*. London: National Institute for Mental Health in England.

Padesky, C. (1995) *Mind over Mood*. New York: Guilford Press.

Paxton, R., Shrubb, S., Griffiths, H., Cameron, L. and Maunder, L. (2000) Tiered approach: matching mental health services to needs. *Journal of Mental Health*, **9**, 137–144.

Richardson, A. (2002) *Graduate Mental Health Workers. The Content and Process of One Year, Full Time Training – A Discussion Paper*. London: Department of Health.

Roth, A. and Fonagy, P. (1996) *What Works for Whom? A Critical Review of Psychotherapy Research.* New York: Guilford Press.

Thompson, K., Strathdee, G. and Woods, A. (eds.) (1997) *Mental Health Services Development Skills Workbook.* London: Sainsbury Centre for Mental Health.

CHAPTER 12

New ways of working in dual diagnosis

Lois Dugmore

Introduction

The role of the nurse consultant working with clients with a dual diagnosis is unique. In the development of the nurse consultant role nurses and other health-care professionals have had to learn to work in new ways, and the development of dual diagnosis services within mainstream services has been controversial.

Historically, mental health services and drug/alcohol teams have worked in individual ways and collaborative practice has been a challenge to existing practices. This chapter will examine the way in which services need to integrate and develop to meet the needs of clients with a dual diagnosis. This chapter will look at strategic development based on national policy and how this can be devolved to local trusts; the role of mapping services; the role of the nurse consultant; and how we address changing practice. This will be discussed both strategically and clinically and will incorporate the role of the nurse consultant in facilitating these changes.

Nurse consultant role

Working with clients with a dual diagnosis is a complex and challenging role. It encompasses skills from both substance misuse and mental health settings used creatively to provide a holistic approach to care. To promote and develop dual diagnosis services requires a culture change in organisations. Within the last decade there has been a proliferation of new roles based on changing practices (Dyson, 1997). The role of the nurse consultant was outlined in *Making a Difference* (Department of Health, 1999a), which highlighted the need for the role of the nurse consultant to provide a career structure for nurses who wished to remain within the clinical care field and to promote the use of advanced clinical skills. The nurse consultant role was developed to improve quality of care and improve outcomes (Department of Health, 1999b). In general, though, there is a lack of clear definition of the role of nurse consultant in the literature (Bent, 2004), which has led to Trusts interpreting the role differently within each organisation. The aim was to provide a 'career framework for nursing and focus on clinical leadership and to strengthen leadership' (Department of Health, 1999b, p. 52). The nurse consultant role is based on five core areas. These are:

- Clinical practice
- Training
- Research
- Supervision
- Strategic

Nurse consultants use their leadership skills to develop care and treatment outcomes based on research practice (Manley, 2000). Within this context the nurse consultant for dual diagnosis has the opportunity to lead and develop clinical practice at both strategic and clinical levels.

Within dual diagnosis services this enables nurse consultants to engage in the development and setting up of dual diagnosis networks both locally and nationally to ensure the development of shared practice. It also empowers nurses to influence change in practice through standard-setting and promoting best practice through shared experience. This has been achieved by the setting up of nurse-led clinics.

The role is vital in supporting change within the health service and meets the needs of clients through the clinical governance agenda. One of the key problems for nurse consultants is that they can be seen as specialists giving advice, and not as part of a team. The role can also be isolated and complex, although this can be alleviated by the use of regular organisational support and supervision. Nurse consultants, through a government directive, are expected to be educated to degree level and to be working towards a Masters degree (Department of Health, 1999b), although nurse education to date has been slow to respond.

Within dual diagnosis the nurse consultant is crucial in creating new ways of working. The *Dual Diagnosis Good Practice Guide* (Department of Health, 2002) cites that the complexity of clinical presentation and social and criminal experience makes diagnosis, care and treatment particularly difficult, with service users being at higher risk of relapse, readmission to hospital and suicide. It recognises the need for effective leadership, rigorous training programmes and a coordinated approach to care. There is, however, a strong political and clinical agenda for change and for the introduction of dual diagnosis services. The National Service Framework (NSF) for Mental Health (Department of Health, 1999b) reported that individuals with substance misuse problems have a higher incidence of mental health problems than the general population. It also notes that one in three rough sleepers have both drug/alcohol and mental health problems. The national guidance makes it clear that supporting someone with a mental health illness and substance misuse problems – alcohol and/or drugs – is one of the biggest challenges facing front line mental health services. This can only be achieved by health and social care community agreeing the needs of the client group whilst incorporating clinical governance and best value requirements, which will provide the impetus to improve standards of care and the transition to a model based on an integrated care pathway and a multi-agency approach.

A joint strategy is necessary in order to:

- Identify the needs of clients with a dual diagnosis.
- Achieve ownership for challenging areas of work affecting primary care, criminal justice, mental health and substance misuse services in the statutory and voluntary sectors.
- Develop an agreed dual diagnosis skills base.
- Measure the level of prevalence of dual diagnosis in local areas.
- Give direction to implement change.
- Meet the demands of the Department of Health (2002) guidelines.
- Identify the resources needed.
- Meet the needs of the client group in a cost-effective manner.
- Develop protocols for practice.
- Deal with medication issues, which are also a prominent feature within mental health (Hamilton, 2000); with increased numbers of individuals using drugs and alcohol, interaction with psychiatric medications is a key issue.

National context

In 2002 the *Dual Diagnosis Good Practice Guide* (Department of Health, 2002) was published to provide guidelines for the development of local services for clients with a dual diagnosis. It states that all services including substance misuse must ensure that clients with severe mental health problems and substance misuse are subject to CPA and have a full risk assessment. It also recommends that specialist teams of dual diagnosis workers should support mainstream mental health services.

It demonstrates the need for definitions to be based on the five SIDDS dimensions of Severity, Informal/formal care, Diagnosis, Disability and Duration. It highlights issues of risk of harm to self or others and of severe self-neglect. Phillips (2000) recognises the need for an effective psychiatric nursing response to assessment and joint clinical management. He also brings attention to the increased rates of violence in dual diagnosis. *Safety First: The National Confidential Inquiry into Suicide and Homicide* (Department of Health, 2001) showed that at least half of all suicides were associated with dual diagnosis.

The 10-year strategy for Substance Misuse (POH, 1998) identifies significant risks for young people using substances being related to psychological problems. *Safety First* (Department of Health, 2001) identifies the need to make provision for dual diagnosis clients within mainstream services. The literature clearly recognises the links between dual diagnosis and the criminal justice system (Phillips, 2000) and the need for focused services. National policy also supports the use of assertive outreach models and teams (Department of Health, 1999). Publications and policies incorporated within a local strategy include:

- The National Drugs Policy, the NSF and the NHS Plan
- Essence of care
- Agenda for change
- NICE guidelines
- Clinical governance and performance frameworks
- CHI reports, audit reports and SSI reports
- Patient surveys
- NIMHE guidelines
- National inquiries
- Good practice guidelines for dual diagnosis

Local primary care, mental health, criminal justice and substance misuse services in the statutory, voluntary and independent sectors need to work together with service users and carers to explore both mental health and substance misuse services to meet individual needs. This requires a locally agreed integrated care model and clearly agreed responsibility for coordinating services at each point in the process in order to ensure that people with a dual diagnosis and the service providers can deliver specialist input on a shared care basis (Simpson *et al.*, 2003; Simpson, in press). Joint planning and commissioning of services specific to clients with a dual diagnosis is essential to provide a comprehensive service to this client group. The coordination of roles between the voluntary and statutory groups is an essential component of this service and fits with the models of care approach through the drug action teams. There is a clear need to work with stakeholders and to learn from audit, complaints and incidents. There will be clear links between providers and improved interfaces.

Developments within dual diagnosis can only take place by the promotion of mainstream services and with a process of cultural change, based on staff training that impacts on all team members. This can only change by looking at models for improvement, and service mapping.

Model for improvement (Langley et al., 1996)

ACT	PLAN
STUDY	DO

This model identifies the changes that need to be made and how the change can be implemented. It looks at setting objectives, asking questions and collecting the data to answer the questions. It completes the collection of data, initially analyses the data and then compares and summarises what has been learnt. It then carries out the plan and analyses the results. The process of mapping the improving services will then be based on Table 12.1.

Another method of mapping is to map the patients' activities and roles. This can be done by identifying the current situation and then modelling on a new system. Activity and role lane mapping in dual diagnosis are set out in Table 12.2.

Critical issues for dual diagnosis are:

- Points of access to services
- Eligibility criteria
- Communication
- Commissioning
- User and carer empowerment/involvement
- Training and education of health care providers
- Strategic development

Table 12.1

Step 1	Identify the target group and the aims of care.
Step 2	Determine how the service will improve the care received by the client group and how the outcomes will be monitored.
Step 3	Look at the problems that clients and carers feel are an issue.
Step 4	Identify staff needs and how to improve/provide training.
Step 5	Pilot training and roll out a programme of training after evaluation and changes to other areas. Set up support links.
Step 6	Implement service improvements.
Step 7	Ensure the service is sustained, and provide feedback to users, carers, staff and commissioners. Look at ways to continue to improve. Advise others.

Table 12.2: Activity and role mapping for dual diagnosis.

Activity/role	Ward team OT/nurse	Drug/alcohol team	Psychology	DR	Housing	CMHT	GP
Joint assessment	✓	✓		✓		✓	
Planned admission	✓	✓		✓		✓	✓
Planned discharge	✓	✓	✓	✓	✓	✓	✓
Emergency admission	✓	✓	✓	✓		✓	✓
Group work	✓	✓	✓	✓		✓	
Individual work	✓	✓	✓	✓	✓	✓	

Changing practice

Historically patients with a dual diagnosis have found themselves moving between mental health and substance misuse services. This led to substance misuse services feeling unable to treat the client until the mental health issues were resolved and the mental health clinicians being unable to engage until the substance misuse issues were resolved. This left the client disengaging with services because of the lack of clarity and engagement by staff. In developing services there is an opportunity to gather client and carer views about services and what they would like to see in place to better meet their needs. Dual diagnosis is complicated but mental health and substance misuse issues are often linked (Littlejohn, 2005). These views serve as the basis on which recommendations should be made for improving existing services on a local basis. Within this context communication is a key area.

Information and improved communication

- A clear definition of dual diagnosis, including the components widely disseminated is essential.
- Service directory in a wide range of modalities. Ensure that the service details collected through the research are added to/adapted for the LAMP directory and new website.

- Existing specialist drug and alcohol helpline/advice services should be promoted for key staff in other agencies – hostels, voluntary agencies, mental health staff.
- Awareness/promotion of each team's and service's roles and referral criteria to ensure that people do not fall through the net and can get the service they need from the most appropriate team.
- Improved support for carers – access to advice, training and better information.

Care pathways and joint working

- The needs of people with a dual diagnosis should be addressed holistically, with a designated care coordinator in the relevant team and by better integration of existing services.
- Develop a core assessment and care protocols – for substance misuse, mental health, learning disability and Asperger's Syndrome, including greater consistency in retaining case responsibility and where necessary transferring people's care between teams.
- Review of guidelines and policies for drug dealing/drug misuse in residential and ward settings and in relation to dealing with challenging behaviours that can be associated with substance misuse, the latter to include maximising assistance to staff from other team colleagues.
- Improve links/liaison between different secondary care teams – each current team in ward and community settings (mental health, learning disability, substance misuse etc.) should nominate individuals on the basis of personal interest as their team specialist(s) in dual diagnosis. This key group should receive support and training and act as a network.
- Improved therapeutic follow up – following discharge from acute inpatient mental health care and inpatient detox, streamlining of 'community care' assessment procedure, improved support/liaison in event of relapse.

Training and development

- Existing good practice needs promotion – local specialist substance misuse formal training, short term part-time secondments, specialist topic reading time, attendance at other teams' team meetings, shadowing, good quality clinical supervision, reduced caseload sizes.
- Engaging staff and clients – increasing confidence and ownership/responsibility, motivational work with users, better 'self-help' information for users,

out of hours advice/support to staff, specialist outreach work to mental health facilities and hostels

■ A training and education strategy for dual diagnosis with a rolling programme for identified 'team specialists' but also available for/targeted at others in the community, residential and ward settings involved in mental health, learning disabilities, substance misuse and Asperger's Syndrome.

■ Partnerships with education institutions for formalised qualifications for dual diagnosis.

Profile of service user group

Within dual diagnosis it is essential to identify the client group. People with a dual diagnosis aged between 18 and 65 years are more vulnerable than those presenting with a single diagnosis. Their prognosis is considered more unpredictable with high levels of service use and disengagement. They are heavy users of inpatient beds and community facilities. They are also more likely to exhibit the following:

■ Childhood abuse (sexual/physical)
■ Increased suicide risk or self-harm
■ Severe mental health problems
■ Homelessness and unsuitable housing
■ Victims of crime
■ Contact with the criminal justice system
■ History of family problems
■ Disengagement with services and non-compliant with treatment
■ Absconding from inpatient facilities
■ Higher levels of violence
■ Physical health problems related to neglect and drug/alcohol use
■ Have not always received appropriate care
≡ Post-traumatic stress/trauma

In Australia in 2003 the Australian National Comorbidity Project published a major review under the auspices of the national mental health and substance misuse strategies. It considered research evidence and clinical studies from the USA, UK and Australia. The authors of this report view the terms 'dual diagnosis' and 'comorbidity' as a reflection of the continuing ambiguity in understanding these complex presentations. They recommended a model developed by Kavanagh *et al.* (2000) that identified six types of dual diagnosis client, which they felt provides a useful framework for conceptualising patterns of dual diagnosis:

Type 1: Clients with psychotic spectrum disorders (schizophrenia, bipolar affective disorder, major depression etc.) who satisfy DSM-IV criteria for substance dependence.

Type 2: Clients with non-psychotic spectrum disorders who satisfy criteria for DSM-IV substance dependence.

Type 3: Clients with a psychotic spectrum disorder who also satisfy DSM-IV criteria for a substance abuse disorder.

Type 4: Clients with non-psychotic spectrum disorders who also satisfy DSM-IV criteria for a substance abuse disorder.

Type 5: Clients with psychotic spectrum disorders who are also using substances in a way that puts them at risk of harm to their physical or mental health.

Type 6: Clients with non-psychotic spectrum disorders who are also using substance in ways that put them at risk of harm to their physical or mental health.

When identifying the needs of the service user group it is clear that one clinical team cannot manage interventions alone. The evidence demonstrates the need for an integrated team approach which engages service users and works within an assertive outreach framework, including:

- Comprehensive assessment including risk
- Care programme approach
- Engagement
- Mental Health Act

Agreeing a care pathway

Integrated care pathways are an based on the current best evidence gained from systematic reviews (Fraser, 2003) as well as information from clinical teams and the client. The advantages are that they bring about quality improvement and are able to track key indicators and processes that look at how the client's care can be improved.

It ensures that care is delivered directly and efficiently to the client. It provides an evaluation process and a team approach.

An integrated care pathway will draw together a team of professionals who will sign up to a specific care pathway that meets the needs of the individual client group in a systematic way.

The integrated care pathway:

- Provides opportunities for improving care delivery
- Enhances multidisciplinary planning and problem solving

- Allows clients and carers to be part of the process
- Provides consistent care
- Ensures interventions are appropriate
- Standardises practice
- Improves outcomes
- Ensures continuity and discharge planning
- Promotes good communication

A care pathway for local services across the health and social care community is set out below. It will be underpinned by shared care protocols and treatment protocols that promote appropriate transfer between services, safe discharge and mechanisms for re-referral. Joint working confidentiality protocols and information sharing protocols will be agreed between all agencies because of the complexity of organisations and the client group.

Education and training

Training and education regarding dual diagnosis and substance misuse has played a small role in education programmes for mental health staff and this needs to be addressed through nurse training. Education and training are key elements in implementing the strategy. This can only be achieved by a robust ongoing system of training and education based on the sharing of key skills. Specialist training and updates will be required in dual diagnosis via the following forums:

- Conferences
- Workshops
- In-house training and updates
- National forums
- Training of mental health professionals
- Regional forums
- Research and development initiatives and training.

Conclusion

Dual diagnosis in itself is a newly defined element in mental health. It requires careful consideration in its placement within existing services and the support of multidisciplinary teams and staff trained in the area of substance misuse to ensure that clients' holistic needs are met.

Nurse consultants have a role to play in the development of services provided they are clear about their own roles and have realistic expectations of their workload management (Bent, 2004). In the development of new ways of working it is essential to identify the key stakeholders to ensure that the process can move forward. Nurse consultants can act as brokers to do this, but stakeholders are the providers of information who can ensure that the process is valid for the service users and clients, which will provide the appropriate outcomes required. The sharing of knowledge and information is essential to ensure that the holistic needs of the client are met, but there is a need for further exploration of this due to the illegal nature of drug use. There is a need for further research based on dual diagnosis and working models.

References

Anon (2000) *Drug Misuse and Mental Health: Learning Lessons on Dual Diagnosis.* Report of the All-Party Parliamentary Drug Misuse Group.

Banerjee, S., Clancy, C. and Crome, I. (eds.) (2000) *Co-existing Problems of Mental Health Disorder and Substance Misuse: an Information Manual.* London: Royal College of Psychiatrists Research Unit. Report to the Department of Health 2001.

Barker, I. (1998) Mental illness and substance misuse. *The Mental Health Review,* **3**(4), 6–13.

Bartels, S. J., Drake, R. E. and Wallach, M. A. (1995). Long-term course of substance use disorders among clients with severe mental illness. *Psychiatric Services,* **46**(3), 248–251.

Bent, J. (2004) How effective and valued are nurse consultants in the UK? *Nursing Times,* **100**(24), 6.04.

Brown, S. (1998) Substance misuse in a chronic psychosis population: prevalence and staff perceptions. *Psychiatric Bulletin,* **22**, 595–598.

Care Programme Approach: Collaborative Practice in Action – Training Package (2000) Directorate of Specialist Mental Health Services.

Carey, K. (1995) Treatment of substance use disorders and schizophrenia. In: *Double Jeopardy: Chronic Mental Illness and Substance Use Disorders* (eds. A. Lehman and L. Dixon). Chur, Switzerland: Harwood Academic.

Conors, G. J., Donnovan, D. M. and DiClimente, C. C. (2001) *Substance Abuse Treatment and the Stages of Change.* New York: Guilford Press.

Crawford, V. (2001) *Co-existing Problems of Mental Health and Substance Misuse ('Dual Diagnosis'): A Review of Relevant Literature*. London: Royal College of Psychiatrists.

Department of Health (1998) *Tackling Drugs to Building a Better Britain. The Government's 10-Year Strategy for Tackling Drug Misuse*. London: HMSO.

Department of Health (1999a) *Making a Difference. Strengthening the Nursing, Midwifery and Health Visiting Contribution to Health and Health Care*. London: HMSO.

Department of Health (1999b) *National Service Framework for Mental Health*. London: HMSO.

Department of Health (2000) *The NHS Plan. A plan for Investment, A Plan for Reform*. London: HMSO.

Department of Health (2001) *Safety First: Five-year Report of the National Confidential Inquiry into Suicide and Homicide by People with Mental Illness*. London: HMSO.

Department of Health (2002) Dual Diagnosis Good Practice Guide. London: HMSO.

Department of Health, Scottish Office Home & Health Department, Welsh Office (1991) *Drug Misuse & Dependence: Guidelines on Clinical Management*. London: HMSO.

Drake, R. E., Mercer-McFadden, C., Mueser, K. T., McHugo, G. J. and Bond, G. R. (1998) A review of integrated mental health and substance abuse treatment for people with dual diagnosis. *Schizophrenia Bulletin*, **24**(4), 589.

Dyson, L. (1997) Advanced nursing roles: their worth in nursing. *Professional Nurse*, **12**(10), 728–732.

Evans, P. D. (2000) *Dual Diagnosis Demonstration Project*: 1 March 1999 to 30 April 2000. The Oxford Homeless Medical Fund.

Farrell, M., Howes, S., Bebbington, P., Brugha, T., Jenkins, R., Lewis, G., Marsden, J., Taylor, C. and Meltzer, H. (2001) Nicotine, alcohol and drug dependence and psychiatric comorbidity. *British Journal of Psychiatry*, **179**, 432–437.

Farrell, M., Howes, S., Taylor, C., Lewis, G., Jenkins, R., Bebbington, P., Jarvis, M., Brugha, T., Gill, B. and Meltzer, H. (1998) Substance misuse and psychiatric co-morbidity: an overview of the OPCS national psychiatric morbidity survey. *Addictive Behaviours*, **23**, 909–918.

Fraser, K. D. (2003) Are home care programs cost-effective? A systematic review of the literature. *Care Management Journals*, **4**(4), 198–201.

Gibbs, M. and Priest, H. M. (1999) Designing and implementing an 'oral diagnosis module: a review of the literature and some preliminary findings. *Nurse Education Today*, **5**, 357–363.

Gibbins, J. (1998) Towards integrated care for patients with dual diagnosis: the Dorset Healthcare NHS Trust experience. *The Mental Health Review*, **3**(4), 25–27.

Gournay, K., Sandford, T., Johnson, S. and Thornicroft, G. (1997) Dual diagnosis of severe mental health problems and substance abuse/dependence: a major priority for mental health nursing. *Journal of Psychiatric and Mental Health Nursing*, **4**, 89.

Gossop, M., Marsden, J. and Stewart, D. (1998) *NTORS at One Year: Changes in Substance Use, Health and Criminal Behaviour One Year After Intake*. London: Department of Health.

Gravestock, S. and Bouras, N. (1995) *Emotional Disorders. Mental Health in Learning Disabilities*. A training pack for staff working with people who have a dual diagnosis of mental health needs & learning disabilities. Chapter 4, pp. 23–29. Brighton: Pavilion Publishing.

Hamilton I. (2000) Dangerous drug interactions. *Nursing Times*, **96**(46), 41.

Health Advisory Service (2001) *Substance Misuse and Mental Health Co-Morbidity (Dual Diagnosis): Standards for Mental Health Services*. London: Health Advisory Service.

ISDD (1996) Dual diagnosis: information for drug workers. Photocopiable fact sheet. *Druglink*, **1**(2).

Johnson, S. (1997) Diagnosis of severe mental illness and substance misuse: a case for specialist services? *British Journal of Psychiatry*, **171**, 205–208.

Kavanagh, D. J., Greenway, L., Jenner, L., Saunders, J. B., White, A., Sorban, J. and Hamilton, G. (2000) Contrasting views and experiences of health professionals on the management of comorbid substance misuse and mental disorders. *Australian and New Zealand Journal of Psychiatry*, **34**, 279–289.

Kessler, R. C., Nelson, C. and McGonagle, K. A. (1996) Epidemiology of co-occurring addictive and mental disorders: implications for prevention and service utilisation. *American Journal of Orthopsychiatry*, **66**(1), 17–31.

Kirchner, J., Owen, R., Nordquist, C. and Fischer, E. (1998) Diagnosis and management of substance use disorders among in-patients with schizophrenia. *Psychiatric Services*, **49**(1), 82–85.

Langley, G. J., Nolan, K. M., Nolan, T. W. *et al.* (1996) *The Improvement Guide A Practical Approach to Enhancing Organisational Performance*. San Francisco: Jossey Bass.

Laurant, C. (2000) Altered image. *Health Service Journal*, Sept 14, p. 18.

Ley, A., Jeffery, D. P., McLaren, S. and Siegfried, N. (2000) Treatment programmes for people with both severe mental illness and substance misuse. *The Cochrane Database of Systematic Reviews*, **4**.

Littlejohn, C. (2005) Links between drug and alcohol misuse and psychiatric conditions. *Nursing Times*, **101**(1), 34.

Manley, K. (2000) Organisational culture and consultant nurse outcome. Part 1: Organisational culture. *Nursing Standard*, **14**(36), 34–38.

Marlatt, G. and Gordon, J. (1985) *Relapse Prevention: Maintenance Strategies in the Treatment of Addictive Disorders*. New York: Guilford Press.

Mathers, D., Ghodrose, A. Caan, A. and Scott, S. (1991) Cannabis use in large sample of acute psychiatric admissions. *British Journal of Addiction*, **86**, 779–784.

Meisson, G., Powell, T., Wituk, S., Girrens, K. and Arteaga, S. (1999) attitudes of alcohol anonymous contact persons towards group participation by persons with a mental illness. *Psychiatric Services*, **50**(8), 1079–1081.

Menezes, P., Johnson, S., Thornicroft, G., Marshall, J., Prosso, A., Bebbington, P. and Kuipers, E. (1996) Drug and alcohol problems among individuals with severe mental illness in South London. *British Journal of Psychiatry*, **168**, 612–619.

Mercer-McFadden, C., Drake, R. E., Clark, R. E., Verven, N., Noorsday, D. L. and Fox, T. S. (1998) *Substance Abuse Treatment for Severe Mental Disorders; A Program Manager's Guide*. New Hampshire-Dartmouth Psychiatric Research Centre.

Miller, W. and Rollnick, S. (1991) *Motivational Interviewing: Preparing People to Change Addictive Behaviour*. New York: Guilford Press.

Moore, R. (2000) *Dual Diagnosis. Mental Health Annual Report of the Director of Public Health*. Leicestershire Health.

Mundin, D., Chrisite, M. M. and Unell, I. (2000) *Dual Diagnosis Services in Leicestershire: A Local Agency Survey in the County of Leicestershire*. A report to the Leicestershire County Council Social Services Department, Adult Mental Health Service.

Murphy, G. G. and Wetzel, R. D. (1990) The lifetime risk of suicide in alcoholism. *Archives of General Psychiatry*, **47**, 383–392.

Naik, P. and Browness, L. (1999) Treatment of psychiatric aspects of alcohol misuse. *Hospital Medicine*, **60**(3), 173–177.

O'Leary, J. (1998). Mental illness, substance abuse and homelessness. *The Mental Health Review*, **3**(4), 25–27.

Orford, J. (1985) *Excessive Appetite; A Psychological View of Addictions*. Chichester: Wiley.

Phillips, P. (2000) Substance misuse, offending and mental illness. *Journal of Psychiatric and Mental Health Nursing*, **7**, 483–489.

Phillips, P. and Johnson, S. (2001) How does drug and alcohol misuse develop among people with a psychotic illness? A literature review. *Social Psychiatry and Psychiatric Epidemiology*, **36**, 269–276.

Prosser, H. (1999) An invisible morbidity? *Psychologist*, **12**(5), 234–237.

Regier, D., Farmer, M., Rae, D., Locke, B., Keith, S., Judd, L. and Goodwin, F. (1990) Co-morbidity of mental disorders with alcohol and other drug abuse: results from the Epidemiologic Catchment Area (ECA) study. *Journal of the American Medical Association*, **264**(19).

Robertson, R. (1998) *Management of Drug Users in the Community*. London: Arnold.

Rostad, P. and Checinski, K. with Ward, M. and McGeachy, O. (eds.) (1999) *Dual Diagnosis: Facing the Challenge. The Care of People with a Dual Diagnosis of Mental Illness and Substance Misuse*. London: Wynne Howard Publishing.

Royal College of Psychiatrists Research Unit (2000) *National Audit of the Management of Violence in Mental Health Settings Final Report: Year 1*. London: Royal College of Psychiatrists.

Ryrie, I. (2000) Coexistent substance use and psychiatric disorders. In: *Working with Serious Mental Illness: a Manual for Clinical Practice* (eds. C. Gamble and G. Brennan). London: Baillière Tindall.

Scott, H., Johnson, S., Menezes, P., Thornicroft, G., Marshall, J., Bindman, J., Bebbington, P., and Kuipers, E. (1998) Substance misuse and risk of aggression and offending among the severely mentally ill. *British Journal of Psychiatry*, **172**, 345–350.

Simpson, A. (in press) Dual diagnosis: shared care and interprofessional practice. In *Dual Diagnosis – Nursing Care and Management* (ed. Rassool, H.). London: Blackwell.

Simpson, A., Miller, C. and Bowers, L. (2003) The history of the Care Programme Approach in England: where did it go wrong? *Journal of Mental Health*, **12**(5), 489–504.

Sims, J. and Lancelot, A. (2001) Mental Illness and substance abuse *Nursing Times*, **97**(39), 36.

Smith, J. and Hucker, S. (1994) Schizophrenia and substance abuse. *British Journal of Psychiatry*, **165**, 13–21.

Solomon, J., Zimberg, S. and Shollar, E. (1993). *Dual Diagnosis; Evaluation, Treatment, Training and Program Development*. New York: Plenum Medical.

Tyler, A. (1986) *Street Drugs: The Facts Explained and Myths Exploded*. London: Hodder and Stoughton.

Ward, M. and Applin, C. (1998) *The Unlearned Lesson – The Role of Alcohol and Drug Misuse in Homicides Perpetrated by People with Mental Health Problems*. London: Wynne Howard Publishing.

Watkins, T. R., Lewellan, A. and Barrett, M. C. (2001) *Dual Diagnosis: An Integrated Approach to Treatment*. New York: Sage.

Weaver, T., Rutter, D., Maden, P., Ward, J., Stimson, G. and Renton, A. (2001) Results of a screening survey for co-morbid substance misuse amongst patients in treatment for psychotic disorders: prevalence and service needs in an inner London borough. *Social Psychiatry and Psychiatric Epidemiology*, **36**, 399–406.

CHAPTER 13

Assertive outreach

James Dooher

Assertive outreach services support people in the community who find it hard to use more traditional mental health services. These services are intended to work more 'assertively' than traditional community support services, and this chapter will explore the comparative differences between the two, their aspirations shortfalls and the interface between assertive outreach and other services.

The approach was developed in the USA as 'Assertive Community Treatment' and is a means of providing intensive care and support to those with severe mental illness who would otherwise be difficult to engage with services. It is characterised by work with clients in their own environment, wherever that may be. This allows services to be provided to people who may not otherwise receive them, where they feel most comfortable. Workers may also visit or accompany clients when they use other services. This is said to promote a two-way engagement that helps to develop trust and rapport between the care provider and the client in a flexible, creative and needs-focused way that enables the delivery of a health and social care package that fits each client's own specific needs.

The Sainsbury Centre for Mental Health considers assertive outreach to be a way of working with an identified client group of severely mentally ill adults who do not effectively engage with mental health services.

Generally, assertive outreach services target adults aged between 18 and approximately 65 with the following:

- A severe and persistent mental disorder (e.g. schizophrenia, major affective disorders) associated with a high level of disability.
- A history of high use of inpatient or intensive home-based care (for example, more than two admissions or more than six months' inpatient care in the past two years).
- Difficulty in maintaining lasting and consenting contact with services.
- Multiple, complex needs including a number of the following: history of violence or persistent offending; significant risk of persistent self-harm or neglect; poor response to previous treatment; dual diagnosis of substance

misuse and serious mental illness; detention under the Mental Health Act (1983).

Services try to improve engagement, increase stability in the lives of service users and their carers/family, reduce hospital admissions and length of stay and improve social functioning whilst being cost-effective.

Historical factors influencing the development of assertive outreach

Following the case of Ben Silcock, who on New Year's Eve 1992 was mauled after entering the lions' enclosure at London Zoo, significant attention has been given to the plight of patients discharged from psychiatric establishments, with particular emphasis upon the quality of aftercare and the responsibilities and accountability of those who provide it. In the same year Jonathan Zito was stabbed to death by Christopher Clunis, a diagnosed 'schizophrenic', in Finsbury Park Station, London, a case which became symbolic of the failures in discharge provision for the mentally ill.

The results of the official inquiry into the Clunis case (Ritchie *et al.*, 1994), identified a combination of a shortage of hospital beds, too few psychiatrists and social workers, and inadequate provision of sheltered housing, day centres and other services as significant factors in this tragedy.

The response from the government of the day was to make inquiries into homicide by people with mental health problems mandatory (Department of Health, 1994) The introduction of mandatory inquiries reflected a rising level of anxiety about the perceived failure of community care policies as expressed through government bodies and the media. Changes in the Mental Health Act were introduced on 1 April 1996, introducing three new elements:

- After-Care Under Supervision (Supervised Discharge).
- Removal of the 28 day limit on returning patients who abscond whilst on section.
- Extending Leave of Absence under Section 17 up to a maximum of 12 months.

These developments were not well received by any of the professional or advocacy bodies in the UK, who were particularly concerned about the conditions which could be imposed on the patient, such as where to live, or whether to attend a day centre or outpatient clinic, and specifically the power to convey people against their wishes to these places.

If a person is detained under Sections 2, 3 or 37 of the Mental Health Act 1983 then no conditions can be imposed on them when they are discharged from hospital. Under existing law conditions can only be imposed on discharge if they are detained on a restriction order under s.37/41, and they are then conditionally discharged.

Section 17 of the Mental Health Act 1983 places a joint legal duty on Health and Social Services to provide after-care for patients who are discharged from hospital if they have been detained under Section 3, Section 37 or Section 37/41 of the Act and are then discharged. Despite this the patient is under no obligation to accept the after-care on offer and has the legal right to refuse it. The consequences of refusal, however, are set out under section 25E(2) of the new Act, as failure to comply with the conditions could lead to being sectioned.

This creates a 'Catch 22' situation where failure to cooperate may lead to compulsory detention.

The Report of the Confidential Inquiry into Homicides and Suicides by Mentally Ill People (Appleby *et al.*, 1999) identified a number of procedural difficulties, such as:

- Failures of communication between professionals
- Lack of clarity about care plans
- Lack of time for face-to-face contact with patients
- Need for additional staff training
- Poor compliance with treatment by patients
- Insufficient use of legal powers to supervise patients at risk
  and made a number of key recommendations:
- Strengthening risk assessment skills in clinical teams
- Increasing face-to-face contact time with patients
- Supporting the development of genuine multidisciplinary teams
- Developing better systems for communication between professionals and between professionals and families
- Raising awareness about appropriate uses of legal powers under the Mental Health Act 1983 through further training
- Ensuring that treatment environments are acceptable for patients

The USA has followed a parallel process and introduced legislation commonly known as 'Kendra's Law', named after Kendra Webdale, a young woman who died in January 1999 after being pushed in front of a New York City subway train by a person who failed to take the medication prescribed for his mental illness.

It provides for assisted outpatient treatment for certain people with mental illness who, in view of their treatment history and present circumstances, are unlikely to survive safely in the community without supervision.

The prescribed treatment is set out in a written treatment plan prepared by a doctor who has examined the individual. The procedure involves a court hearing in which all the evidence, including testimony from the doctor, and, if desired, from the person alleged to need treatment, is considered. If the court determines that the individual meets the criteria for assisted outpatient treatment (AOT), an order is issued to the director of a hospital licensed or operated by the Office of Mental Health (OMH). The initial order is effective for up to six months and can be extended for successive periods of up to one year. The legislation also establishes a procedure for admission to an inpatient setting in cases where the patient fails to comply with the ordered treatment and poses a risk of harm.

The drive for the development of assertive outreach in the UK was driven by Standards 4 and 5 of the National Service Framework for Mental Health (1999), Services for Severe Mental Illness. This 10-year strategy was further strengthened by the publication in 2000 of the NHS Plan, which demonstrated a commitment to delivering this vision. The NHS Plan target on Assertive Outreach Services states that:

> There are a small number of people who are difficult to engage. They are very high users of services, and often suffer from a dual diagnosis of substance use and serious mental illness. A small proportion also have a history of offending. Services to provide assertive outreach and intensive input seven days a week are required to sustain engagement with services and to protect patient and public.

Standard 4 proposes that all mental health service users on the Care Programme Approach (CPA) should receive care that optimises engagement, prevents or anticipates crisis, and reduces risk. The service users must have a copy of a written care plan that includes the action to be taken in a crisis by the service user themselves, their carers, and their care coordinators. This care plan should advise GPs how they should respond if a service user needs additional help. The care plan should be regularly reviewed by the care coordinator, and service users must be able to access services 24 hours a day, 365 days a year.

Standard 5 proposes that each service user who is assessed as requiring a period of care away from their home, should have timely access to an appropriate hospital bed or alternative place, which is in the least restrictive environment consistent with the need to protect both the service user and the public, and as close to the person's home as possible.

In addition, the service user must receive a copy of a written after care plan agreed upon discharge, which sets out the care and rehabilitation to be provided, identifies the care coordinator, and specifies the action to be taken in a crisis.

What this means in reality is that assertive outreach services engage with the high-risk severely mentally ill (SMI) client group who have complex needs and are perhaps resistant to contacting services. Assertive outreach proactively reaches out to clients in their own territory in the community, assesses need comprehensively, develops individually tailored care packages and effectively coordinates care across agencies. In theory this optimises the recovery potential of clients by delivering clinical interventions that enhance client functioning.

The success of this aspiration relies upon a collaborative, holistic approach with the service users' interests at the centre of professional thinking and decision making. However the central paradox with assertive outreach concerns the ethical dilemma of providing services which the user does not want. Therefore the acts of beneficence and non-malificance are often delivered through the guiding principle of advocacy, and the professional's interpretation of the client 's best interest.

If the client's mental illness is exacerbated by ambivalence or avoidant behaviours, such as refusal to take prescribed medication, resulting in repeated, disruptive and distressing relapses necessitating compulsory admission, then the choice to maintain this chosen lifestyle may be restricted by proposed changes to the new Mental Health Act.

Community Treatment Orders (CTOs) are proposed within the new act, and it will clearly fall under the responsibility of assertive outreach teams to coordinate their implementation. This draft bill has been the subject of much debate and its implementation will have a direct effect upon the role, function, responsibilities and perceptions of assertive outreach teams.

The Chair of the National Assertive Outreach Forum, Mike Firn (2004), identifies the tensions for staff working within assertive outreach teams and suggests that opinion is clearly divided about the potential value of CTOs and the ethical effects on practice when implementing them.

> Working alongside someone you have got to know well and like, and having to wait, once they have discontinued medication, while they deteriorate slowly to the point of warranting compulsory readmission becomes increasingly difficult. Especially as this so often follows a predictable course, destroying relationships, losing accommodation, running personal risks, alienating family and unravelling all the preceding year's rehabilitative gains. (Firn, 2004, p. 1)

Rethink (2004) identifies the draft bill as creating the new possibility of treatment in the community. They suggest that the 1983 Mental Health Act identifies hospital treatment rather than treatment in the community if they are going to be treated compulsorily. They conclude that the number of people detained under the act has always been limited by the number of hospital beds, and go on to warn that 'with the possibility of treatment in the community, this limit will no longer exist, so more people could be treated compulsorily'.

Mental Health Alliance (2004) believes that the development of CTOs is a misplaced response to concern about public safety, and that the personal and human rights of individuals are being inappropriately eroded as a result. They suggest that it is most unlikely that the Bill will fully meet the requirements of the Human Rights Act and it is certain that it fails to meet internationally accepted standards in both the Council of Europe and the United Nations.

Clearly from these perspectives assertive outreach workers may be placed in a difficult position, and the success of their efforts will rely on the composition and expertise within the team.

The Department of Health's *Policy Implementation Guide (PIG) for Assertive Outreach*, sets out the range of interventions, and the composition of multidisciplinary teams required to deliver them, underpinned by adherence to the Care Programme Approach.

A prerequisite for the composition of an assertive outreach team is sufficient Care Coordinators (CCs) to support its envisaged caseload based on its local population and its health needs analysis. The PIG indicates, for example, that a population of 250,000 will have approximately 90 service users who would benefit from this approach at any one time; thus the team will need to provide 8–9 CCs carrying CPA responsibility for 10–12 service users each. This ratio of CCs to service users is not absolutely defined, but a ratio of 1:10 is considered appropriate. CCs are generally professionally qualified mental health workers whose work is limited to purely assertive outreach. In addition, sufficient numbers of professionally qualified and trained support staff are needed to deliver a broad range of interventions:

- Assertive engagement
- Frequent contact
- Attention to basics of daily living
- Family work, and 'concordance' therapy
- Support and intervention to family/carer and significant others
- Medication
- Psychological formulation and interventions (e.g. cognitive behavioural therapy (CBT))
- Treatment of comorbidities
- Social systems interventions (e.g. housing, finance, occupation, social networks)
- Attention to service users' physical health
- Help in accessing local services and educational, training and employment opportunities
- Relapse prevention (e.g. medication)
- Crisis situations
- Suicide awareness/prevention techniques
- Needs assessment
- Multi-agency working
- Age-, culture- and gender-sensitive interventions
- Risk assessment and management

■ Interventions under the Mental Health Act

The development of multidisciplinary teams to deliver this agenda with the most complex and difficult to engage client groups is not an easy one, and the investment in their growth has been criticised for not meeting the desired outcomes or expectations. For example, Thornicroft *et al.* (1998) published 10 report papers, which appeared to show that intensive case management produced no better outcomes than standard care, and the UK 700 study (UK 700, 1999) showed that assertive outreach treatment teams do not make significant difference compared with standard community treatment teams. Although the Royal College of Psychiatrists (2003) suggested that American studies of ACT have demonstrated reduced hospital bed use, and UK studies have not replicated these findings, a review of the latest literature would contest this. As a contrast, there is a range of research from the USA (Test and Stein, 1978; Cohen, 1999) where assertive community treatment (assertive outreach) is rapidly becoming the standard for care of persons with severe and persistent mental illness who are living in the community (Bustillo *et al.*, 2001; Phillips *et al.*, 2001) In addition there is a wealth of supportive literature from the UK which endorses the principles of assertive outreach (Burns *et al.*, 2001; Greatley and Ford, 2002; Jeffery *et al.*, 2004; Marshall, 2004; Pharoah *et al.*, 2004; Reda *et al.*, 2004; Tyrer *et al.*, 2004). Sainsbury Centre chief executive Matt Muijen is quoted as saying

> People with severe mental illnesses are often isolated from their communities. Most do not have a job, and many lack the friendships that most of us consider a fundamental part of normal life. Those from black and minority ethnic groups often experience double discrimination. Assertive outreach teams can help to combat this exclusion and enable people to rebuild their lives. (Greatley and Ford, 2002)

The style of delivery and make up of assertive outreach services

The objectives of an assertive outreach service are specific and complex, and as already indicated, the priority of any team is to provide support for adults aged between 18 and approximately 65 with a severe and persistent mental disorder associated with a high level of disability. Dealing with people who have difficulty in maintaining lasting and consenting contact with services, and who demonstrate multiple and complex needs, requires a skill mix and experience base which goes beyond that of the well-intentioned social and community support initiatives currently in place. The composition of the team, and the allocation of roles within it, are fundamental considerations for successful assertive outreach. Staff members should have dedicated responsibilities for assertive outreach. This discreet and ring-fenced role prevents competing priorities from diluting this type of service. An adequate skill mix within the team, and strong links with other mental health services together with a good general knowledge of local resources, will promote the likelihood of success.

People with a history of violence or persistent offending, or who are at risk of persistent self-harm or neglect, require specialized approaches and those based within a framework of multidisciplinary cooperation and teamwork are considered the most suitable.

The operational demands may be achieved through a range of interventions listed below.

Assessment

The initial multidisciplinary screening should ensure the appropriateness of the referral for the service user. Followed by a comprehensive, multidisciplinary, culturally competent, needs assessment, including a physical health assessment where appropriate, and risk assessment in all cases.

A plan of care which is agreed by the team and, where possible, the service user, should then be produced, together with a statement of needs which identifies the service user's strengths, goals and aspirations.

Continuity of care is assured by a team approach with each service user assigned a care coordinator who has overall responsibility for ensuring appropriate assessment, care and review. The allocation of this important role should be cognizant of the individual team members' strengths and the relationship that person has with the service user, being mindful of factors such as age, culture and gender, for example.

One of the advantages of this type of service is its responsiveness and flexibility to meet changing need. This process is assisted by regular review, even on a daily basis, that incorporates for example risk, medication, response to interventions, reassessment, planning and evaluation.

It is recommended that weekly review meetings with a consultant psychiatrist, where action is agreed and changes in treatment are discussed by the whole team, should form part of the monitoring process. In addition, care plans should be formally reviewed at least six monthly. These timetabled reviews benefit from a service user focus and include family/carer/people important to the service user in review of care plan.

The high prevalence of diagnosed psychosis in certain cultural groups emphasizes the importance of developing a culturally competent service, and 24 hour access to translation services should be available.

Interventions

The following interventions should be provided.

Assertive engagement is provided through giving a high priority in both the initial stages of engagement and the roll-out of care with a persistent approach to engagement through repeated attempts at contact through tenacity, creativity and innovation rather than more aggressive and disempowering strategies (Dooher and Byrt, 2003, 2004).

A team should have the capacity to visit seven days a week, respond rapidly to changes in need and provide intensive support in the community. It should produce a care plan to address all aspects of daily living so as to raise independence and achieve the recovery process through the frequency of contact and practical support, such as help with shopping, domestic work, cleaning and improving living conditions and budgeting.

This will enhance the service users' ability to survive in their own environment and these survival skills should be embedded into the daily living skills training of service users. This will empower and provide real choices to the clients.

This level of involvement may not be sustainable over longer periods, and it is important to consider the range of familial and social support mechanisms available to enable service users to improve their living conditions. This may be achieved through family therapy, psycho-education or simple practical support.

The issue of concordance and compliance with medication is a contentious one which produces passionate debate whenever raised. It is expected that teams will play a key role in the delivery and administration of medication to service users who require intensive monitoring, promoting concordance through participation and involvement in decision making and the monitoring of positive and negative effects of the medication. This may be achieved through validated self-rating scales such as the LUNSERS (Liverpool University Neuroleptic Side Effect Rating Scale (Day, 1995) and links with hospital and local pharmacies

Cognitive Behavioural Therapy (CBT) has been identified as the therapy of choice and has a proven track record (British Psychological Society, 2002; Williams, 2001a,b; Williams and Garland, 2002; Williams and Whitfield, 2001). CBT has proved very useful as a psychological intervention for psychotic experiences, Substance misuse, depression, suicidal thoughts and anxiety disorders. The main assumption behind CBT is that psychological difficulties depend on how people think or interpret events (cognitions), how people respond to these events (behaviour), and how it makes them feel (emotions). CBT aims to break the cycle between thoughts, feelings and behaviours by helping people to learn more useful ways of thinking and coping. A range of techniques should be available within the team and used appropriately.

The links between mind and body extend beyond the individual, and assertive outreach recognizes the importance of social systems interventions, whereby the maintenance and expansion of social networks and peer contact are emphasized. This is considered to reduce social isolation and provide lasting non-medicalised support which we all rely upon. In addition, attention to service users' physical health is important (help in keeping appointments with the client's GP for example) and the team provides a useful role in health promotion and access to general screening. Physical health problems, including nutritional and dental needs, should be identified and addressed. Help and encouragement should be given to the service user to access health services, education, training and employment. Developing the service users' skills and promoting their aspirations are additional long-term pillars of a successful life and may be seen as enabling one's optimum potential to be achieved.

These factors will reduce the likelihood of relapse and the close relationship between the care coordinator and the client will ensure that early warning signs of relapse are recognized and that a plan is in place, already developed. This plan should be agreed with the service user and their family and carers. It should be kept on file and will reduce the severity of relapse should it occur.

Where relapse does occur a joint assessment should take place between assertive outreach teams, crisis teams and acute care teams, where appropriate, to ensure that the least restrictive and stigmatizing setting for care is arranged. Avoidance of hospitalisation is desirable and intensive support in the community should be provided wherever possible.

If inpatient care is required, the care coordinator should maintain contact during the stay and be involved in decision making to promote continuity and involvement with the discharge plans.

Assertive outreach should continue indefinitely whilst evidence of health gain is evident, although where recovery is progressive transfer to a community mental health team providing less intensive intervention will be appropriate.

Conclusion

The treatment of people in their home environment is generally preferred to institutional care by patients and professional staff alike, and the development of assertive outreach must be seen as a positive development. The questions raised by professionals objecting to the powers and responsibilities of compulsory treatment are obviated by the fact that it is these very same professionals who have the responsibility of implementing the proposed actions. As such they will have the ability to sanction their own actions and thus minimise any transgression of service user rights. The degree of coercion therefore rests entirely within the hands of the professionals and we look to them to ensure sensible safeguards for civil liberties. There are no absolute or simple answers to these issues. There is, however, a place for judicious use of compulsory community treatment for our patient population for the protection of themselves and the public, and the professionals' role is to execute exactly that: a professional, educated, evidence-based, expert intervention, to ensure the least restrictive opportunities for clients to live a full and optimum existence in the community.

References

Appleby, L., Shaw, J., Amos, T. *et al.* (1999) *Safer Services. Report of the National Confidential Inquiry into Suicide and Homicide by People with Mental Illness.* London: Department of Health.

British Psychological Society (2002) *Understanding Mental Illness – Recent Advances in Understanding Mental Illness and Psychotic Experiences.* British Psychological Society: Division of Clinical Psychology.

Burns, T., Knapp, M., Catty, J., Healey, A., Henderson, J. and Watt, H. (2001) Home treatment for mental health problems: a systematic review. *Health Technology Assessment*, **5**(15).

Bustillo, J. R., Lauriello, J., Horan, W.P. and Keith, S. J. (2001) The psychosocial treatment of schizophrenia: an update. *American Journal of Psychiatry*, **158**, 163–175.

Cohen, N. L. (ed.) (1999) *Psychiatric Outreach to the Mentally Ill*, pp. 47–64. New Directions for Mental Health Services, No. 52: The Jossey-Bass Social and Behavioural Sciences CVs. San Francisco, CA.

Day, J. C., Wood, G., Dewey, M. and Bentall, R.P. (1995)A self-rating scale for measuring neuroleptic side-effects. Validation in a group of schizophrenic patients. *British Journal of Psychiatry*, **166**, 650–653.

Department of Health (1994) *Guidance on the Discharge of Mentally Disordered People and Their Continuing Care in the Community.* London: Department of Health.

Dooher, J. and Byrt, R. (2003) *Empowerment and Participation. Power, Influence and Control in Contemporary Healthcare.* Salisbury: Quay Books.

Dooher, J. and Byrt, R. (2004) *Empowerment and Health Service Users.* Salisbury: Quay Books.

Firn, M. (2004) *Memorandum from the National Forum for Assertive Outreach (DMH 406).* Submission to the Joint Parliamentary Scrutinising Committee of the Draft Mental Health Bill 2004: The proposal for community treatment orders (non-resident orders). London: Department of Health.

Greatley, A. and Ford, R. (2002) *Out of the Maze. Reaching and Supporting Londoners with Severe Mental Health Problems.* London: Sainsbury Centre for Mental Health/King's Fund.

Jeffery, D. P., Ley, A., McLaren, S. and Siegfried, N. (2004) Psychosocial treatment programmes for people with both severe mental illness and substance misuse (Cochrane Review). In: *The Cochrane Library*, Issue 1, 2004. Chichester: John Wiley & Sons.

Marshall, M., Gray, A., Lockwood, A. and Green, R. (2004) Case management for people with severe mental disorders. In: *The Cochrane Library*, Issue 1, Chichester: John Wiley & Sons.

Mental Health Alliance (2004) *Mental Health Alliance Submission to the Joint Scrutiny the Draft Mental Health Bill.* London: Mental Health Alliance.

Department of Health (2000) *The NHS Plan. A plan for Investment, A Plan for Reform.* London: HMSO.

Pharoah, F. M., Rathbone, J., Mari, J. J. and Streiner, D. (2004) Family intervention for schizophrenia. In: *The Cochrane Library*, Issue 1. Chichester: John Wiley & Sons.

Phillips, S. D., Burns, B. J., Edgar, E. R., Mueser, K. T., Linkins, K. W., Rosenheck, R. A,. *et al.* (2001) Moving assertive community treatment into standard practice. *Psychiatric Services*, **52**, 771–779.

Reda, S. and Makhoul, S. (2004) Prompts to encourage appointment attendance for people with serious mental illness. In: *The Cochrane Library*, Issue 1, 2004. Chichester: John Wiley & Sons.

Rethink (2004) The Draft Mental Health Bill 2004: Quick reference guide
`http://www.rethink.org/news+campaigns/campaigns/mental-health-bill/quick-reference-mhb.doc.`

Ritchie, J., Dick, D. and Lingham, R. (1994) *The Report of the Inquiry into the Care and Treatment of Christopher Clunis.* London: HMSO.

Royal College of Psychiatrists (2003) *A quarter of assertive outreach patients compulsorily hospitalised.* Press release, 1 August.

Test, M. A. and Stein, L. I. (1978) The clinical rationale for community treatment; review of the literature. In: *Alternatives to Mental Hospital Treatment* (eds. L. I. Stein and M. A. Test). New York: Plenum.

Thornicroft, G. and Goldberg, D. (1998) *Has Community Care Failed?* Maudsley discussion papers 1–10. London: Institute of Psychiatry.

Tyrer, P., Coid, J., Simmonds, S., Joseph, P. and Marriott, S. (2004) Community mental health teams (CMHTs) for people with severe mental illnesses and disordered personality. In: *The Cochrane Library*, Issue 1. Chichester: John Wiley & Sons.

UK 700 Group (1999) Comparison of intensive and standard case management for patients with psychosis. Rationale of the trial. *British Journal of Psychiatry*, **174**, 74–78.

Williams, C. J. (2001a) *Overcoming Depression: A Five Areas Approach.* London: Arnold.

Williams, C. J. (2001b) Use of written cognitive-behavioural therapy self-help materials to treat depression. *Advances in Psychiatric Treatment*, **7**, 233–240.

Williams, C. J. and Garland, A. (2002) A cognitive-behavioural therapy assessment model for use in everyday clinical practice. *Advances in Psychiatric Treatment*, **8**, 172–179.

Williams, C. J. and Whitfield, G. (2001) Written and computer-based self-help treatments for depression. *British Medical Bulletin*, **57**, 133–144.

CHAPTER 14

Early intervention in psychosis

Martin Fahy

Introduction

There has been a growing interest amongst mental health workers and research-ers internationally and within the UK in the concept of intervening early in psychosis. Preventive interventions in early psychosis are a relatively new area for most clinicians working within mental health. In recent years, there has been increasing confidence that preventive interventions for psychotic disorders are becoming a realistic proposition in clinical settings (Birchwood *et al.*, 1998).

Current standard approaches to psychotic disorder typically delay treat-ment until the disorder is established, usually initiated in the context of high-risk incidents such as suicide attempts or aggressive or disorganised behaviour. Treatment is generally focused on acute phases of illness with intensive long-term follow-up confined to the most complex severe cases in the later phases of illness. Around one out of every 100 young people will experience a psychotic episode. The prospects of short-term recovery in this group are good: with sustained treatment over 80% of individuals achieve remission of symptoms from their first episode of psychosis within six months (Lieberman *et al.*, 1993).

With the resurgence of interest in both psychopharmacological and psy-chotherapeutic treatments of people with psychotic illnesses in recent years, advances in the long-term clinical management of schizophrenia have shown that the skilled application of current therapeutic strategies may provide sub-stantial benefits (Falloon *et al.*, 1998). Comprehensive programmes for the detection and treatment of early psychosis, which support the needs of young people with early psychosis, carry the important function of promoting recovery, independence, equity and self-sufficiency and facilitating the uptake of social, educational and employment opportunities by young people.

Schizophrenia remains one of the most debilitating and inherently complex illnesses, given the progressive nature of this illness and its severity. Despite the introduction of newer treatments which challenge traditional notions of schizophrenia as a deteriorating illness, the so-called Kraepelian viewpoint, the prognosis remains poor for far too many people. First episode psychosis is still potentially a devastating happening for young people and their families (Hegarty *et al.*, 1994; McGlashan, 1998).

Several authors have suggested (Wyatt, 1991) that untreated psychosis can be biologically toxic and is responsible for long-term morbidity. The evidence suggests that treating individuals with schizophrenia early in the course of their illness decreases their long-term morbidity. Early intervention may help prevent the often significant biological, social and psychological deterioration that can occur in the early years following the onset of a psychotic disorder. Significant delays before effective treatment is initiated can have serious consequences in the medium and long term (Loebel *et al.*, 1992).

Perkins and Repper (1998) comment that public concern for the safety and general well being of people with mental health is high, but it is not necessarily reflected in commitment by those responsible for allocating public monies to fund services and develop mental health services. They point out the shortfalls with respect to mental health funding in comparison to funding made available for physical health services. In particular, they draw attention to the disparity in funding available to provide specialist treatments for people with severe mental illness in comparison to their counterparts with severe physical health problems.

Benefits of intervening early

There are many potential benefits to early intervention and treatment in psychotic illness:

- Reduced morbidity
- Promotes rapid recovery
- Improved long-term prognosis
- Preservation of social skills
- Preservation of family and social support/networks
- Decreased need for hospitalisation (delays in treatment associated with substantially high health care cost)
- Longer untreated illness associated within longer first and second admissions

First episodes typically occur in late adolescence, when a person's sense of self and developmental pathway are most likely to be threatened, and this is often when the patient is most vulnerable to secondary morbidity in the form of depression or anxiety disorders. Longer periods of untreated psychosis have consistently been shown to be related to poorer long-term outcome.

The idea of secondary prevention in psychosis has been gathering momentum over the last decade (Birchwood, 2000; McGorry, 1998; Falloon, 1992). The question has been raised whether the positive results in somatic medicine with early diagnosis of disorders such as cancer, heart diseases etc. can be replicated within the field of psychiatry.

Why intervene early in psychosis?

In most cases, the delay between the onset of psychotic symptoms and first treatment is surprisingly long. Treatment 'lag' time or duration of untreated psychosis (DUP) to first presentation and treatment after onset of frank psychotic symptoms ranges from one to two years on average. The longer individuals with psychosis remains untreated, the greater the opportunity for serious physical and social harm, DUP prior to treatment has been linked to poor long-term outcome.

Reasons that contribute towards treatment lags include:

- Lack of clear pathways from primary to secondary care
- Lack of clarity of information where to seek assistance
- Denial or non-recognition of symptoms by families/carers and friends
- Stigma and fear of mental illness, the negative stereotypes of mental illness
- Culturally insensitive services/language barriers/failure to recognise ethnicity in determining pathways to care
- Services not geared to manage early psychosis or pre-psychosis; lack of 24 hour crisis support
- Homeless people
- People with alcohol or drug problems
- Comorbidity – co-occurrence with psychosis of a variety of problems is well documented
- Location of services – these are frequently located within large inpatient psychiatric facilities, and young people are often alarmed by this
- Inaccessible or non-responsive services – failure to follow up new referrals or ensure engagement with services
- Non-youth-focused services

There are numerous studies suggesting that early intervention can radically effect later outcome (McGorry, 1998; McGlashan, 1998; Falloon, 1992; Birchwood and Smith, 1992). Evidence indicates that the early phase is critical.

Ten to 15% of people with psychosis do commit suicide and the risk of this is greatest early in the illness (two-thirds of suicides occur within the first five years).

If services step in *intensively* at this early stage, the evidence is overwhelming. Mental health services need to be proactive, concentrating efforts much earlier, rather than adopting the traditional 'wait and see' approach to who becomes chronically ill and whose illness turns out to be benign.

The early psychosis paradigm

Early intervention strategies in first-episode psychosis include one or more of the following aims: (a) reduce the duration of untreated psychosis; (b) provide comprehensive expert treatment of the first episode of psychosis; (c) reduce the duration of active psychosis In the first episode and beyond; and (d) maximise recovery, community involvement, and quality of life (McGorry, 1998). A more radical subset of the 'early intervention movement' has proposed that intervention could be possible before the first episode of psychosis (Yung and McGorry, 1997).

Focus 1: Pre-psychotic phase

Most, if not all, psychotic episodes are preceded by prodromal changes or changes in subjective experience and behaviour. For most clinicians and researchers, preoccupied with the advanced phases of this disorder, such an idea has remained a pipedream. The changes that occur during the prodromal phase have been broadly characterised by Hafner and colleagues (1995). These and other studies (Jones *et al.*, 1993) have shown that although diagnostic specificity and ultimately potentially effective treatment comes with the later onset of positive psychotic symptoms, most of the disabling consequences of the underlying disorder emerge and manifest well prior to this phase. In particular, deficits in social functioning occur predominantly during the prodromal phase and prior to formal treatment by specialist mental health teams.

Focus 2: Reducing DUP services

Most psychotic episodes in which severe symptoms of mental illness, such as delusion, hallucinations or severe thought disorder are present, are often subject to long treatment delays. This is reported to be on average between one and two years. Identification of first episode psychosis can lead to better long-term prognosis. Reducing DUP is theoretically beneficial by slowing or preventing the neurobiological deficit processes linked to symptom formulation in the early course of psychosis (Lieberman *et al.*, 1993).

Focus 3: First-episode services and the critical period

Unlike Focus 1 and Focus 2, Focus 3 applies itself most specifically to health care professionals who are based within mainstream mental health services, where the immediate possibility of preventively orientated treatment arises, which can begin upon the first episode of psychosis and the subsequent recovery and the 'critical' period of the early months and years which follow.

The basic principles behind this focus are:

- Youth friendly-streaming of first episode patients away from the chronically ill
- Development of a phase-specific approach which targets early treatment during the early phase of psychosis
- Development of future strategies to prevent or abort impending episodes/ cooperation of psychological and medical approaches
- Providing a broad range of treatments from psychopharmacological to psychotherapeutic treatments
- Offering intensive consistent support and follow-up during the first one to three years of the illness

Models of early intervention in psychosis

Early intervention services should provide an extensive case management service to young people experiencing a first episode of psychosis, focusing on psychosocial, vocational and family interventions. Early intervention sevices should ideally consist of a specialised mental health team providing individual tailored evidence-based interventions to people aged 14–35 in the early stages of psychosis. The team should consist of a mix of mental health workers including psychiatric nurses, social workers, occupational therapists, psychologists, psychiatrists, support workers and youth and community workers.

The service should take direct referrals from community mental health teams, child and adolescent services, primary care services, crisis teams, forensic services, other mental health services and acute medical services (including accident and emergency), and from youth agencies, education and other community-based youth agencies.

Skills/knowledge base essential for early intervention team workers:

- A youth-focused worker would be essential
- Workers with specific vocational training and awareness of local services
- Developed links with local drug and alcohol services
- Services need to be community-based
- Access to both training and supervision for psycho-social interventions and cognitive behavioural techniques for all team members
- Development of operational 'seamless' care pathways for young people from child and adolescent services through to adult-based services
- The developments of real alternatives to admission to acute generic adult mental beds
- Streaming people with first episode psychosis away from the chronically ill
- The establishment of purpose-built youth-focused inpatient facilities for the 16–25 age groups
- Clear links between local forensics services (possible entry point to the service in crisis)
- Consideration to gender- and cultural-sensitive issues with respect to team composition, ensuring where possible that culturally specific issues can be catered for
- Adopting a policy of family-based engagement, recognising the needs of the family as a unit and its importance in the wider treatment context
- 24 hour access to support and advice in the event of crisis
- The adoption of the team concept to ensure a consistent approach to cover sickness, holidays etc. (avoiding over-dependence on one worker)
- Establish clear links with primary care-based services/provide training in better detection of early psychosis

Recovery in psychosis

Recovery as a term can encompass a number of ideas and concepts; it describes a personal journey for people with mental health problems. Turner describes this as a constant struggle for people who have lived the experience of mental distress. The reaction of many mental health professionals to people who describe themselves, as 'recovering' is often to reappraise or deny their diagnosis. All too often, professionals question the validity of the original diagnosis rather than accept that the person has made a recovery. It would be very limiting to judge recovery in terms of time spent in services.

Strauss and Carpenter (1974) advance this point by highlighting the potential flaws in adopting single outcome measures such as hospitalisation or treatment compliance as sole indicators of improved social functioning. They suggest that with the advancements being made in treatment and outcomes for people with schizophrenia, alternative methods of measuring social functioning and recovery need to include employment, leisure activity and occupational performance rather than solely symptom reduction.

The primary aim of practitioners who promote recovery is to support people to take back control of their illness and to make real choices based on objective information and a developing sense of self worth. This can be achieved by providing access to information that will assist people to make choices concerning their illness and treatment. Individuals should be expert in their own mental distress and should be accorded all the rights and responsibilities that the wider general public enjoy.

Double (2002) suggested that the government's NSF for mental health and its agenda to modernise mental health services has given a new direction for mental health policy. The impetus so far has been given to the development of the newer community treatment teams: assertive outreach, crisis resolution and home treatment teams, and EIS. These initiatives are to be welcomed, yet many staff working within mental health services are demoralised, under pressure and exhausted by the workload and the constant change and restructuring of services. Mental health practice and training are currently dominated by approaches that emphasise medical diagnosis and the use of physical treatments. In order to counteract this, training in psychosocial interventions (PSI) will help to refocus mental health workers, encouraging what Double called the bio-psychosocial approach – a more complete assessment of people's mental health problems and recognition of the social and psychological aspects of those problems. This approach considers the whole person: their life and circumstances and not simply their brain. More training programmes for mental health workers are required in order to raise knowledge levels and create an improved understanding of people with severe mental illness. If mental health workers do not receive the correct training, the newer services may actually make things worse for service users rather than better.

Mental health problems are common and widely misunderstood. At any one time, one adult in six has a mental health problem of some sort (Mental Health and Social Exclusion, 2003). These include a wide spectrum of conditions, from anxiety to psychotic disorders. The precise nature and impact of these conditions varies significantly from individual to individual. They are rarely static during a person's life, and change, disappear and reappear. Mental health problems often coexist with other problems, such as substance misuse, homelessness, poor physical health and learning disabilities.

Maj (2002) points out that schizophrenia in particular is characterised by chronicity and it is commonly perceived that patients with this diagnosis will never achieve a full restitution of mental functioning. In his work he cautions mental health workers about focusing their efforts solely on either the acute phase of the illness or the long-term management of the illness. Instead, he views the illness as requiring continuous and integrated approaches from onset to recovery. A range of risk factors influence the development of mental health problems. These include socio-economic disadvantage, homelessness, neighbourhood violence and crime, unemployment, poor educational attainment, being a member of a minority group or being a lone parent or teenage mother.

What Maj (2002) describes as an unexpected consequence of community care is that disabilities that do not prevent a person from remaining in hospital could prevent a person from remaining in the community. Disabilities in interpersonal skills and vocational skills diminish the patient's capacity to fulfil culturally determined adult roles in society. If the patient remains disabled it is inappropriate to call that a successful outcome. Early intervention services need to create an optimistic positive approach to all people who use mental health services. The vast majority have real prospects of recovery if they are supported by appropriate services, driven by the right values and attitudes.

Working with families and carers

Barbato *et al.* (2000) points out that there has been considerable attention paid to the family environment as a significant factor in the onset and course of psychosis. Brown's (1985) findings suggested that clients with a diagnosis of psychosis returning to their families following an acute episode of their illness faired worse in terms of relapse rate than those who remained in care or lived alone. He suggested that clients living with critical or over-involved relatives were more prone to relapse (this over-critical or highly sensitive family reaction to serious illness was classified as high expressed emotion (EE)). Falloon *et al.* (1982), Hogarty (1986) and Leff and Kuipers (2002) take this notion further, supporting Brown's (1995) findings: that clients living with critical or over-involved relatives were more prone to relapse than those clients who did not. However, when the family intervention was offered consistently over a fixed period of time a reduction in relapse rate was achieved.

These family interventions were based on broad psycho-educational and or behavioural approaches aimed at improving communication or problem-solving techniques within the family unit. Fadden (1998), in her review of family interventions, indicated that effective family interventions can result in a fourfold reduction in relapse rate.

Birchwood (2000) highlighted the phenomenon of carer stress brought on by caring for a person with psychosis, suggesting that this was a normal reaction to coping with a relative with a severe illness like psychosis. He suggested that the impact on having to care for a relative with psychosis is likely to be severe and to contribute to EE levels within the family unit. In comparison, Fadden and

Kuipers' (1987) research into families and psychosis has examined this issue and has found that families frequently describe a sense of burden and stress that the carer role imposes upon them.

Birchwood (2000) expanded on this carer response as a normal initial reaction to the changing role which carers undergo from relative to carer, their reactions ranging from bewilderment to denial, anxiety and shock as they adjust to a new and often unexpected care-giving role. Most carers will have a limited comprehension initially of what the future holds and will often make assumptions that this illness is a temporary problem. They are often unaware of the extended time period required for social recovery and will quickly become frustrated with the perceived lack of progress the client is making.

Summary

The development of early intervention in psychosis services represents an exciting opportunity for young people, carers and professionals in the UK. Early intervention in psychosis is recognised as a major priority in the National Service Framework for Mental Health (Department of Health, 1999). The NHS Plan (Department of Health, 2000) outlined the requirement for 50 early intervention teams to be in place nationally by 2004. The NHS Plan specifies that teams will provide a service for young people aged 14–35 during the first three years of a psychotic illness. Early treatment is crucial because the first few years of psychosis carry the highest risk of serious physical and social harm.

The early intervention service should provide an extensive case management service to young people experiencing a first episode of psychosis, focusing on psychosocial, vocational and family interventions. Early identification and treatment of symptoms is seen as crucial to longer-term outcome.

Psychosis can be a debilitating illness with far-reaching implications for individuals and their families. It can affect all aspects of life – education and employment, relationships and social functioning, and physical and mental well being. Without support and adequate care, psychosis can place a heavy burden on the person, his or her carers and family. The establishment of these services represents an opportunity to build on current service provision and understanding of psychosis and to modernise current service provision for this client group. This will demand collaboration within the NHS and between the social services, education and youth services, the voluntary sector, youth offending teams, probation, prisons, and housing providers.

References

Barbato, A. (2000) Family interventions in schizophrenia and related disorders: critical review of clinical trials. *Acta Psychiatrica Scandinavica*, **102**, 81–97.

Birchwood, M. (2000) *Early Intervention in Psychosis: a Guide to the Concepts, Evidence and Interventions*. Chichester: Wiley.

Birchwood, M. and Smith, J. (1987) Expressed emotion and first episode of schizophrenia. *British Journal of Psychiatry*, **151**, 859–860.

Birchwood, M., Hallett, S. and Preston, M. (1998) *Schizophrenia: An integrated Approach to Research and Treatment*. Harlow: Longman.

Birchwood, M., Todd, P. and Jackson, C. (1998) Early intervention in psychosis. *British Journal of Psychiatry*, **172**, 2–5.

Brown, G. (1985) The discovery of expressed emotion: induction or deduction? In *Expressed Emotion in Families* (eds. J. Leff and C. Vaughn), pp. 7–25. New York: Guilford.

Chattergree, A. and Liberman, J. (1999) Studies of biological variable in first episode of schizophrenia: a comparative review. In: *The Recognition and Management of Early Psychosis* (eds. P. D. McGorry and H. J. Jackson). Cambridge: Cambridge University Press.

Double, D. (2002) Redressing the imbalance. *Mental Health Today*, September.

Fadden, G. (1998) Family intervention. In *Serious Mental Health Problems in the Community: Policy, Practice and Research* (eds. C. Brooker and J. Repper). London: Baillière Tindall.

Fadden, G. and Kuipers, I. (1987) The burden of care: the impact of functional psychiatric illness on the patient's family. *British Journal of Psychiatry*, **150**, 285–292.

Falloon, I. R. M. (1992) Early intervention for the first episode of Schizophrenia: a preliminary exploration. *Psychiatry*, **55**, 4–15.

Falloon, I. (1995) *Family Management of Schizophrenia*. Baltimore: Johns Hopkins University Press.

Falloon, I. R. H., Boyd, J. L., McGill, C. W., Ranzani, J., Moss, H. B. and Gilderman, A. M. (1982) Family management in the prevention of exacerbation of schizophrenia. *New England Journal of Medicine*, **306**, 1437–1440.

Falloon, I. R. H., Coverdale, J. H., Laidlaw, T. M., Merry, S., Kydd, R. R., Morosini, P. and The OTP Collaborative Group (1998) Early intervention for schizophrenic disorders. *British Journal of Psychiatry*, **172**, 33–38

Garety, P., Fowler, D., Kuipers, E., Freeman, D., Dunn, G., Bebbington, P., Hadley, C. and Jones, S. (1997) The London and East Anglia randomised controlled trial of cognitive behaviour therapy for psychosis II: Predictors of outcome. *British Journal of Psychiatry*, **171**, 420–426.

Hafner, H., Nowotny, B., Loffler, W., van der Heiden, W. and Maurer, K. (1995) When and how does schizophrenia produce social deficits? *European Archives of Psychiatry and Clinical Neuroscience*, **246**, 17–28.

Harris, N., Williams, S. and Bradshaw, T. (eds.) (2002) *Psychosocial Interventions for People with Schizophrenia*. Basingstoke: Palgrave Macmillan.

Hegarty, J., Baldessarini, R. J. and Tohen, M. *et al.* (1994) One hundred years of schizophrenia: a meta-analysis of the outcome literature. *American Journal of Psychiatry*, **151**, 1409–1416.

Jones, P. B., Bebbington, P., Foerster, A., Lewis, S. W., Murray, R. M., Russell, A., Sham, P. C., Toone, B. K. and Wilkins, S. (1993) Premorbid social underachievement in schizophrenia: results from the Camberwell Collaborative Psychosis Study. *British Journal of Psychiatry*, **162**, 65–71.

Krapelian, E. (1896/1997) Dementia Praecox. In *The Clinical Roots of the Schizophrenia Concept* (eds. J. Cutting and M. Shepherd), pp.13–24. Cambridge: University Press.

Larsen, T. K., Johannessen, J. O. and Opjordsmoen, S. (1998) First-episode schizophrenia with long duration of untreated psychosis. *British Journal of Psychiatry*, **172**, 45–52.

Leff, J. and Kuipers, E. (2002) *Family Work for Schizophrenia: A Practical Guide*, 2nd edn. London: Gaskell.

Lieberman, J. A., Jody, D., Gheisler, S., Alvir, J., Loebel, A., Szymanski, S., Woerner, M. and Borenstein, M. (1993) Time course and biologic correlates of treatment response in first episode schizophrenia. *Archives of General Psychiatry*, **50**, 369–376.

Lincoln, C. and McGorry, P. (1999) Pathways to care in early psychosis: clinical and consumer perspectives. In: *The Recognition and Management of Early Psychosis* (eds. P. D. McGorry and H. J. Jackson). Cambridge: Cambridge University Press.

Loebel, A., Lieberman, J. A., Alvir, J. M. *et al.* (1992) Duration of psychosis and outcome in first-episode schizophrenia. *American Journal of Psychiatry*, 149, 1183–1188.

Maj, M. (2002) *Schizophrenia*, 2nd edn. Chichester: Wiley.

Mason, P., Harrison, G., Glazebrook, C., Medley, I., Dalkin, T. and Croudace, T. (1995) Characteristics of outcome in schizophrenia at 13 years. *British Journal of Psychiatry*, **167**, 596–603.

McEvoy, J. P., Hogarty, G. E. and Steingard, S. (1991) Optimal dose of neuroleptic in acute schizophrenia: a controlled study of the neuroleptic threshold and higher haloperidol dose. *Archives of General Psychiatry*, **48**, 739–745.

McGlashan, T. H. (1998) Early detection and intervention of schizophrenia: rationale and research. *British Journal of Psychiatry*, **172**, 3–6.

McGorry, P. (1998) Preventive strategies in early psychosis: verging on reality. *British Journal of Psychiatry*, **172**, 1–2.

Perkins, R. and Repper, J. (1998) *Dilemmas in Community Mental Health Practice Choice or Control*. Radcliffe Medical Press.

Power, P., Elkins, K., Adlard, S., Curry, C., McGorry, C. and Harrigan S. (1998) Analysis of the initial treatment phase in first-episode psychosis. *British Journal of Psychiatry*, **172**, 71–76.

Social Exclusion Unit (2003) *Mental Health and Social Exclusion*. Consultation Document, Office of the Deputy Prime Minister.

Strauss, M. D. and Carpenter, W. (1974) The prediction of outcome in schizophrenia II: Relationships between predictor and outcome variables. A report from the WHO International Pilot Study of Schizophrenia. *Archives of General Psychiatry*, **31**.

Turner, D. (2002) Mapping the routes to recovery. *Mental Health Today*, July.

Wyatt, R. J. (1991) Neuroleptics and the natural cause of schizophrenia. *Schizophrenia Bulletin*, **24**, 78–85

Wyatt, R. J., Damiani, L. M. and Henter, I. D. (1998) First episode schizophrenia. *British Journal of Psychiatry*, **172**, 77–83

Yung, A. R., Phillips, L. J., McGorry, P. D., McFarland, C. A., Francey, S., Harrigan, S., Patton, G. C., and Jackson, H. J. (1998) Prediction of psychosis. *British Journal of Psychiatry*, **172**, 14–20.

Bibliography

Department of Health (1999) *National Service Framework for Mental Health. Modern Standards and Service Models*. London: HMSO.

Department of Health (2000) *The Mental Health Policy Implementation Guide. Adult Acute Inpatient Care Provision*. London: HMSO.

Department of Health (2000) *The NHS Plan*. London: HMSO.

Department of Health (2000) *The Mental Health Policy Implementation Guide. Community Mental Health Teams*. London: HMSO.

Department of Health (2003) *Mental Health Policy Implementation Guide. Dual Diagnosis Good Practice Guide*. London: HMSO.

Haddock, G. and Slade, P. (1996) *Cognitive-Behavioural Interventions with Psychotic Disorders*. London: Routledge.

Gamble, C. and Brennan, G. (2000) *Working with Serious Mental Illness: A Manual for Clinical Practice*. London: Baillière Tindall.

Lincoln, C. and McGorry, P. (1999) Pathways to care in early psychosis: clinical and consumer perspectives. In *The Recognition and Management of Early Psychosis* (eds. P. D. McGorry and H. J. Jackson). Cambridge: Cambridge University Press.

Mason, P., Harrison, G., Glazebrook, C., Medley, I., Dalkin, T. and Croudace, T. (1995) Characteristics of outcome in schizophrenia at 13 years. *British Journal of Psychiatry*, **167**, 596–603.

McEvoy J. P., Hogarty, G. E. and Steingard, S. (1991) Optimal dose of neuroleptics in acute schizophrenia: a controlled study of the neuroleptics threshold and higher haloperidol dose. *Archives of General Psychiatry*, **48**, 739–745.

Power, P., Elkins, K., Adlard, S., Curry, C., McGorry, C. and Harrigan, S. (1998) Analysis of the initial treatment phase in first-episode psychosis. *British Journal of Psychiatry*, **172**.

Index